ITALIAN DRAWINGS

FROM
THE COLLECTION
OF
DUKE ROBERTO FERRETTI

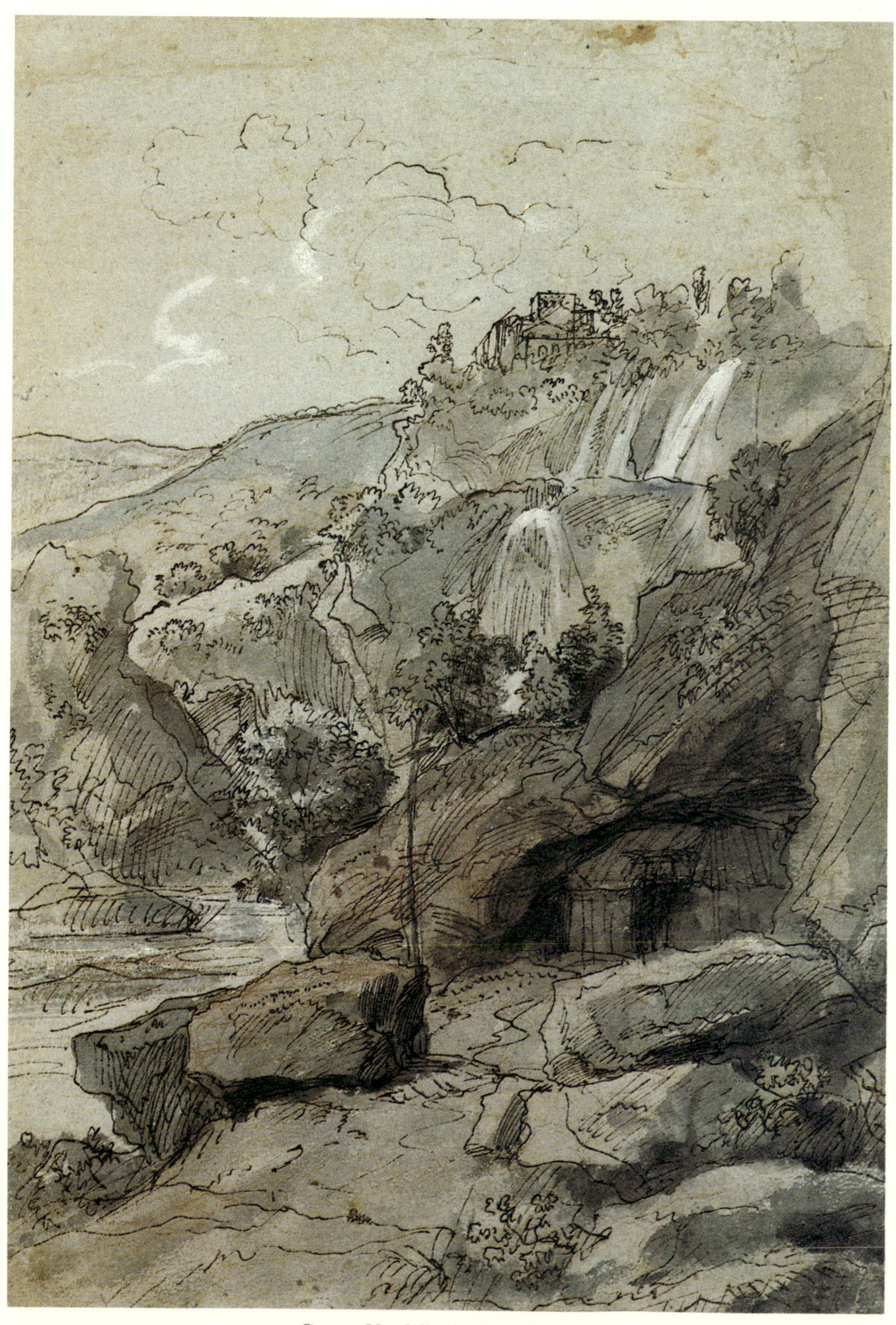

54 Gaspar Van Wittel, *The Falls at Tivoli*

On the cover: 10 Francesco Salviati, *Portrait Study of a Boy Wearing a Cap*

ITALIAN DRAWINGS

FROM
THE COLLECTION
OF
DUKE ROBERTO FERRETTI

* * *

DAVID McTAVISH

·

ART GALLERY OF ONTARIO
MUSÉE DES BEAUX-ARTS DE L'ONTARIO
TORONTO, CANADA

———

Art Gallery of Ontario, Toronto
OCTOBER 26, 1985 – JANUARY 5, 1986

·

The Pierpont Morgan Library, New York
FEBRUARY 14 – APRIL 20, 1986

* * *

The Art Gallery of Ontario gratefully acknowledges the
generous support of Chubb Insurance Company of Canada.

The Art Gallery of Ontario is generously funded by
the Ontario Ministry of Citizenship and Culture;
the Municipality of Metropolitan Toronto; and the
Museum Assistance Programmes of the National
Museums of Canada.

Printed in Canada

CANADIAN CATALOGUING IN
PUBLICATION DATA

McTavish, David.
   Italian drawings from the collection of Duke Roberto Ferretti

Catalogue to accompany an exhibition held at the Art Gallery
of Ontario, Oct. 26, 1985-Jan. 5, 1986, and The Pierpont
Morgan Library, New York, Feb. 14-Apr. 20, 1986.
Bibliography: p.
ISBN 0-919777-21-X

1. Drawing, Italian—Private collections—Ontario—Toronto—
Exhibitions. 2. Ferretti, Roberto—Art collections—Exhibitions.
I. Art Gallery of Ontario. II. The Pierpont Morgan Library.
III. Title.

NC255.M28 1985   741.945'074'0113541   C85-099601-5

TABLE OF CONTENTS

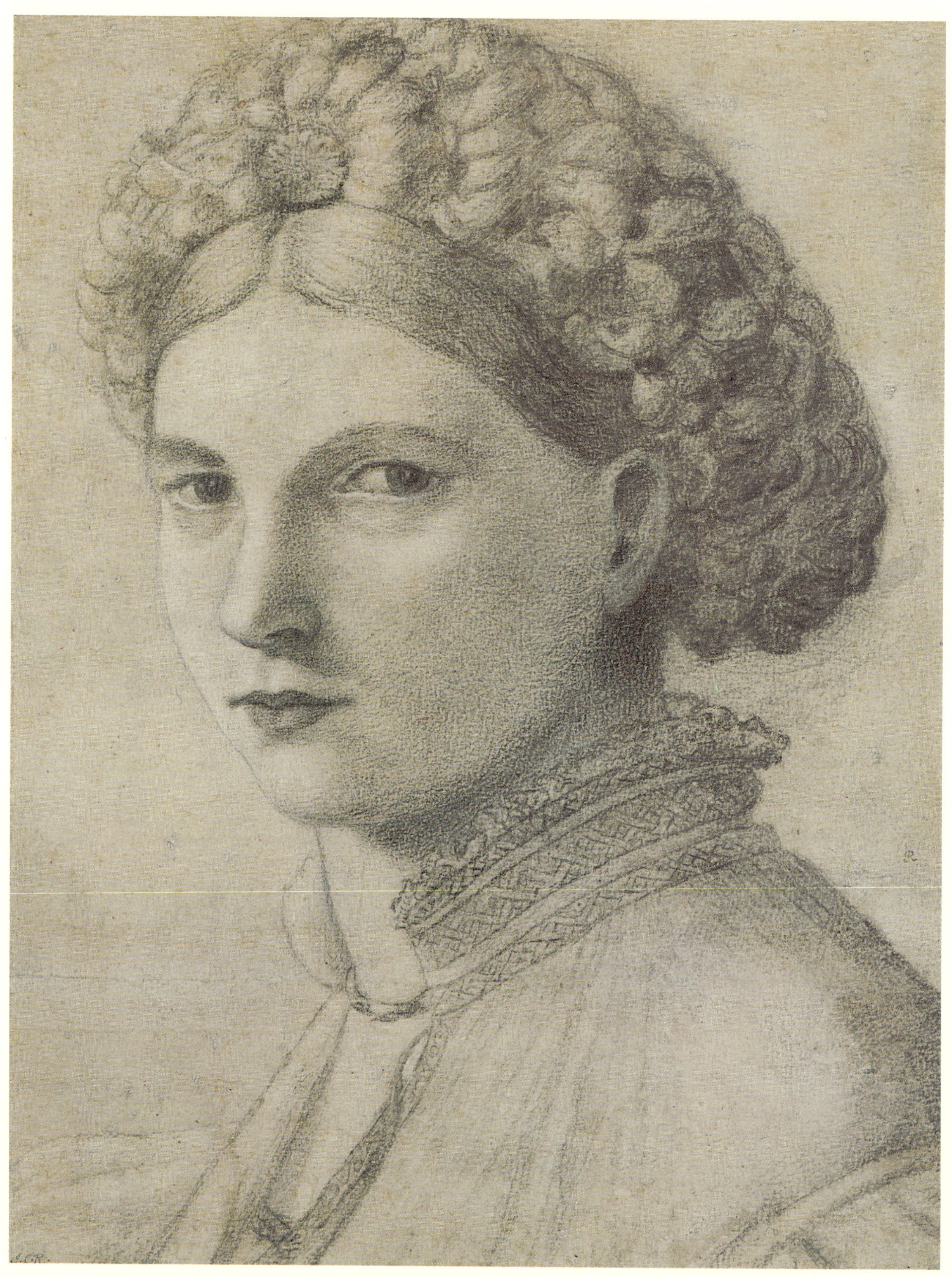

9 Andrea Previtali, *Portrait of a Young Lady, Bust Length*

PREFACE

AT a time when works of quality have become increasingly scarce on the art market, it is an unusual pleasure to present to the public a significant collection of Old Master drawings, only recently assembled by a single *amateur*. Duke Ferretti, a Canadian citizen but at home in many parts of the world, has been systematically collecting drawings for little more than ten years, yet during that time he has put together a collection remarkable for its representation and its high quality. As Dr. McTavish explains in his introduction, collecting is an instinct which the Duke has possessed since boyhood, but just in the last few years has he focussed that impulse on Old Master drawings from the sixteenth to eighteenth century of his homeland. Although Duke Ferretti, in his characteristically modest way, would be the first to admit that there are gaps in the collection, he has managed to acquire drawings by many of the most celebrated masters of the major Italian schools, and he has also succeeded – more significantly – in securing works of considerable historical importance and of great intrinsic beauty. Apart from the sheer pleasure that the contemplation of such intimate works of art affords, a substantial number of the drawings offer glimpses into the past and into other worlds; for many of these sheets are preparatory studies for major works of art in other media – works in some cases unexecuted or now lost. That a seemingly modest sheet of paper can be the nexus in a whole range of associations is clearly an abiding interest of the owner, and sometimes an informing principle in the acquisition of more pieces. In the end, however, it is the aesthetic quality that distinguishes this collection, by far the larger part of which is here shown to the public for the first time.

The Art Gallery of Ontario has been privileged to share this exhibition with The Pierpont Morgan Library in New York. Duke Ferretti has strong associations with both institutions. Since he began collecting Italian drawings, he has closely followed the exhibitions held in New York and the many publications of the Morgan Library, including their journal, *Master Drawings*. The staffs of the departments of drawings there and in Toronto have keenly enjoyed the study and connoisseurship of Italian drawings with the Duke.

We are grateful to David McTavish of Queen's University in Kingston for proposing the exhibition and, in consultation with the collector, for making the present selection of drawings from a much larger whole. In writing the catalogue he has had access to Duke Ferretti's own extensive research, which in turn has been aided by the contributions of many specialists in the field. Together they would like to acknowledge the generous assistance, of many sorts, of Noel Annesley, James Byam Shaw, Giulio Bora, Ileana Chiappini, Luigi Dania, Mimi Cazort, Diane DeGrazia, Ursula Fischer-Pace, Filippo Giochi, Catherine Monbeig Goguel, Luigi Grassi, John Gere, Rupert Hodge, Catherine Johnston, Chandler Kirwin, Denis Mahon, Charles McCordquodale, Jörg Martin Merz, Jennifer Montagu, Antonella Pampalone, Philip Pouncey, Simonetta Prosperi Valenti Rodini, Stella Rudolph Mellini, Giancarlo Sestieri, Julian Stock, Francis Russell, Nicholas Turner, Françoise Viatte, Mary Newcome Schleier and Eric Schleier.

At the Art Gallery of Ontario, the Curator of Prints and Drawings, Katharine Lochnan, and her assistant, Brenda Rix, have been responsible for overseeing the realization of the exhibition and its catalogue. Catherine Van Baren has edited the catalogue, which has been designed by Richard Male. The author would like to thank Mabel Burns for typing the manuscript and his wife Anndale for assistance throughout the entire undertaking. At the Morgan Library, Cara D. Denison, William W. Robinson, Felice Stampfle, and Priscilla Barker have been particularly helpful in planning the exhibition and the catalogue.

In Toronto we are delighted that Chubb Insurance Company of Canada has agreed to act as corporate sponsor of the exhibition and we should like to acknowledge our gratitude for their generous support.

Our greatest debt is of course to Duke Roberto Ferretti whose generosity and whose understanding and good-humoured patience have made him an exemplary lender.

Charles Ryskamp
Director, The Pierpont Morgan Library

William J. Withrow
Director, Art Gallery of Ontario

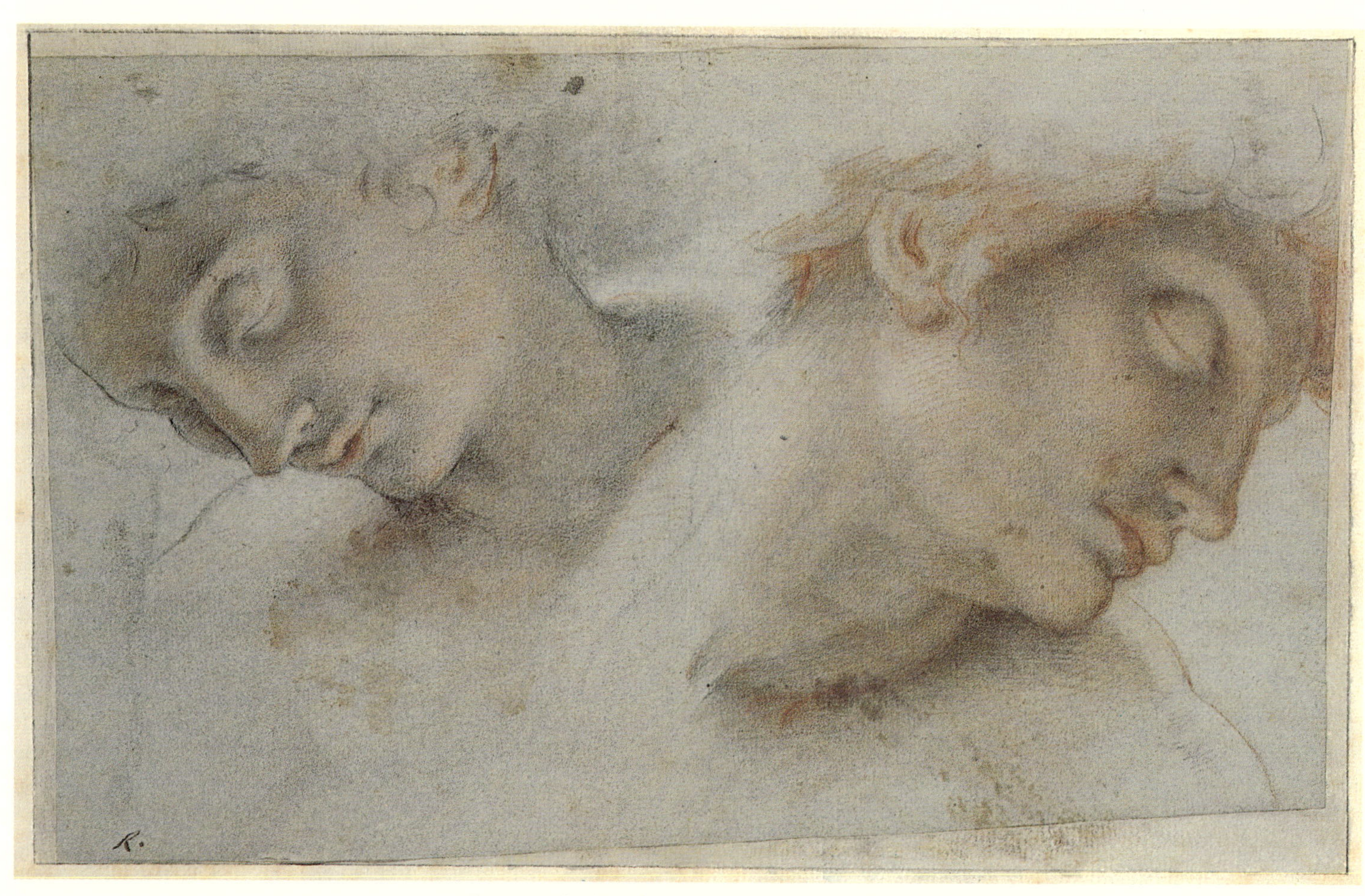

24 Pomarancio, *Two Studies of a Head with Eyes Closed*

IT is a great pleasure for me to be able to meet my friends' request and write a short foreword to this catalogue. First I wish to express my deepest gratitude to all those who have helped me with their valuable advice over the years. The world of Old Master drawings is a small one, and the relationship between experts, collectors, and dealers is far easier than is generally the case in the art world. Scholars are patient and forthcoming with their advice, and the newcomer, benefiting from their kindness, slowly improves his connoisseurship. On the other hand the collector may come across a drawing which is also of major interest to the expert; an ideal collaboration ensues at this point.

I would like to address a few words of advice to anyone who is interested in drawings but who has not yet started a serious collection: do not give any consideration at all to the written material that deals with Old Master drawings as a purely commercial venture, subject to periodical increases of value. Sometimes the collector comes across a drawing which gives him a sudden rush of feeling, as if the spark of genius that was present at its moment of creation still exists today, a spark that continues to reveal the exceptional skill and power of the artist. This is the drawing that he will be happy to acquire and study, and that he will always cherish. No other reason for collecting drawings is equally important.

In recent times I have given in to temptation and bought some high priced sheets. Nevertheless the main part of my collection consists of drawings purchased slowly and reasonably, and these drawings are equally dear to me. Even today, in my opinion, a good and interesting collection can be formed at a not impossible price.

Public and private collections sometimes overlook certain periods and schools, and research is more difficult in such areas. There is much to be explored for those who will have the privilege to find what is still undiscovered. Since much of the world of Old Master drawings is still dimly lit, the collector may be rewarded by an unexpected and thrilling discovery. Even if such an event is rare, the pleasant possibility of a lucky find is always there.

In addition to the preceding considerations, collecting Old Master drawings is a highly stimulating activity with its own intrinsic rewards. Foremost is the consequent training of the mind, since a profound and detailed knowledge is required in even the minor branches of art history. And the newcomer will be forced to brush up on long-forgotten knowledge of such various subjects as mythology, ancient history, holy scripture, literature, heraldry, chronicles, and the study of emblems.

From time to time, just to be able to unravel a difficult subject gives great enjoyment and leads to the right attribution of a drawing. But how can one describe the overwhelming pleasure reserved for the collector who has succeeded in establishing a link between a drawing and a finished work of art? In some cases the discovery rewards a patient research, one which often originates in passionate discussion. In others, it is just the result of chance. In both cases the fortunate collector will be overjoyed and ready to continue devoting many more hours to the study of other drawings.

I would like to end my foreword by wishing that this exhibition of my beloved drawings, besides bringing to the public some unpublished sheets and much new research, will encourage visitors to deepen their interest in Old Master drawings. Should this happen, I will be very happy indeed; even more so will be my friends, who have organized the show with such great skill and competent care, and who deserve much praise and gratitude.

Roberto Ferretti di Castelferretto

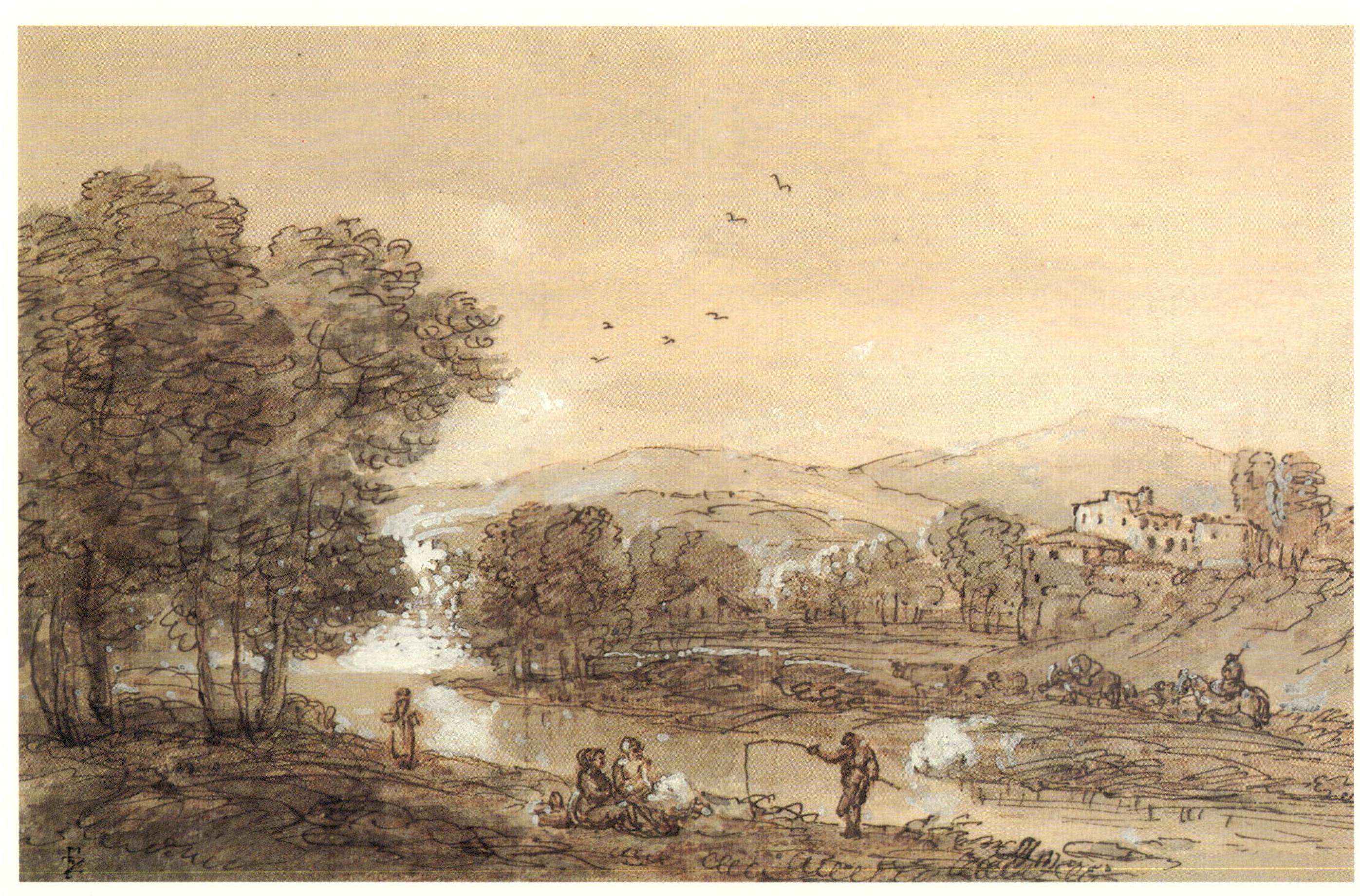

64 Francesco Zuccarelli, *A River Landscape with Fisherfolk and Drovers, a Farm on a Bluff Beyond*

INTRODUCTION

THE drawings in this exhibition have almost all been collected by Duke Roberto Ferretti within the last ten years, yet they reflect the interests of a lifetime. Duke Ferretti has acquired the majority of the drawings in the London salerooms where he normally bids for himself, sitting near the front so as not to be unduly influenced by the activities of the other participants. The decisions are his own, and if he seeks advice he usually does so after a drawing has been acquired, not before. It is natural, then, that to some extent the collection reflects the vagaries of the recent art market; none the less, to an impressive degree Duke Ferretti has succeeded in finding outstanding examples of the work of the artists who interest him most. Understandably, these are Italian artists, or artists who have worked principally in Italy, from the Renaissance onwards. There are no sheets from the Quattrocento or from periods previous to it in the collection, but there are some good nineteenth-century Italian drawings, although they have not been included on the present occasion. In fact the exhibition accurately represents the strengths of the collection: it begins with the school of Raphael at approximately 1520 and extends to the collapse of the old order during the Napoleonic occupation of Italy at the end of the eighteenth century.

Roberto Ferretti grew up in an environment rich with historical and cultural connections. Both his parents were amateur painters, and winters spent in Milan and summers in Ancona brought him into daily contact with a wide range of contemporary cultural activities and with a seemingly inexhaustible fund of historical associations. In Ancona the historical dimension loomed especially large: it was both immediate and extremely personal. There, in the beautiful city overlooking the Adriatic Sea was the family's sixteenth-century *palazzo*, and there too was a heritage of family accomplishments dating back to the later Middle Ages. Over the centuries the Ferretti family had contributed substantially not only to the political and economic life of the community, but also to its cultural and spiritual life. One member of the family, the Franciscan Gabriele Ferretti, had in 1489 been declared venerable by Pope Innocent VIII, and Carlo Crivelli's full-length portrait of the Beato Gabriele Ferretti in ecstasy, which for centuries was in the church of San Francesco in Alto, Ancona, now hangs in the National Gallery, London. The portrait of another monk, the Dominican Angelo Ferretti, was painted in the guise of St. Peter Martyr by Lorenzo Lotto. Done in 1549, immediately after Lotto had moved to the Marches—where he remained for the rest of his life—the portrait is sometimes identified with one in the Fogg Art Museum at Harvard, but more likely the picture is now lost.

Only a few years later, Pellegrino Tibaldi executed frescoes in the recently completed palace, built for another and more public Angelo Ferretti (1506-1574), an extremely successful businessman, who late in his life contributed a galley to the fleet that defeated the Turks at Lepanto. Until recently it had been widely held that Tibaldi was also responsible for the design of the palace, but it is much more probable that the papal architect, Antonio da Sangallo the Younger, was instead involved. Certainly Sangallo executed plans for a villa commissioned by the same Angelo Ferretti, and built just outside Ancona, but today largely destroyed. The palace, as one of the city's most commodious edifices, was home to Charles Borromeo when from 1561-65 he was governor of Ancona, and even today there is one room which is usually called the *Camera di San Carlo*. In the eighteenth century the palace underwent major renovations and additions, no doubt under the supervision of Luigi Vanvitelli. A newly discovered drawing for such renovations is included in the exhibition (see no. 61).

Roberto Ferretti responds to this heritage with pride and benevolent detachment, and treats it not as a burden but frequently as an intellectual challenge. Even as a youth he began to doubt that Pellegrino Tibaldi was the architect of his family's *palazzo*, and more recently he has been responsible for systematically organizing the vast Ferretti archives. At an early age he acquired the means, such as the mastery of languages, to deal with history and related matters as vital, almost palpable forces. During the war years membership in the Noble Guard at the Vatican and legal studies at the University of Florence offered new experiences, as did, during the ensuing years, business interests in many parts of the world.

These concerns enriched but did not supplant his earlier curiosity about history and the visual arts: everything was retained and exercised in an accurate memory. Shortly after the war, Roberto Ferretti met Bernard Berenson; and when the great connoisseur asked him if on his next trip to Ancona he would transcribe the poignant epitaph in Ancona cathedral of Beato Giannelli—the devoted monk who, rather than see his demented brother put in chains, lived with him for years alone in a cave on Monte Cornero— Ferretti had no need of going to the cathedral, but could quote the inscription on the spot.[1]

Members of his immediate family were not active collectors, but even at age ten Roberto Ferretti was purchasing antiquarian books, at prices which now seem preposterously low. Later he began to buy old furniture and on trips abroad with his wife to acquire fine pieces of oriental porcelain. Although he inherited one important drawing, a sheet of St. Anthony by Guercino (not in the exhibition), the collection of drawings began in fact under casual circumstances. Possessing some small, but very attractive, antique frames, Duke Ferretti decided to buy some drawings to hang in them. One of the sheets turned out to be by the eighteenth-century Bolognese artist, Donato Creti. It was not long before the London auction houses were casting an irresistible spell over the incipient collector, and he was organizing his business interests, which now extended to Canada, in such a way as to allow regular attendance at the sales of Old Master drawings in the early summer and late autumn. At first he acquired drawings from several schools, including some Flemish and French sheets and a small sketchbook by George Romney, but soon the Italian school, about which he was already well informed, began to receive almost exclusive attention.

If the nature of a collection can be said to reveal something about the personality of its owner, the present selection would suggest an abiding interest in people. The human figure predominates, often idealized to some extent and often involved in some extraordinary event; but if the drawings exhibit such features, in doing so, they also reiterate the primary concerns of Italian art in general. One of the remarkable aspects of the collection is the number of arresting studies of heads, beginning with the restrained examples by Sogliani (no. 1) and Previtali (no. 9), continuing with the colouristic interests of Barocci (no. 23) and Pomarancio (no. 24), and the refined sensibility of Reni (no. 28) and Cortona (no. 32), and ending with the sympathetic naturalism of the head of an old man by Sebastiano Ricci (no. 56) and the alert glance of the youth by Giovanni Battista Tiepolo (no. 59). A number of other drawings are distinguished by their direct connections with significant structures of a larger nature, such as the Palazzo del Te in Mantua (no. 3) and the church of San Sigismondo in Cremona (no. 8), or the Palazzo Farnese (no. 11) and the churches of Trinità dei Monti (no. 20) and San Giovanni in Laterano (no. 24) in Rome, or the Palazzo Pamphili at Valmontone (no. 45) just outside Rome, and the Schloss at Veitshöchheim (no. 62) outside Würzburg. There is also a small but harmonious group of landscapes (nos. 47, 53, 54, 64, 65), where, however, the human element is never far away. It is perhaps revealing that among the landscape artists, two were non-Italian (Claude: no. 47, and Van Wittel: nos. 53-54), though they made Italian landscape their principal subject, and indeed helped to define that landscape for the artistic imagination. Altogether, then, the collection is characterized by its human content, and by its associations of personalities and places— enhanced throughout by high quality which, while it should not be taken for granted, speaks eloquently for itself and requires no special explanation here.

David McTavish
Guest Curator and Associate Professor of Art History,
Queen's University, Kingston

---

[1] The inscription reads:
SOLUS IN OCCULTIS DEGENS HYERONIMUS ANTRIS
  HIC RECUBO MONTIS ACCOLA CHYMERICI
UNDE MARE ET TERRAS TENEBROSAQUE AERA CERNO
  ET VIDEO COELUM–QUOD COLO–SYDEREUM

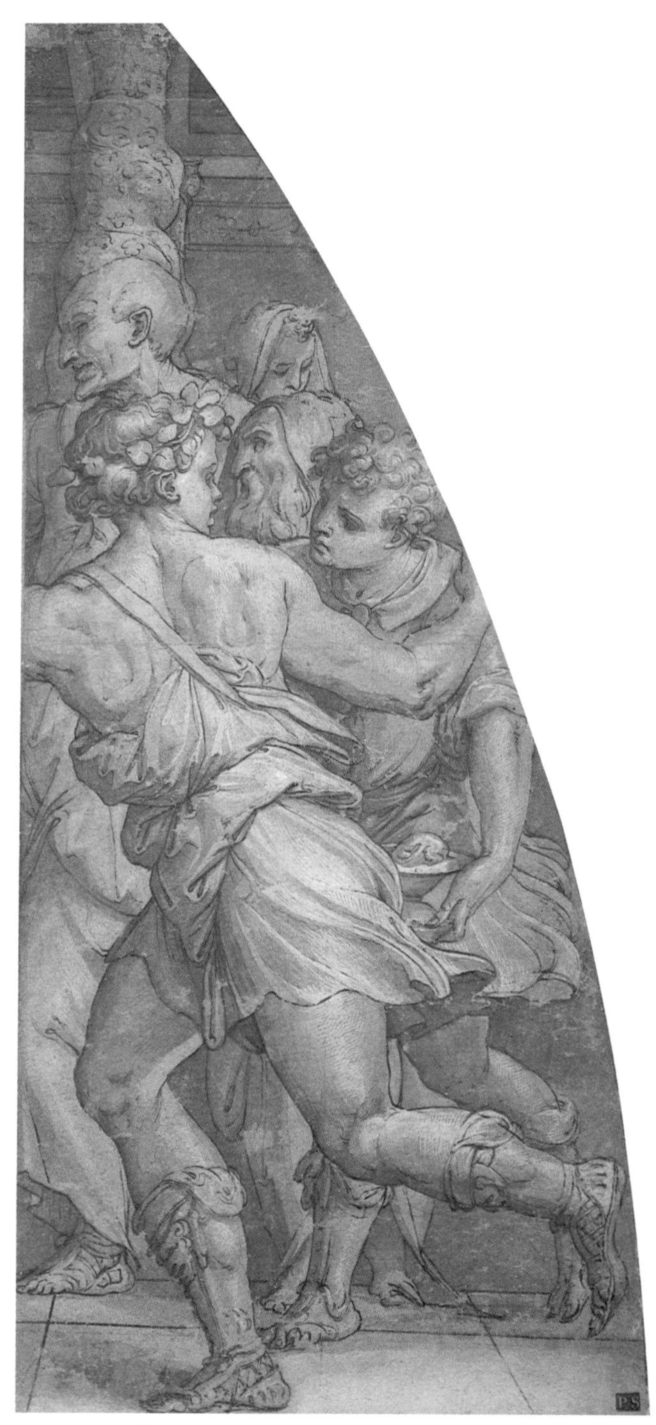

13 Giorgio Vasari, *A Running Youth*

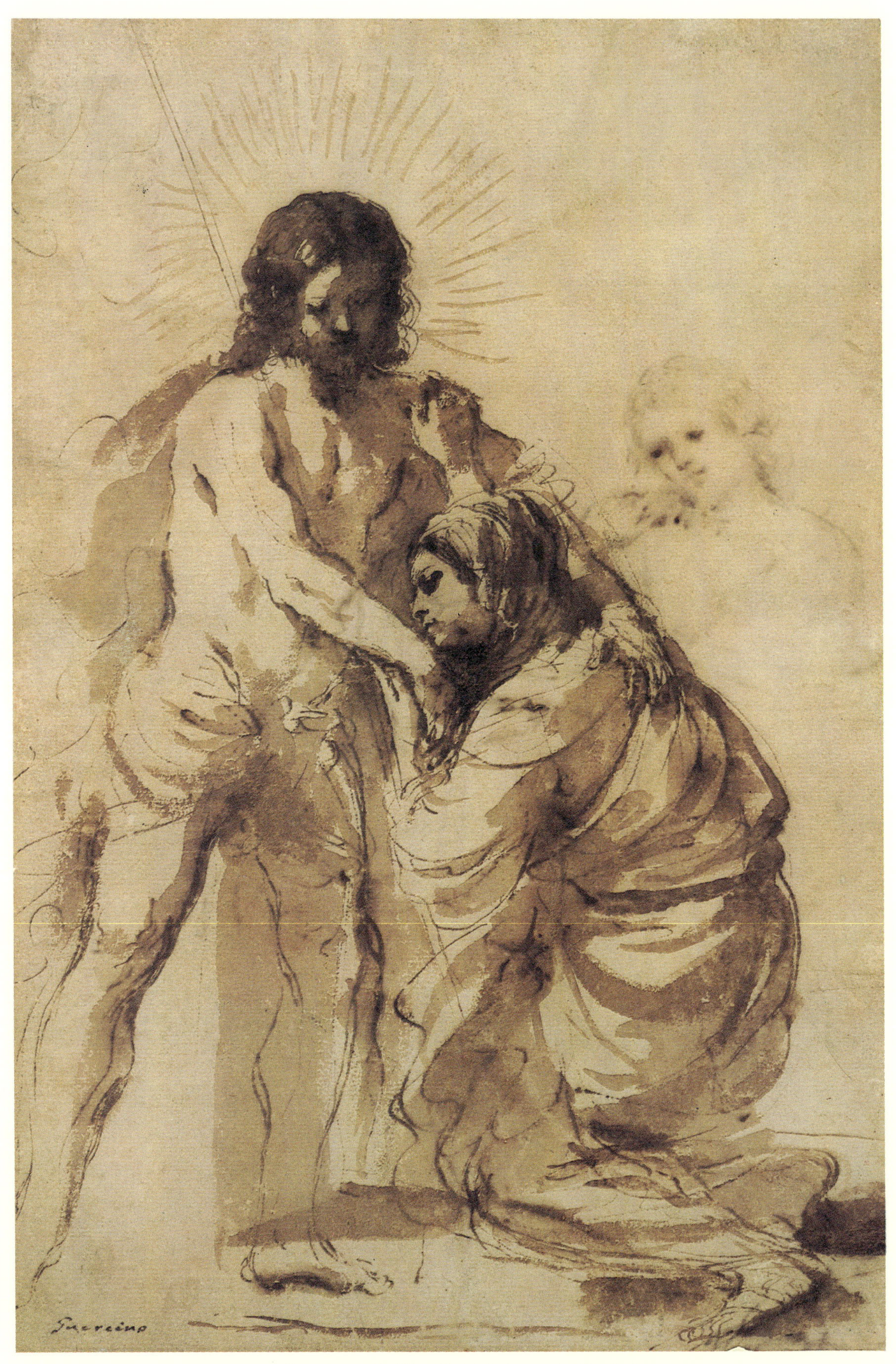

29 Guercino, *The Risen Christ Appearing to His Mother*

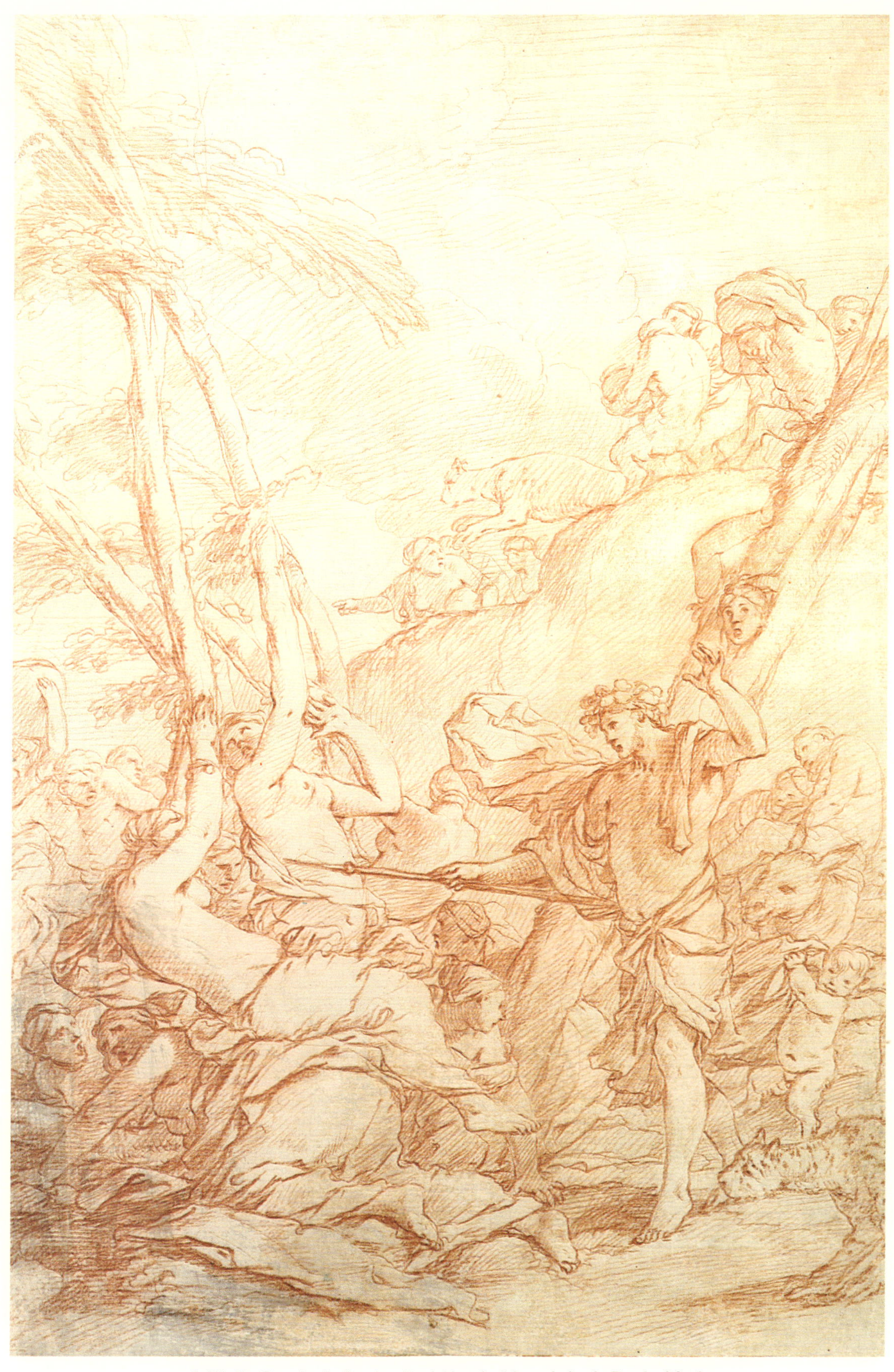

48 Giulio Carpioni, *Bacchus Punishing the Maenads for the Death of Orpheus*

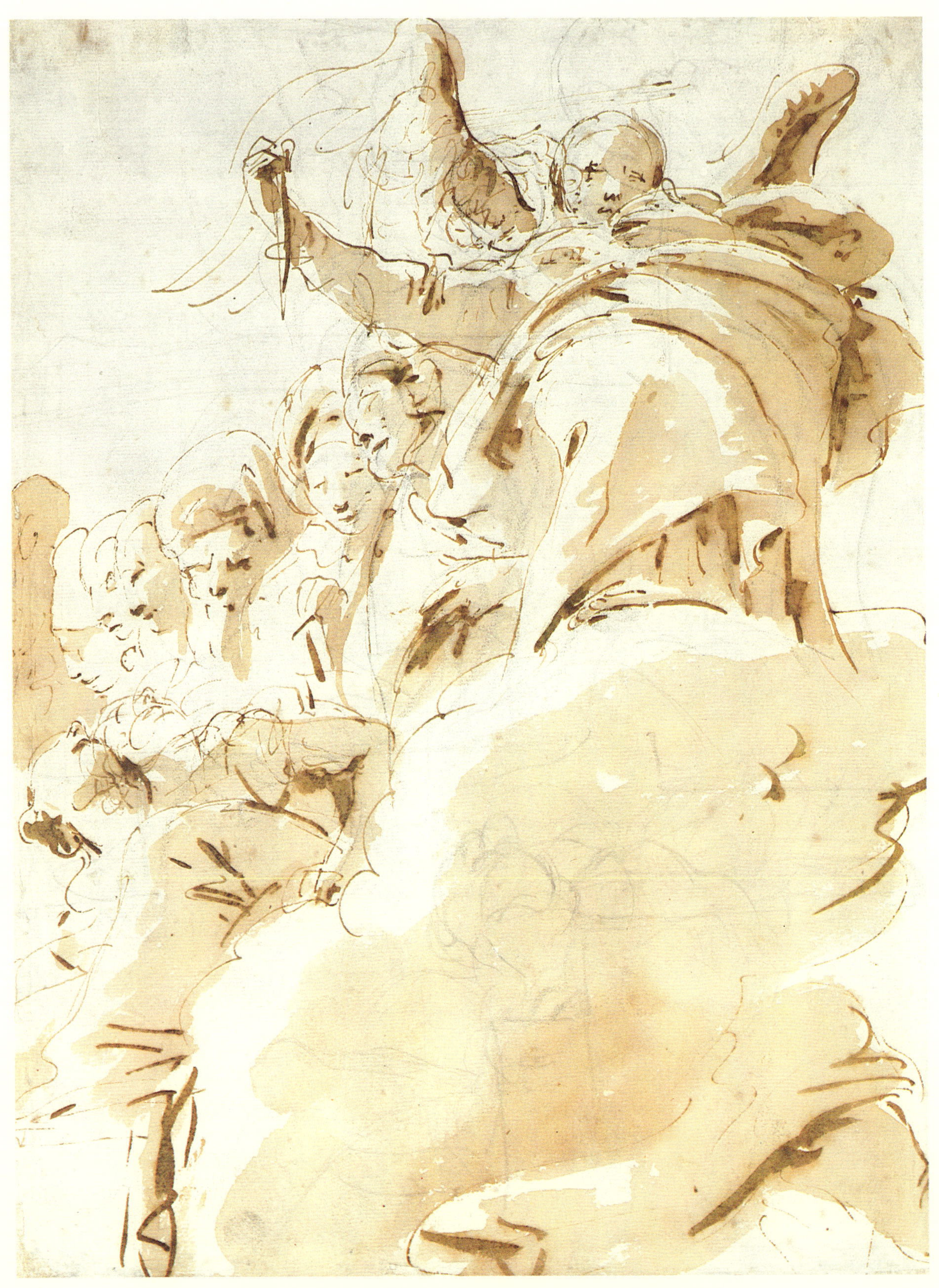

57 Giovanni Battista Tiepolo, *A Winged Deity and Other Figures on Clouds*

CATALOGUE

Giovanni Antonio Sogliani

Florence 1492 – 1544 Florence

1 *Study of the Head of a Young Woman
in Profile to the Right*

Black chalk on brownish paper. 205 x 164 mm

Literature: B. Berenson, *The Drawings of the Florentine Painters,*
New York, 1903, no. 2736 (and later editions).

Provenance: Earl of Warwick (Lugt 2600); Christie's, London,
20 May 1896, lot 18 (as Fra Bartolommeo); Sir J.C. Robinson
(Lugt 1433); Sir Herbert Cook; Christie's, London, 11 December 1979, lot 31.

Although sold at auction in 1896 with an attribution to Fra
Bartolommeo, in 1903 the drawing was published by Berenson
as the work of Sogliani. Recently the head has been tentatively
connected with the flying angel in the upper left of Sogliani's
altarpiece, the *Disputà on the Immaculate Conception,* Florence
(fig. 1a).[1] While the features of the angel are more pointed in
the painting, the general facial type, the inclination of the head,
and the fall of light are similar.

The *Disputà on the Immaculate Conception* no doubt dates from
the 1520s.[2] According to Vasari, the altarpiece was commissioned by Giovanni Serristori who died before its completion.
Serristori's heir, Alamanno di Iacopo Salviati, took over the
commission and gave the finished painting to the monastic
church of San Luca, where it was placed on the high altar.[3] The
lower part of the altarpiece shows the recumbent figure of Adam
and six standing saints who hold scrolls and books with inscriptions referring to the Immaculate Conception; above, in clouds,
God the Father presents the Immacolata, surrounded by
angels. Vasari claims that the altarpiece's numerous heads are
wonderful, the best that Sogliani ever painted.[4]

Berenson lists numerous drawings for the altarpiece, executed either in metalpoint or in Sogliani's favourite black
chalk.[5]

On the *verso* of the present sheet there is visible through the
backing a study of a draped right arm holding a small book.

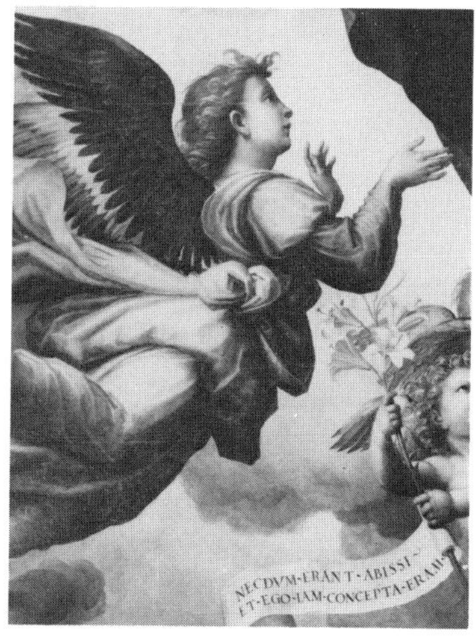

fig. 1a G.A. Sogliani, *Disputà on the Immaculate
Conception* (detail), oil on canvas, on deposit
Accademia, Florence.

1 *Important Italian and French Drawings,* Christie's, London, 11 December 1979,
lot 31.

2 B. Degenhart in Thieme-Becker, XXXI, 1937, p. 213; W. and E. Paatz,
Die Kirchen von Florenz, Frankfurt, 1940, I, pp. 400, 404; II, 1941, pp. 598-99.

3 Vasari, V, pp. 130-1. In 1734 the painting was transferred to the church of San
Bonifazio, then about 1870 to the Galleria of the Arcispedale di Santa Maria
Nuova. In 1900 the picture passed to the Uffizi and is now on deposit in the
Accademia *(Gli Uffizi: Catalogo Generale,* Florence, 1979, P 1614).

4 *Ibid.*, p. 130: *"un numero infinito di figure, dove sono alcune teste miracolose e le
migliori che facesse mai.''*

5 B. Berenson, *The Drawings of the Florentine Painters,* Chicago and London, 1938:
nos. 2539, 2540, 2564[B], 2598, 2620, 2621, 2639, 2648, 2656, 2667, 2669, 2704
(all in the Uffizi), and 2743 (Christ Church, Oxford).

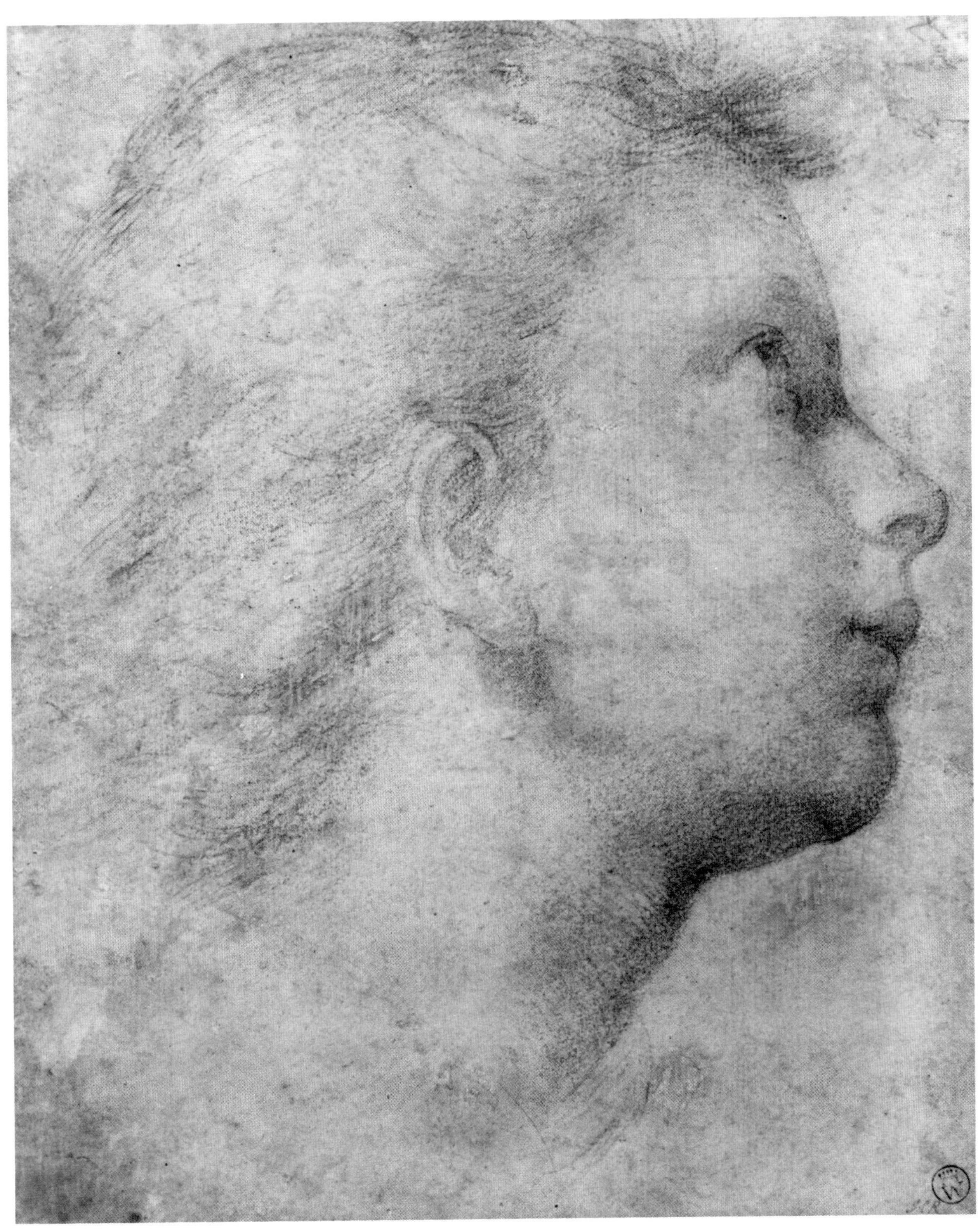

Polidoro Caldara
called Polidoro da Caravaggio

Caravaggio 1490/1500 – 1543? Messina

2 *A Cavalry Battle*

Red chalk. Some slight stains. 202 x 284 mm. Inscribed in red chalk on the *verso: d'mà Prop[?] d'Raffael. d Vr^no* and *C.*[3]

Provenance: Christie's, London, 13 December 1984, lot 33.

This recently discovered drawing has not been connected with any known work by Polidoro. It represents a subject frequently undertaken by Renaissance artists – pre-eminently by Leonardo da Vinci in his *Battle of Anghiari* in Florence, but also by artists in Rome, where numerous classical reliefs of similar subjects provided abundant inspiration. Polidoro, who was trained by Raphael, would have known such depictions of rearing horses, twisting riders, and fallen foot soldiers, as the *Battle of Constantine,* executed by Raphael's pupils Giulio Romano and Giovanni Francesco Penni in the Sala di Costantino of the Vatican between 1520 and 1524. He may also have known an earlier drawing by Raphael himself at Chatsworth of a cavalry encounter executed for an unidentified commission, and recently published by John Gere.[1] That Polidoro was interested in antique representations of equestrian subjects is suggested by a red chalk drawing in Berlin which is generally attributed to the artist and is after a damaged classical relief of a rearing horse and rider.[2]

The subject of the present sheet would be appropriate for a façade fresco, a popular type of sixteenth-century painting. In Rome this type of painting usually simulated classical relief sculpture, and Polidoro's façade frescoes rank among the out-standing examples of the genre. The majority of Polidoro's façade frescoes are now lost, but an anonymous drawing in Turin, after a façade evidently by Polidoro in the Piazzo dei Caprettari, Rome, shows a similar, if more planar, battle scene.[3] It is one of the perplexing aspects of Polidoro's *oeuvre,* that although a considerable number of his drawings survive, very few can be directly related to his known façade frescoes. Thus the exact nature of the preparatory drawings for Polidoro's most celebrated paintings cannot be securely documented.

While the subject may be fitting for a façade decoration, other aspects of the drawing are perhaps less suitable. In particular, the drawing's extremely pictorial appearance – cast shadows on the ground and sun-drenched surfaces which all but obliterate contours – seems ill-suited to translation into mono-chromatic fresco intended to simulate relief sculpture. Yet such draughtsmanship, with extensive areas of vigorous diagonal hatching, was employed in part by Polidoro even in anatomical studies,[4] and he may well have used it in preparatory studies for façade frescoes too. Where line is more conspicuous, as in the mane of the horse to the left of centre, it is supple and expressive.

The chronology of Polidoro's drawings is vexed by the scarcity of securely documented examples. Although the present sheet has been said to be among Polidoro's earliest,[5] the masterful assurance of the draughtsmanship may well argue for a considerably later date.

1 No. 57; J.A. Gere, *Il Manierismo a Roma, I Disegni dei Maestri,* Milan, 1971, pl. 1, p. 81, who suggests that the drawing may be an early idea for the *Battle of Constantine.*

2 Kupferstichkabinett, Staatliche Museen, no. 20723; A. Marabottini, *Polidoro da Caravaggio,* Rome, 1969, I, p. 343, no. 184, II, pl. CXXI, 1; and Gere, *op.cit.,* p. 66, no. 9, p. 88.

3 Biblioteca Reale, no. 15841; Marabottini, *op.cit.,* I, p. 356, no. 9, II, pl. CXXX. Vasari, V, p. 145: *"alla piazza della Dogana allato a S. Eustachio una facciata di battaglie."*

4 Eg. in the subsidiary areas of red chalk studies of a male torso and left arm in the British Museum: P. Pouncey and J.A. Gere, *Italian Drawings…in the British Museum, Raphael and his Circle,* London, 1962, pp. 120-21, nos. 208-9, pls. 176-77.

5 *Important Old Master Drawings,* Christie's, London, 13 December 1984, lot 33.

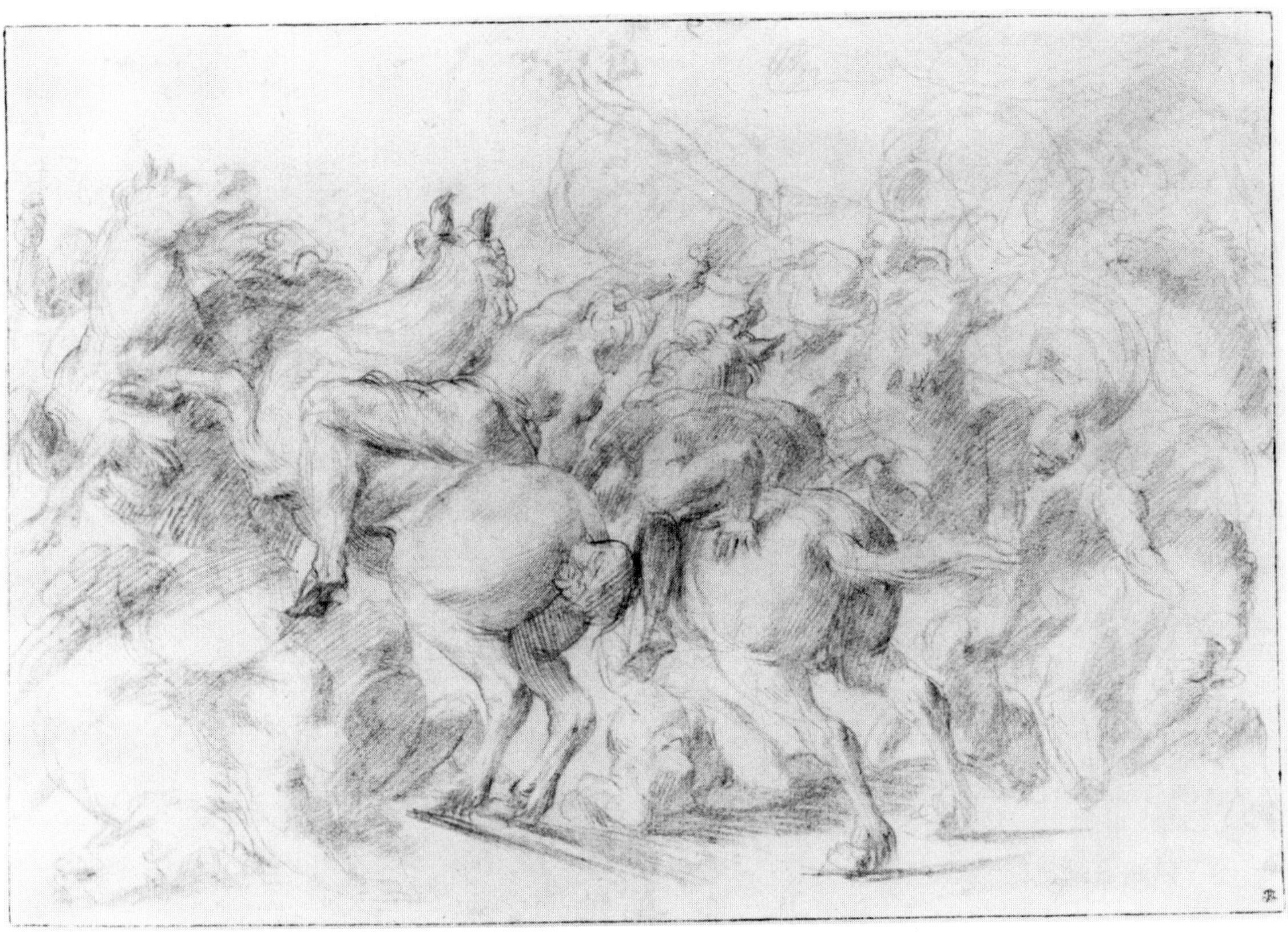

Giulio Pippi
called Giulio Romano

Rome ca. 1499 – 1546 Mantua

3 *Victory, Janus, Chronos and Gaea*

Pen and brown ink and wash over black chalk, in part squared in black chalk. A triangular area at the middle right made up. 370 x 313 mm. Inscribed in brown ink on the *verso: fⁿ. 34 Nᵒ 30/di Giulio Romano – /buon disegno*

Literature: F. Hartt, *Giulio Romano,* New Haven, 1958, I, pp. 159, 299, no. 210, II, fig. 349; E. Verheyen, *The Palazzo del Te in Mantua: Images of Love and Politics,* Baltimore and London, 1977, p. 128.

Provenance: Sir Peter Lely (Lugt. 2092); Dr. Mead (according to an inscription on the backing: *'from Dr. Meads Collⁿ'*), John Barnard (Lugt. 1420; his inscription *No. 570/14¾x12½'*); Sir Joshua Reynolds (Lugt. 2364); Weimar, Grand-Ducal Collection, until 1918; continental collector; Christie's London, 7 April 1981, lot 48.

Apart from a small number of figure studies in chalk, the numerous surviving drawings by Giulio Romano are of two distinct types: quick exploratory sketches in pen and ink (and occasionally slight wash), and carefully finished studies in pen and ink and ample wash. The present drawing falls into the latter category and has been identified by Frederick Hartt as a *modello* for the frescoed vault of the Sala dei Giganti in the Palazzo del Te, Mantua (fig. 3a).[1] Hartt lists two other drawings for the vault: a rapid drawing of Jupiter hurling the thunderbolt, formerly in the Ellesmere Collection and now in a private collection; and a large *modello* in the Louvre of Diana, Neptune, Minerva and other gods.[2] A fourth drawing, a study of one of the giants crushed under boulders for the west wall of the room, was identified by Samuel Woodburn in the Lawrence Gallery; it was sold at auction with drawings from the Ellesmere Collection in 1972 and is now in a private Swiss collection.[3]

The continuous walls and vaulted ceiling of the Sala dei Giganti, situated at one corner of the Palazzo del Te, represent the Fall of the Giants, described by Ovid in the first book of the *Metamorphoses*. The execution of the frescoes commenced in 1532, but was still not finished in 1534, the last year in which Giulio's participation in the decoration of the Palazzo del Te is documented. Vasari declared that no one was ever likely to see a painted work more horrible and frightful or more natural than this room; and Gregorio Comanini, writing at the end of the century, asserted that the Sala dei Giganti was the main reason why so many foreigners visited Mantua.[4]

Although the room was designed by Giulio Romano, the execution of the frescoes was principally entrusted to Rinaldo Mantovano, using the master's elaborate drawings.[5] The only significant difference between the present drawing and the finished fresco is that in the fresco the figure of Victory has been moved to the right, above the head of Chronos. No doubt the area at the left of the drawing was left blank because it directly corresponded to the already finished right-hand part of the large drawing now in the Louvre.

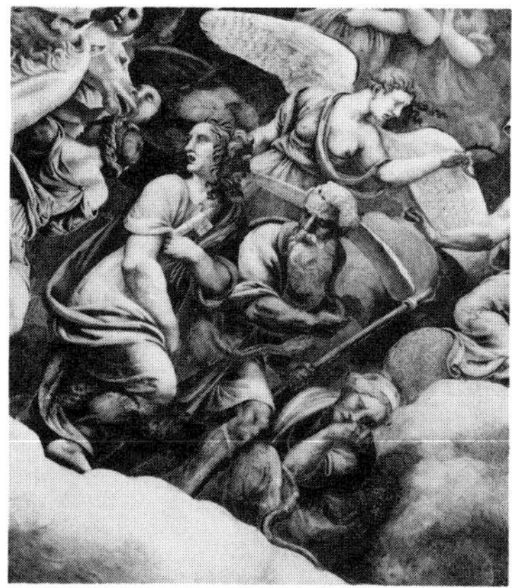

fig. 3a Giulio Romano, detail of vault of the Sala dei Giganti, fresco, Palazzo del Te, Mantua.

1 Hartt, *op. cit.*

2 *Ibid.,* pp. 159, 299, nos. 208, 209, figs. 350, 348. For the drawing in the Louvre, also see *Autour de Raphael,* catalogue by R. Bacou, Cabinet des Dessins, Musée du Louvre, Paris, 1983, pp. 53-4, no. 57, repr.

3 Sotheby's, London, 5 December 1972, lot 43 (repr.); and E. Verheyen, *The Palazzo del Te in Mantua: Images of Love and Politics,* Baltimore and London, 1977, p. 128, fig. 76. What appears to be a copy is at Windsor: A.E. Popham and J. Wilde, *The Italian Drawings of the XV and XVI Centuries...at Windsor Castle,* London, 1949, p. 237, no. 363; exhibited as autograph in *Splendours of the Gonzaga,* Victoria and Albert Museum, London, 1981, p. 189, no. 167, pl. 88a.

4 Vasari, V, p. 543: *"Onde non si pensi alcuno vedere mai opera di pennello piú orribile e spaventosa, né piú naturale di questa;"* Il Figino ovvero del fine della pittura, Mantua, 1591, p. 25; cited in E. Verheyen, *op cit.,* p. 54.

5 Vasari, V, p. 544. Documentary evidence shows that Rinaldo was assisted by Fermo da Caravaggio and Luca da Faenza (Il Figurino): Verheyen, *op. cit.,* docs. no. 66, 77, and 95.

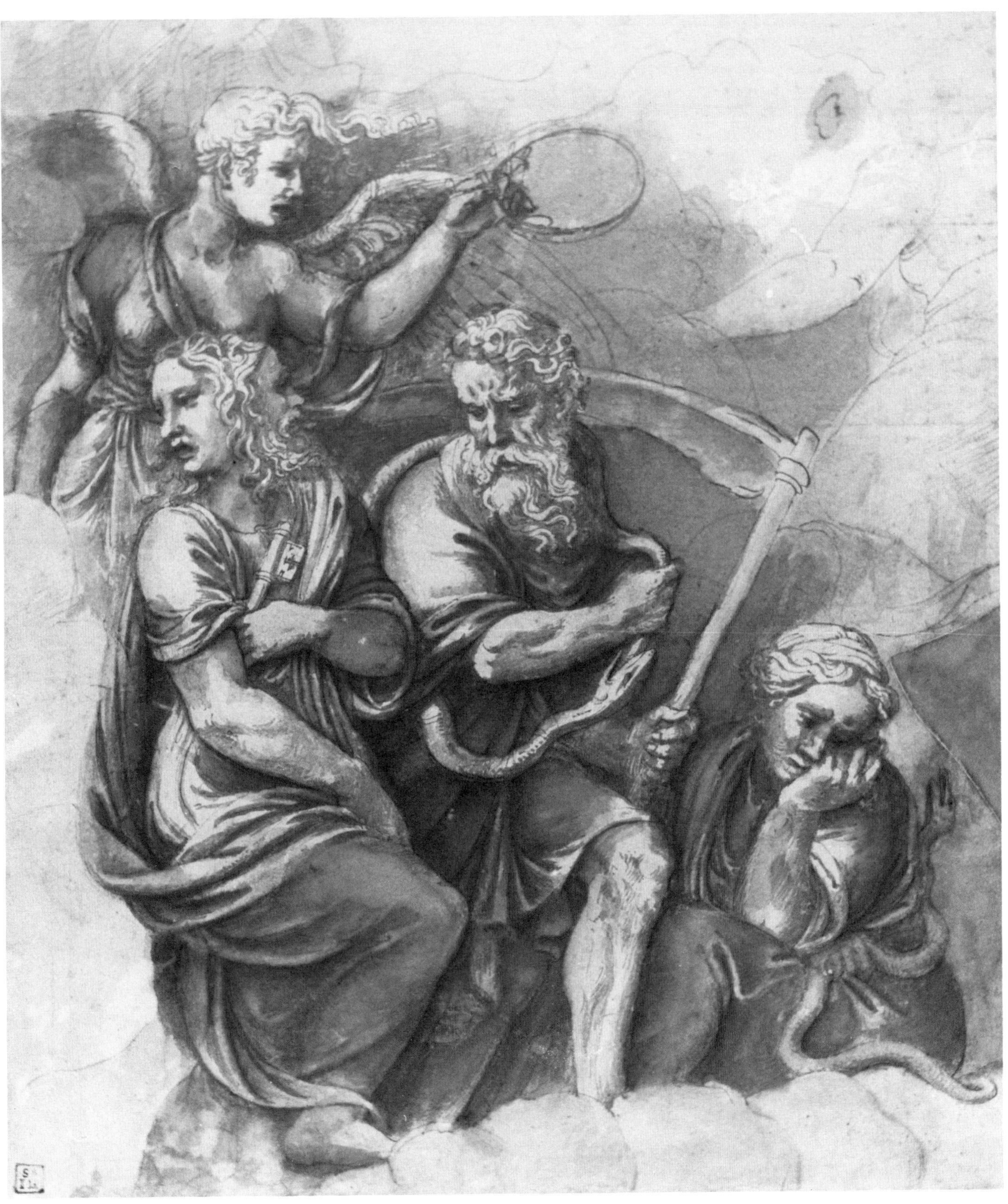

Girolamo Francesco Maria Mazzola
called Parmigianino

Parma 1503 – 1540 Casalmaggiore

4   *The Adoration of the Shepherds (recto);*
    Group of Putti Playing (verso)

Black chalk with white heightening *(recto)*; red chalk, in places over stylus; head at right pricked for transfer and a corresponding area on the reverse rubbed with black chalk. Repairs along top and bottom edges. 230 x 163 mm

Exhibited: D. DeGrazia, *Correggio and His Legacy: Sixteenth-Century Emilian Drawings,* National Gallery of Art, Washington 1984, pp. 150-1, no. 40.

Provenance: Timothy Clifford; Christie's, London, 8 July 1975, lot 10; Baron Hatvany; Christie's, London, 24 June 1980, lot 11.

This drawing has been generally dated to ca. 1522-24, that is, toward the end of Parmigianino's first period in Parma, before he moved to Rome in 1524. While it is difficult to be absolutely certain with drawings, it seems that the study on the present *recto* was executed before the *verso,* otherwise Parmigianino would have begun a new drawing on a side, the *recto,* already marred by the blackening at the upper left. This blackening was applied in order to transfer the image of the single putto's head on the other side of the sheet. This head has also been pricked for transfer. The drawing has been cropped at the bottom (of the *recto*) and probably at the right.

The drawing on the *recto* shows Mary, at least two child angels, a shepherd with a staff, and two bearded men, one of whom is no doubt Joseph (with his head propped on his clenched hand), in a high beamed room through which a heavenly light descends. No known painting by Parmigianino relates to this composition, although at least two pictures from early in his career feature the Holy Family in the company of child angels.[1] Some years later Parmigianino repeated the rudi-

ments of the composition in a more finished drawing of the *Nativity* (at Chatsworth), which was subsequently engraved, perhaps by Fagiuoli.[2]

The drawings on the *verso* have been associated with Parmigianino's fresco decorations in the Rocca at Fontanellato, near Parma.[3] Executed about 1522-24, the frescoes in the extant *stufetta* show scenes from the story of Diana and Actaeon in the lunettes and playful putti and foliage in the spandrels of the vault. A drawing in The Pierpont Morgan Library reveals that at one stage Parmigianino considered placing the scenes of Diana and Actaeon in the spandrels.[4] It has also been proposed that putti were then to appear in the lunettes, and that the group of putti in the present drawing was destined for such a location.[5] There is, however, no conclusive proof that Parmigianino intended putti for the lunettes, nor is the present group of putti well suited for translation into the shape of either a lunette or a spandrel. More persuasive, then, is Diane DeGrazia's recent proposal that the drawing should be connected with a double-sided sheet at Berlin which includes horizontal bands of putti and Diana and Actaeon on the *recto* and Europa and the bull on the *verso.*[6] Popham hypothesized that the Berlin drawing was undertaken for decorations in another room at Fontanellato, where the paintings would appear in a frieze around the walls, instead of on the ceiling.[7]

The single, more fully realized head of a putto at the right of the sheet does, however, provide closer ties with the frescoes at Fontanellato as executed; it resembles the putto in the spandrel to the right of the scenes with a nymph pursued by hunters. This head seems to be repeated, in summary form in pen and ink, in a sheet of quick sketches by Parmigianino (in Ottawa).[8]

---

1 Courtauld Institute Galleries, London (ex Seilern collection) and the Prado. It is worth noting that Correggio's drawing at Cambridge, usually associated with *La Notte,* also represents the *Adoration of the Shepherds* with small angels present at the manger. Although the altarpiece is usually dated to the late 1520s, the contract was drawn up on 14 October 1522, and the drawing may be from approximately that time (A.E. Popham, *Correggio's Drawings,* London, 1957, pp. 79-81, 163-64, no. 72, pl. LXXXVI.)

2 A.E. Popham, *Catalogue of the Drawings of Parmigianino,* New Haven and London, 1971, I, p. 212, no. 732, III, pl. 243.

3 Christie's sales catalogues, 8 July 1975, lot 10 and 24 June 1980, lot 11.

4 Popham, *op.cit.,* I, p. 123, no. 313, II, pl. 31.

5 Christie's sales catalogues, see note 3.

6 *Correggio and His Legacy: Sixteenth-Century Emilian Drawings,* National Gallery of Art, Washington, 1984, p. 150.

7 Popham, *op.cit.,* I, p. 47, no. 12, II, pl. 30.

8 Popham, *op.cit.,* I, p. 127, no. 328, II, pl. 13.

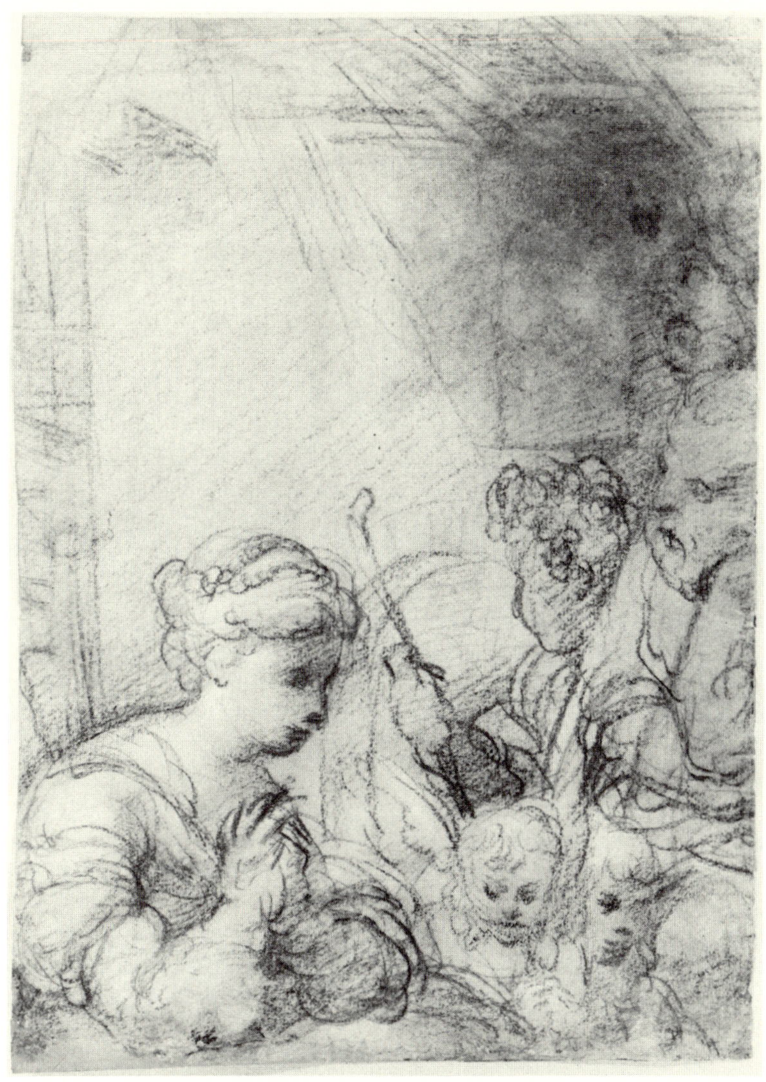

recto

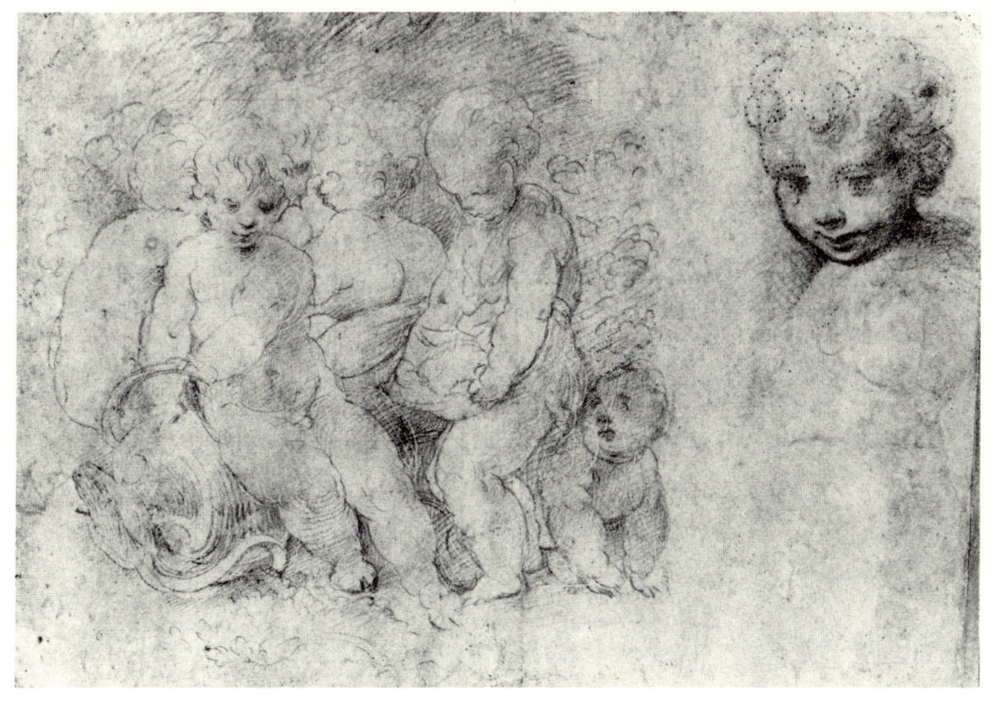

verso

Girolamo Francesco Maria Mazzola
called Parmigianino

Parma 1503 – 1540 Casalmaggiore

5 *Study of a Standing Youth (recto); A Seated Woman Asleep, attended by a Putto (verso)*

Red chalk *(recto)*, black chalk over stylus indications *(verso)*. On two rejoined sections of a single sheet; two small sections made up. 303 x 123 mm

Provenance: Sir Peter Lely (Lugt 2092); Jonathan Richardson, Senior (Lugt 2184); Sir Joshua Reynolds (Lugt 2364); Dr. H. Wellesley; Sotheby's, 2 July 1866, lot 1269; Christie's, London, 23 March 1982, lot 11.

Parmigianino drew on both sides of this sheet, which was cut and rejoined evidently by the artist himself, only to be taken apart and re-assembled again, probably in the eighteenth century. It would seem that Parmigianino first drew the red-chalk male figure on the *recto,* then cut the sheet across the middle, perhaps in order to redraw the legs. In any event, as the drawing is now assembled it is clear not only that an extra left leg is included but also that the alignment of the other legs (especially the model's right leg) and the rest of the body is not entirely consistent. The lower part of the drawing was then attached to the left of the upper part and the *verso* used for a different subject in black chalk. In this state the area immediately below the bent elbow of the male model constituted the lower right corner of the sheet, a place where it was not uncommon for collectors to place their marks. Since the marks of Sir Peter Lely (1618-1680) and Jonathan Richardson, Senior (1665-1745) are located in that corner, it is probable that the sheet was still arranged in that manner under their ownerships. Since the mark of Sir Joshua Reynolds (1723-1792) appears in the lower right corner as the sheet

appears today, it is possible that the sheet had been re-arranged by the time of his ownership, or that Reynolds himself was responsible for the reconstitution. In the latter process a strip along the centre of the *verso* was lost.

Neither the drawing on the *recto* nor that on the *verso* has been directly connected with any painting by Parmigianino. It has been remarked that the pose of the male model recalls the figure of John the Baptist in Parmigianino's early altarpiece at Bardi (ca. 1521),[1] but this is only in general terms. As well, the pose has been compared to a figure in a pen and ink drawing at Darmstadt, which A.E. Popham has associated with Joseph of Arimathea in Parmigianino's two etchings of the *Entombment.*[2] In fact, the present drawing closely resembles the pose of Joseph of Arimathea in the second of the two etchings, where the saint is shown at the left in reverse, heavily draped, bearded and holding the crown of thorns over the dead Christ's head. In addition, a double-sided, red chalk drawing in the British Museum with various figure studies for the *Entombments* includes a detail of a leg which is analogous in style to the present drawing.[3] It is not known exactly when the etchings were made, but most authorities date them to the Roman or Bolognese periods.[4] In any case, Popham has concluded that Parmigianino may well have made use of earlier drawings in their preparation.[5] In the present instance it is possible to detect the influence of Raphael, particularly in the hatching and cross-hatching of the modelling of the legs. This would most likely point to a date during Parmigianino's Roman period, 1524-27.

1 *Important Old Master Drawings,* Christie's London, 23 March 1982, lot 11, p. 10.

2 *Ibid.* For the drawing in Darmstadt (A.E. 1403), see A.E. Popham, *Catalogue of the Drawings of Parmigianino,* New Haven and London, 1971, I, p. 62, no. 62, II, pl. 159; the two etchings are Bartsch XVI, p.8, 5, and XVIII, p. 300, 46 (Popham, *op.cit.,* I, figs. 28 and 29); the latter convincingly restored to Parmigianino by K. Oberhuber, 'Parmigianino als Radierer,' *Alte und moderne Kunste,* VIII, 1963, p. 36.

3 Inv. no. 1905-11-10-12; Popham, *op.cit.,* I, pp. 94-95, no. 196, II, pl. 163.

4 Popham, *op.cit.,* I, p. 14.

5 *Ibid.*

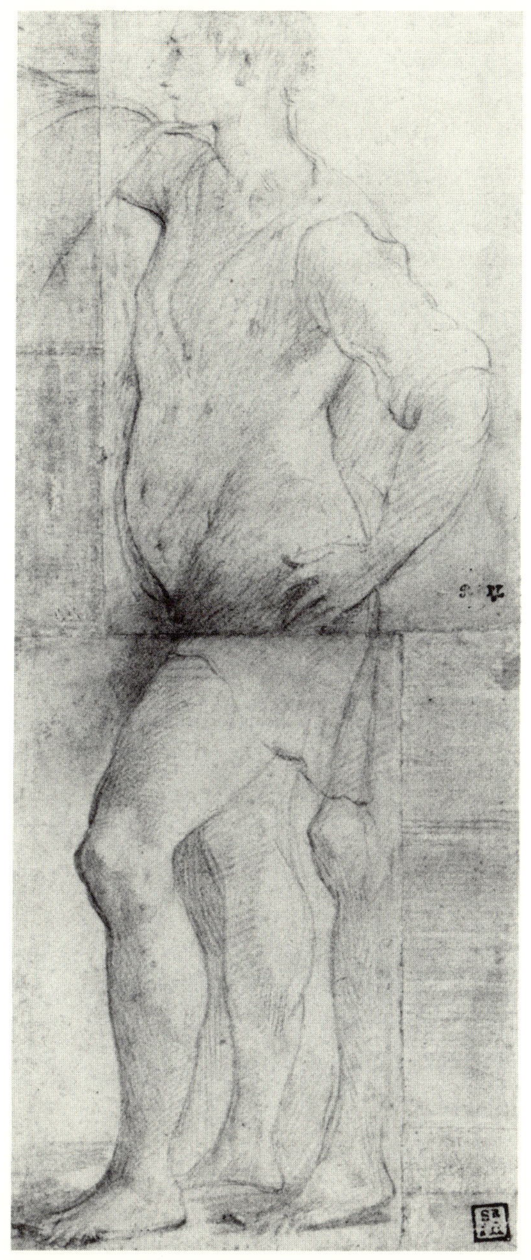

recto

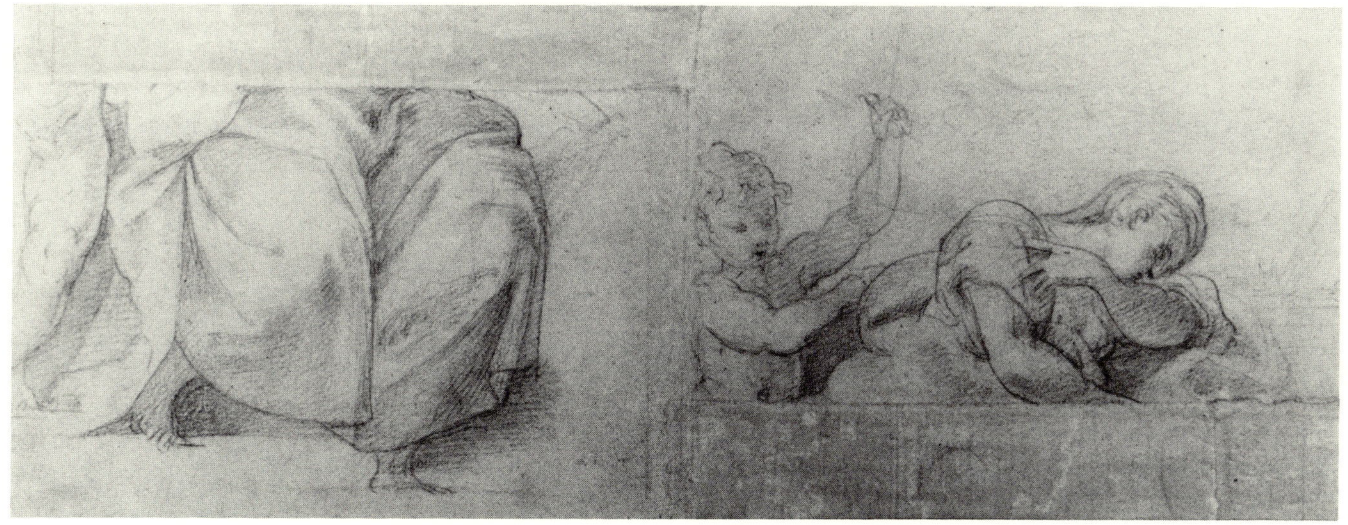

verso

Girolamo Francesco Maria Mazzola called Parmigianino

Parma 1503 – 1540 Casalmaggiore

6 *The Holy Family with Saint Elizabeth and the Infant Baptist*

Pen and brown ink and wash heightened with white over black chalk on greenish prepared paper. Laid down. Stains.
162 x 119 mm

Exhibited: Drawings by Old Masters, Royal Academy, London, 1953, no. 72; *Old Master Drawings from Chatsworth,* Manchester City Art Gallery, Manchester, 1961, no. 44; *Old Master Drawings from Chatsworth,* catalogue entries by A.E. Popham, National Gallery of Art, Washington, etc. 1962-63, no. 45; *Old Master Drawings from Chatsworth,* catalogue reprinted from Washington, 1962-63 above, Royal Academy, London, 1969, no. 45.

Literature: A.E. Popham, *Catalogue of the Drawings of Parmigianino,* New Haven and London, 1971, I, p. 212, no. 733, and pl. 249.

Provenance: Sir Peter Lely (Lugt 2092); William, 2nd Duke of Devonshire (Lugt 718); Chatsworth no. 805; Christie's, London, 3 July 1984, lot 33.

This intimate domestic scene with an aged Elizabeth and her son, John the Baptist, greeting their kinsmen, the Christ Child and his mother is not directly related to any known painting by Parmigianino. A.E. Popham has pointed out the similarities between the composition, with a figure standing in the doorway at the back, and Parmigianino's *Mystic Marriage of St. Catherine,* formerly in the collection of Lord Normanton and now in the National Gallery, London.[1] The painting has been dated to the second half of the 1520s, either when Parmigianino was in Rome or, after the Sack, in Bologna. The twisting pose of John the Baptist in the drawing is intriguingly close to the Christ Child in Michelangelo's *Medici Madonna,* begun in Florence during the same years.

---

1 *Catalogue of the Drawings of Parmigianino,* I, p. 212, no. 733.

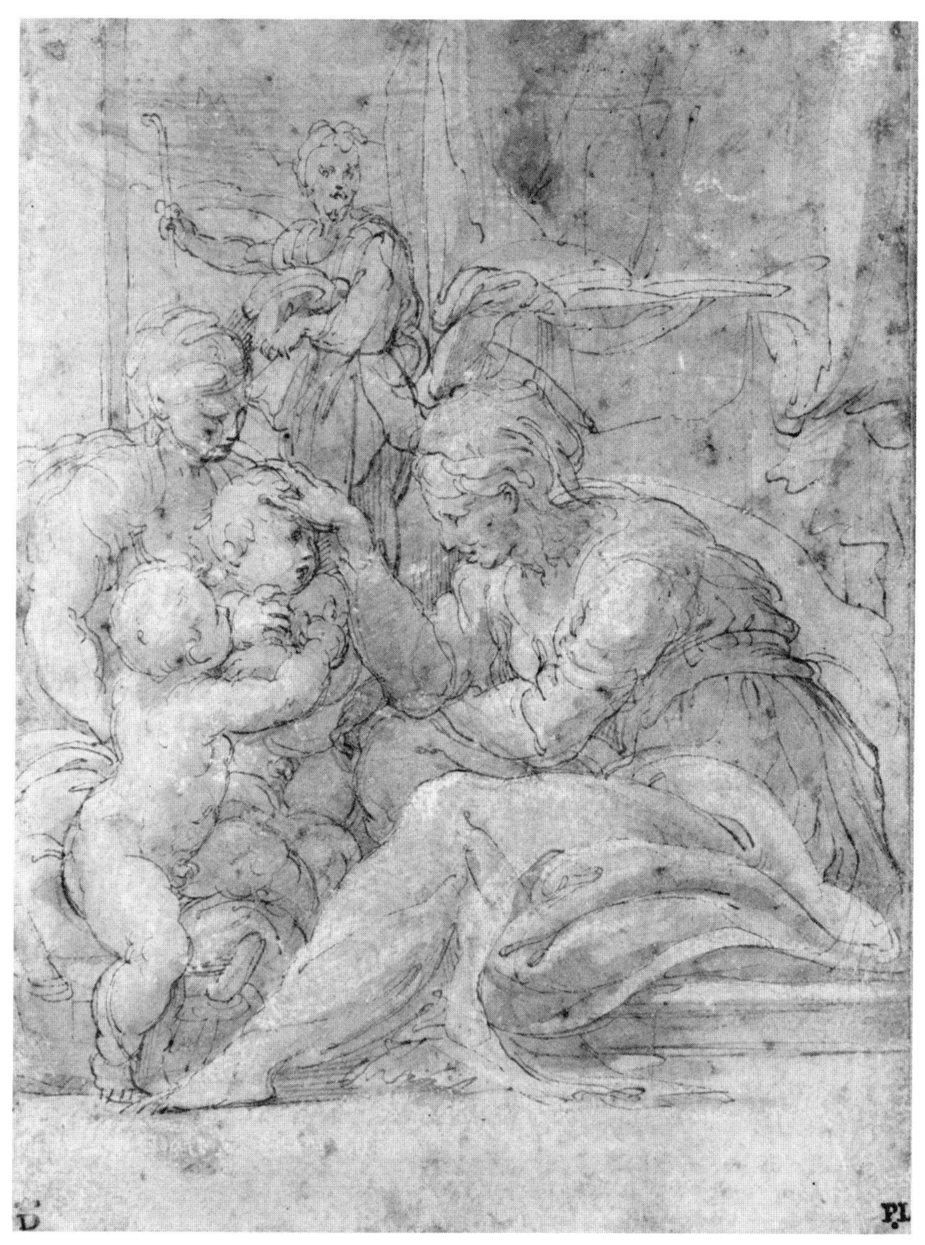

Nicolò dell'Abate

Modena 1509 or 1512 – 1571 France

7 *Two Putti, One with the Veil of Veronica, the Other with the Standard of the Resurrection*

Black chalk heightened with white (some oxidation) on light grey paper. 113 x 171 mm. Inscribed on *verso* in ink: *nicolo Abate, detto Dell'abbate, o messor Nicolo/Da Modena 1512-, pitt: arch:–/Discipl di Beggarelli/Scuola di Bologna.* In pencil: *Labatti,* and in brown ink: *BAF.* Other inscriptions in brown ink scored through.

Exhibited: D. DeGrazia, *Correggio and His Legacy: Sixteenth-Century Emilian Drawings,* National Gallery of Art, Washington, 1984, pp. 248-49, no. 81, repr.

Literature: S. Béguin, ''Contributions à l'étude des rapports des artistes Emiliens et Bellifontains,'' *Le arti a Bologna e in Emilia dal XVI al XVII secolo,* ed. A. Emiliani, Bologna, 1982, p. 56, fig. 72.

Provenance: North American collector (according to Christie's 1979); Christie's, London, 10 July 1979, lot 162; Christie's, London, 8 July 1980, lot 19.

This drawing was identified by Sylvie Béguin as a preparatory study for the frescoes on the vault of the chapel of the Château of Fleury-en-Bière in France. The frescoes were painted after 1552, when Nicolò dell'Abate left Bologna to accept Henry II's invitation to work in France with Primaticcio, and probably before 1558 when Cosme Clausse, secretary of finance and the patron, died.[1] Although only a few fragments of the vault survive, the appearance of the frescoes can be ascertained from engravings made by Antoine Garnier in 1646 (fig. 7a).[2] In the fresco, the head of the angel with the standard was turned to the right, his wings were shown in a more horizontal position and his legs more frontally. Included in the drawing are *pentimenti* anticipating the change in the position of the wings. Other *pentimenti* indicate that the putto at the left originally looked upward to the second angel, and that this inclination of the head was then replaced by a downward gaze, which was retained in the fresco.

Other drawings for the chapel at Fleury-en Bière are at Stockholm and in the Louvre.[3] Although these drawings reflect, to varying degrees, both the continuing influence of Parmigianino and the recent contacts with Primaticcio, they are, nonetheless, characteristically imbued with Nicolò's delicate and slightly nervous refinement.

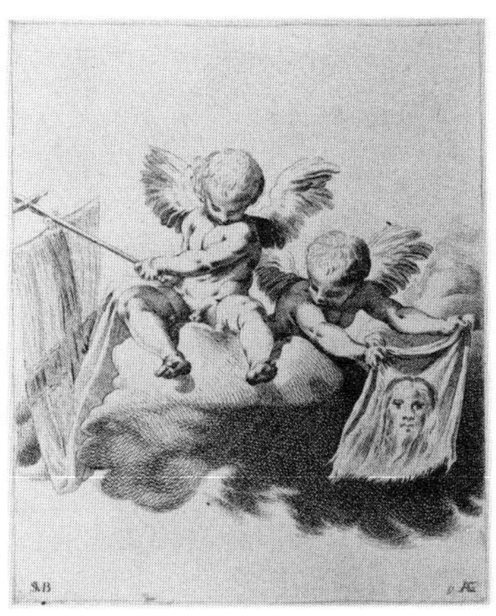

fig. 7a Antoine Garnier after Nicolò dell'Abate, *Angels with the Veil of Veronica and the Standard of the Resurrection,* engraving, Metropolitan Museum of Art, New York.

1 L. Dimier, *Le Primatice,* Paris, 1900, pp. 173-74, n. 2. The frescoes include Cosme Clausse's namesake, Saint Cosmos.

2 Garnier made seventeen engravings, as after Primaticcio, but Dimier (*ibid.*) showed that Nicolò dell'Abate was instead the original artist.

3 Stockholm 844/1863 (P. Bjurström, *French Drawings, Sixteenth and Seventeenth Centuries,* Stockholm, 1976, no. 2, repr.) and Louvre, Inv. 5828, 5837, 5842, 5843. For these drawings see S. Béguin, ''Contributions à l'étude des rapports des artistes Emiliens et Bellifontains,'' *Le arti a Bologna e in Emilia dal XVI al XVII secolo,* ed. A. Emiliani, Bologna, 1982, p. 60, n. 53.

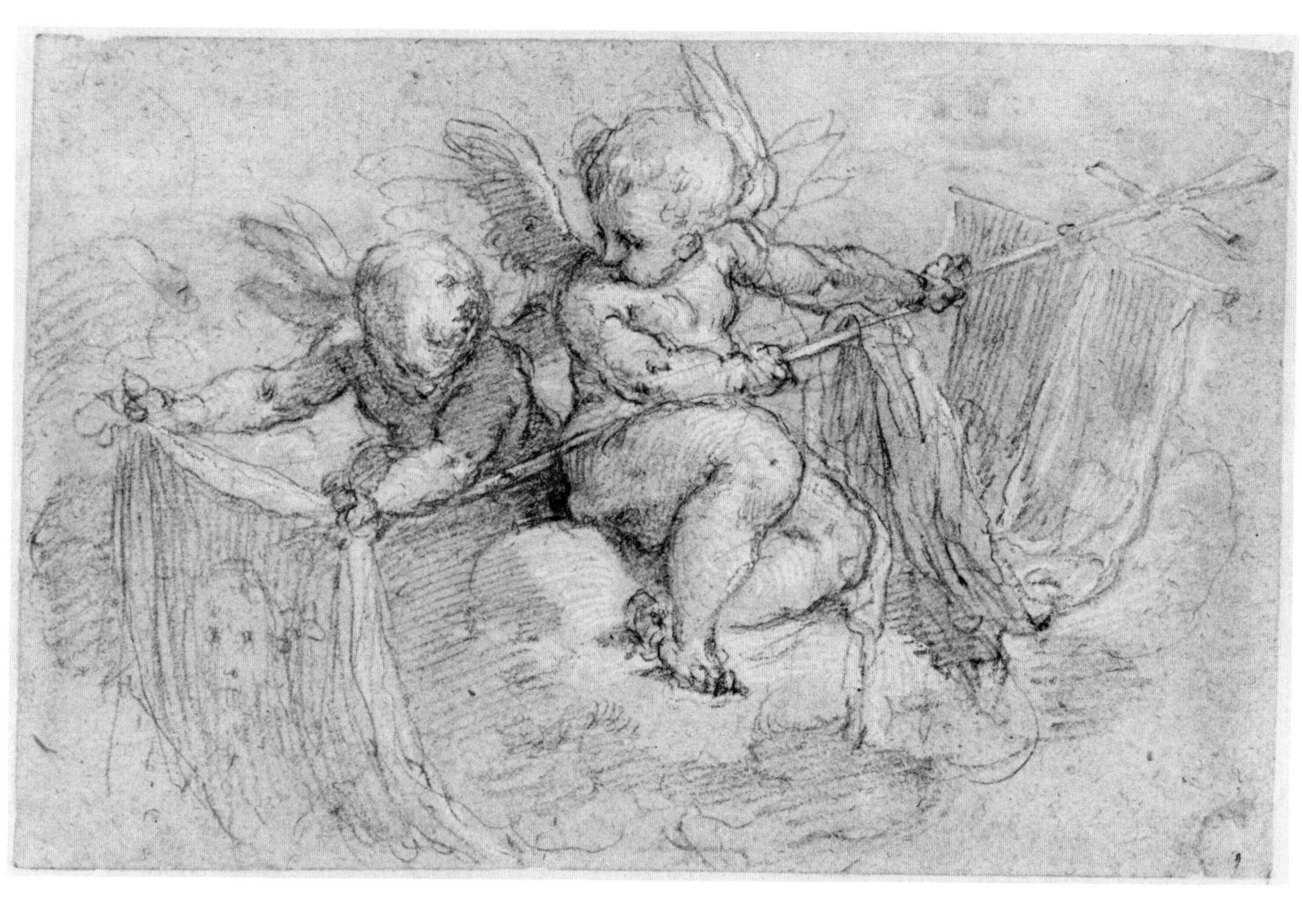

Giulio Campi

Cremona ca.1500 – 1572 Cremona

8   *Seated Apostle*

Black chalk, heightened with white, squared in black chalk on blue grey paper. Stains and wrinkles. 198 x 254 mm

Exhibited: D. DeGrazia, *Correggio and His Legacy: Sixteenth-Century Emilian Drawings,* National Gallery of Art, Washington, 1984, pp. 282-84, no. 94, repr.

Literature: M. Di Giampaolo, "Giulio Campi: ancora due disegni per San Sigismondo," *Prospettiva,* 8, 1977, p. 55-6, fig. 7; G. Godi and G. Cirollo, *Studi su Giulio Campi,* Milan, 1978, pp. 44-45, pl. 37.

Provenance: Finarte, Milan, Asta di disegni dal XVI al XVIII *secolo,* 122, December 1971, lot 68, pl. XXIII (as Primaticcio, according to Di Giampaolo, *op.cit.*).

Mario Di Giampaolo identified this drawing, which had previously been attributed to Primaticcio, as a study for one of the apostles in Giulio Campi's *Pentecost,* on the vault of the nave of San Sigismondo, Cremona (fig. 8a).[1] Signed and dated 1557, the fresco shows the Virgin and the apostles on the edge of an octagonal opening, seen from below. Either standing or reclining, the figures look and gesture upward to another feigned opening, a large oculus, through which a brilliant radiance and the tongues of fire descend (Acts 2: 1-4).

A small drawing in pen and ink in Bergamo indicates that Giulio Campi had considered another architectural setting for the *Pentecost,* with a balustrade and Solomonic columns perspectivally rising above a square opening and supporting an entablature, which frames the descending dove of the Holy Spirit.[2] The rejection of this system of *quadratura* in favour of the present arrangement, a circular opening above an octagon, suggests the influence of Correggio's frescoes in the dome of the cathedral of Parma. The similarities between Giulio Campi's gesticulating apostles and those by Correggio in the Duomo, Parma, have already been noted by Adolfo Venturi.[3] Indeed the present apostle, seated with one leg extended and seen *di sotto in sù,* reflects a type frequently found in Correggio's *oeuvre.*[4] In addition, Diane DeGrazia has detected connections between the soft *sfumato* of the black and white chalk of this drawing and of sheets by Correggio.[5] Entirely distinctive of Giulio Campi, however, are the dense cross-hatching of the drapery and the parallel, slat-like strokes of the background. A drawing in the Uffizi for two of the other reclining apostles, similarly seen from below, displays in an even more emphatic manner Giulio Campi's peculiar cross-hatching.[6]

On the verso of the drawing is a fragment of a large head, not yet connected with any painting.

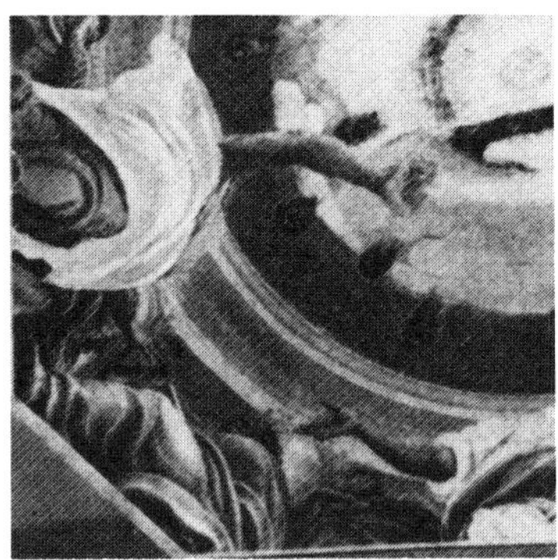

fig. 8a Giulio Campi, *Pentecost* (detail), fresco, S. Sigismondo, Cremona.

---

1   M. Di Giampaolo, *op. cit.*

2   Accademia Carrara, no. 1236: G. Bora, "Note Cremonesi, I: Camillo Boccaccino, Le Proposte," *Paragone,* XXV, 295, 1974, p. 60, pl. 63a.

3   Venturi, IX, 6, p. 856.

4   *E.g.* a drawing in the British Museum (1946-7-13-631) of a sibyl for S. Giovanni Evangelista, Parma.

5   *Correggio and His Legacy: Sixteenth-Century Emilian Drawings,* Washington, 1984, p. 284.

6   n. 17398 F.: Bora, *op.cit.*, p. 60, pl. 63b. Formerly classified as Vincenzo Campi, the drawing was recognized as Giulio Campi's by S. Zamboni.

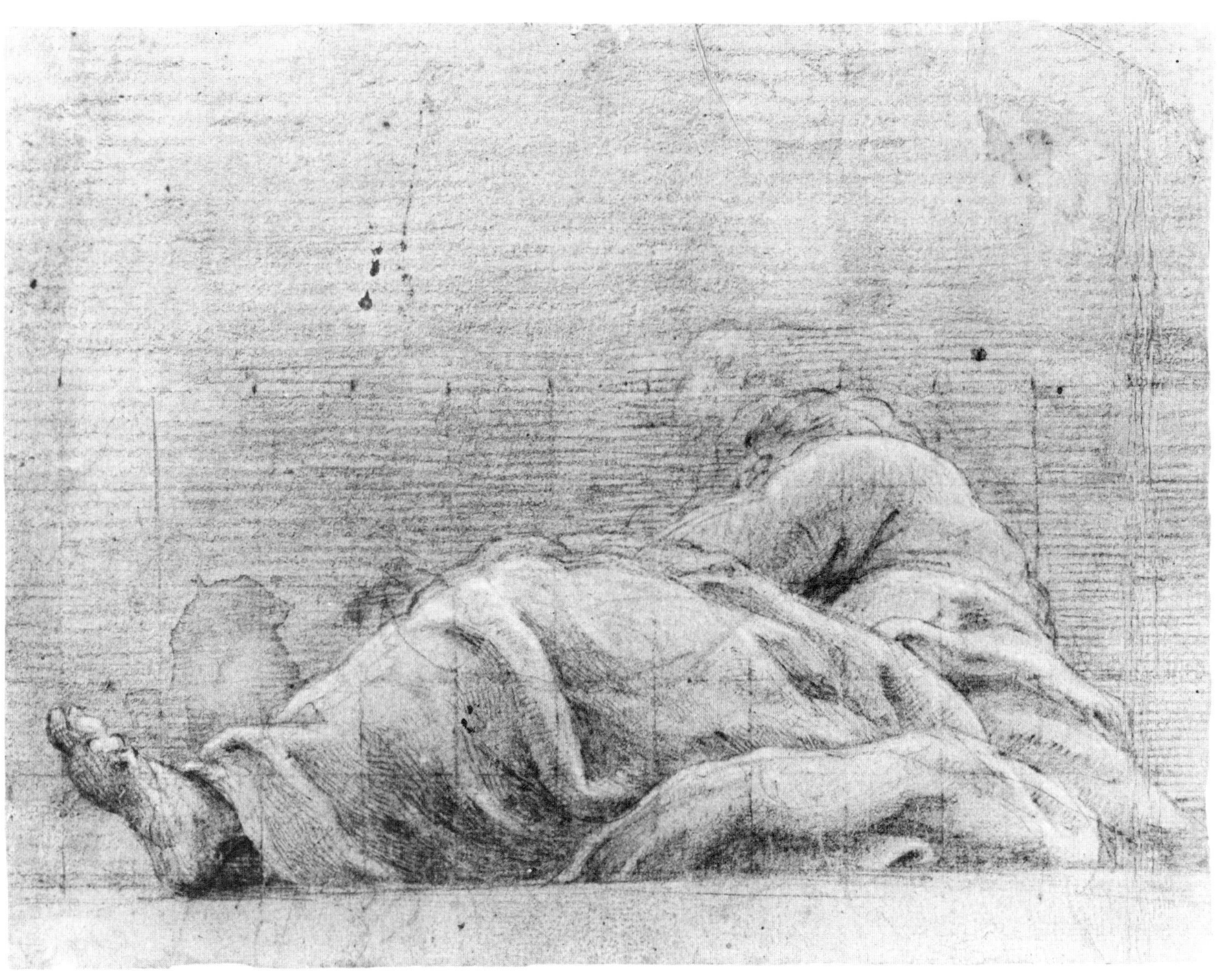

Andrea Previtali

Berbenno? ca.1480 – 1528 Bergamo

9 *Portrait of a Young Lady, Bust Length*

Black chalk on grey paper. Some stains and foxing. 350 x 257 mm

Exhibited: Guildhall, London, 1895; *Exhibition of Italian Art,* Royal Academy, London, 1930, (Commemorative Catalogue, ed. Lord Balniel and K. Clark, London, 1931, p. 267, no. 861, as ''Attributed to Lorenzo Lotto.'').

Literature: [J. P. Heseltine]. *Original Drawings by Old Masters of the Schools of North Italy in the collection of J. P. H.,* London, 1906, no. 15, repr. (as Lorenzo Lotto); D. von Hadeln, *Venezianische Zeichnungen des Quattrocento,* Berlin, 1925, p. 65, pl. 85 (as Andrea Previtali); A. Venturi, ''Scelta di rari disegni nei musei d'Europa,'' *L'Arte,* XXXIX, 1926, pp. 10-13, fig. 12 (as Lorenzo Lotto); *idem., Studi dal Vero,* Milan, 1927, p. 268, fig. 168 (as Lorenzo Lotto); C. Holmes, ''Recent Acquisitions at Trafalgar Square,'' *Burlington Magazine,* LI, 1927, p. 113 (as Lorenzo Lotto); Venturi, 1929, 9, IV, p. 87, fig. 78 (as Lorenzo Lotto); Ottinger, *Belvedere,* IX, 2, 1930, (as Lorenzo Lotto); A. E. Popham, *Italian Drawings Exhibited at the R.A., Burlington House, 1930,* London, 1931, no. 259, pl. CCXXVIa (as ''attributed to Lorenzo Lotto''); Tietzes, 1944, pp. 241-42, A 1373; A. Banti-A. Boschetto, *Lorenzo Lotto,* Florence [1953] p. 83, under no. 87 (reject attribution to Lotto); F. Heinemann, *Giovanni Bellini e i Belliniani,* Venice [1962], I, p. 146, S. 381, II, fig. 525; J. Meyer zur Capellen, *Andrea Previtali,* Inaugural-Dissertation, Würzburg, 1972, pp. 90-1, 193, no. Z3.

Provenance: Jonathan Richardson, Sen. (Lugt 2184); John, Duke of Argyl; T. Philipe, 21-23 May 1798, lot 164 (as Sebastiano del Piombo, 'lightly and delicately touched'); The 2nd Viscount Palmerston (d. 1801) and by descent to Hon. Evelyn Ashley; Christie's, 24 April 1891, lot 179 (as Sebastiano del Piombo); Sir J. C. Robinson (Lugt 1433); Christie's, 12 May 1902, lot 194 (as Lorenzo Lotto); J. P. Heseltine (Lugt 1507); Henry Oppenheimer; Christie's, 13 July 1936, lot 154 (as Andrea Previtali); purchased from Matthiesen, 1943; Baron Hatvany; Christie's, London, 24 June 1980, lot 10 (as Andrea Previtali).

This unidentified young lady wears a blouse with embroidered collar and a *schuffa* or headdress made of hair and other materials, fashionable in the 1520s and 1530s, and said to have been popularized by Isabella d'Este.[1] While the attribution of this sheet has not been conclusively settled, there seems to be general agreement that the drawing was executed in Northern Italy, probably in or around Bergamo in the 1520s. Whereas in the eighteenth and nineteenth centuries the drawing was given to Sebastiano del Piombo, in the Sir J. C. Robinson sale of 1902 it was ascribed to Lorenzo Lotto, whose work was just then becoming better known, as a result of Berenson's pioneering study. The attribution to Lotto was supported by Adolfo

Venturi and Sir Charles Holmes, among others; although already in 1925 Detlev von Hadeln had proposed an àttribution to Andrea Previtali, a pupil of Giovanni Bellini, who worked mainly in Bergamo and who on one occasion at least shared a commission with Lotto.[2] This attribution has been generally, if somewhat grudgingly, accepted in more recent publications.[3]

The problem of attribution is frustrated by the fact that the drawing does not relate closely to any known painting, and that there are very few comparable drawings. However, enough is now known about Lotto's drawings, various though they may be, to make a direct link with that artist seem unlikely; most conspicuously the present drawing lacks Lotto's peculiarly animated line, which can be alternately sinuous, gnarled or abrupt.[4] Instead, the head is executed, despite the concentrated expression, in a more relaxed and generalized manner, and indeed, as such, affords telling comparisons with the paintings by Previtali. Detlev von Hadeln, in first publishing the drawing as by Previtali, compared the head to such details in Previtali's work as the portrait of Agnese Casotti in the *Madonna Casotti* in the Accademia Carrara, Bergamo.[5] The Tietzes, focussing only on the similarities of the headdresses, considered the comparison too general, but in fact, the smooth and abstracted rendering of the volumes and the slow-moving, very gentle quality of the line are typical features of Previtali's figures. Unfortunately there are no reliably attributed portrait drawings by Previtali to serve as comparisons, and so the attribution can scarcely be considered more than tentative until fresh evidence is forthcoming.

1 See *Splendours of the Gonzaga,* Victoria and Albert Museum, London, 1981, p. 161 (entry by J. T. Martineau).

2 In SS. Stefano e Domenico, Bergamo; M. A. Michiel, [D. J. Morelli], *Notizia d'Opere di Disegno,* 2nd ed., ed. G. Frizzoni, Bologna, 1884, p. 132. See also C. Cohen, ''The 'Modello' for a Lost Work by Lorenzo Lotto,'' *Master Drawings,* XIII, 1975, pp. 131-35; and W. R. Rearick, ''Lorenzo Lotto: The Drawings, 1500-1525,'' *Lorenzo Lotto,* Atti del Convegno Internazionale di Studi per il V Centenario della Nascità, ed. P. Zampetti and V. Sgarbi, Treviso, 1981, pp. 26-28, figs. 4-5.

3 Tietzes, p. 242, A 1373, although they list the drawing under Previtali, conclude that ''this beautiful drawing has to remain anonymous for the time being;'' Heinemann, *op. cit.,* I, p. 146, S. 381, considers the drawing is *''forse troppo monumentale per il Previtali,''* and he adds a question mark after Previtali's name in the caption to fig. 525. W. R. Rearick, *Tiziano e il Disegno Veneziano del suo tempo,* Gabinetto Disegni e Stampe degli Uffizi, Florence, 1976, p. 34, evidently rejects the attribution, although he does not mention the drawing by name.

4 P. Pouncey, *Lotto disegnatore,* Vicenza, 1965; W. R. Rearick, *op. cit.,* pp. 23-36, figs. 1-16. The present portrait is not included in either of these studies or in the monographs on Lotto by Berenson, and G. Mariani Canova. A. Banti and A. Boschetto, *op. cit.,* p. 83, under no. 87, reject the attribution to Lorenzo Lotto.

5 No. 491, dated about 1520: F. Rossi, *Accademia Carrara, Bergamo,* Bergamo, 1979, p. 147, repr. p. 152. See also Previtali's *Family Group against Coastal Landscape,* Conte Moroni collection, Bergamo, repr. B. Berenson, *Italian Pictures of the Renaissance, Venetian School,* London, n.d., II, pl. 754.

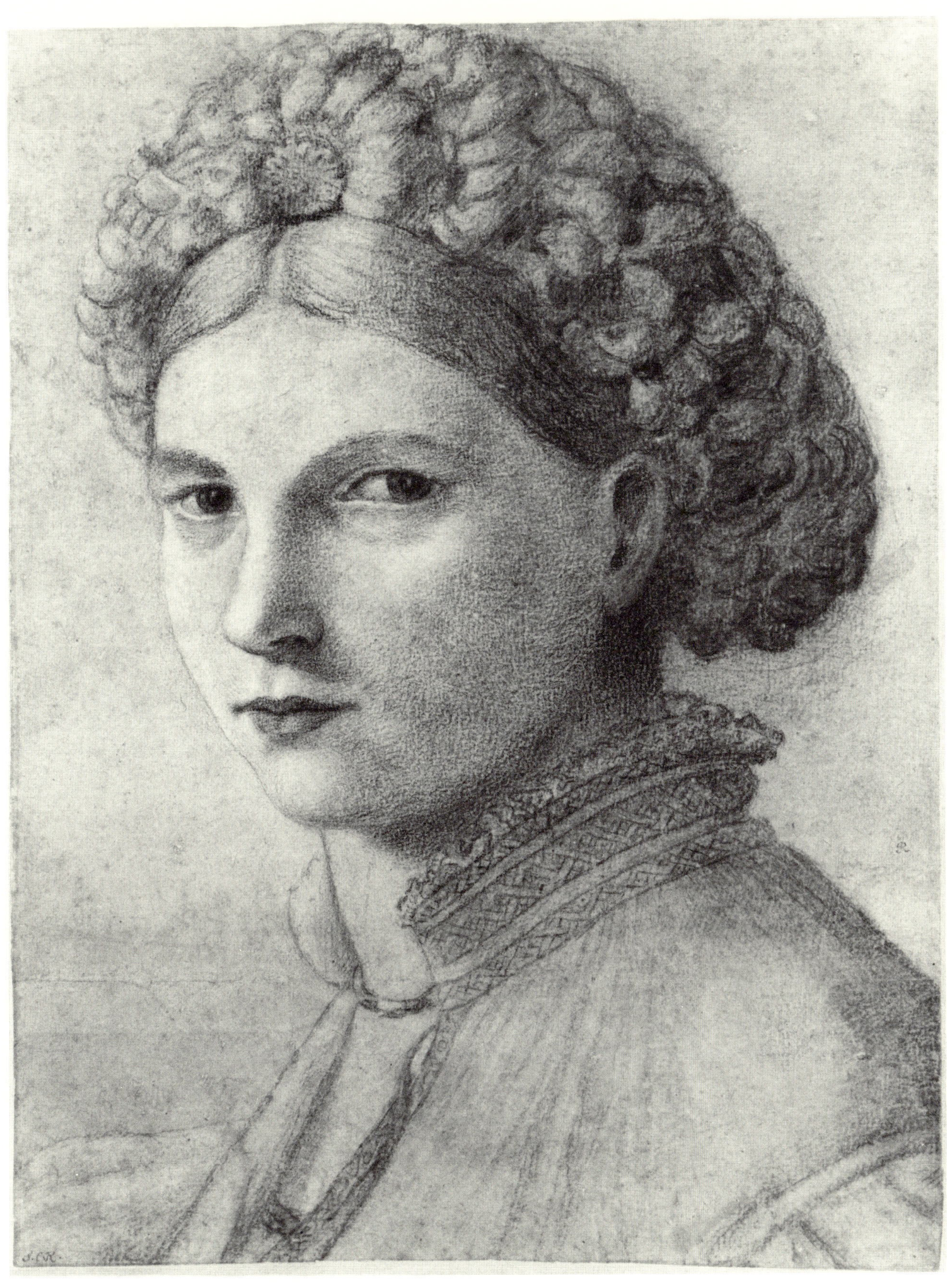

Francesco de' Rossi
called Francesco Salviati

Florence 1510 – 1563 Rome

10 *Portrait Study of a Boy Wearing a Cap*

Red chalk. Laid down. Stains and foxing. 168 x 124 mm

Literature: P. Ward-Jackson, *Victoria and Albert Catalogues, Italian Drawings, Volume One: 14th-16th century,* London, 1979, p. 139, under no. 280.

Provenance: William, 2nd Duke of Devonshire (Lugt 718); Chatsworth no. 12; Christie's, London, 3 July 1984, lot. 42.

The attribution of this drawing to Francesco Salviati is traditional. The hatching and cross-hatching in red chalk reflect the artist's training in Florence, especially his contacts during the second half of the 1520s with Andrea del Sarto.[1] Francesco Salviati has not, however, endeavoured to be as consistent as Andrea del Sarto in the use of line to define three-dimensional form. In the present drawing, Salviati's contours are sinuous and often engagingly decorative; and in certain areas, such as the face, he has stumped or possibly dampened the chalk to produce a soft and continuous tone. In technique the drawing is comparable to sheets of a mother and child by Francesco Salviati in the Ashmolean Museum and the Louvre which are directly related to designs by Andrea del Sarto, and like these drawings the present example should be dated to the early 1530s.[2]

In view of the high degree of finish and of the inclusion of the detailed background, the drawing was almost certainly intended as an independent work of art. The drapery behind the sitter is a device that appears in a number of Francesco Salviati's portraits, such as the reasonably early *Portrait of Young Man from the Santacroce Family* in Vienna. A similar red chalk drawing of a boy by Salviati remains at Chatsworth, while other portrait studies of youths by the artist are in the Uffizi and the Victoria and Albert Museum.[3]

1 Francesco Salviati was in Andrea del Sarto's workshop during 1529-30, but had earlier studied drawings by the master, supplied to him by Vasari (Vasari, VII, pp. 8, 10).

2 H. Macandrew, *Ashmolean Museum, Oxford, Catalogue of the Collection of Drawings, Volume III, Italian Schools: Supplement,* Oxford, 1980, p. 283, no. 681; C. Monbeig-Goguel, *Inventaire Général des Dessins Italiens, Vasari et son Temps,* Paris, 1972, p. 108, no. 127 (Inv. 2727).

3 Chatsworth, no. 13, 168 x 111 mm (exhibited in *Between Renaissance and Baroque, European Art 1520-1600,* City of Manchester Art Gallery, Manchester, 1965, p. 111, no. 375); Uffizi, no. 15211 F, red chalk on rose paper, 160 x 118 mm; Victoria and Albert Museum, Dyce 186, black chalk, 270 x 216 mm (P.W. Jackson, *Victoria and Albert Catalogues, Italian Drawings, Volume One: 14th-16th century,* London, 1979, pp. 136-39, no. 280).

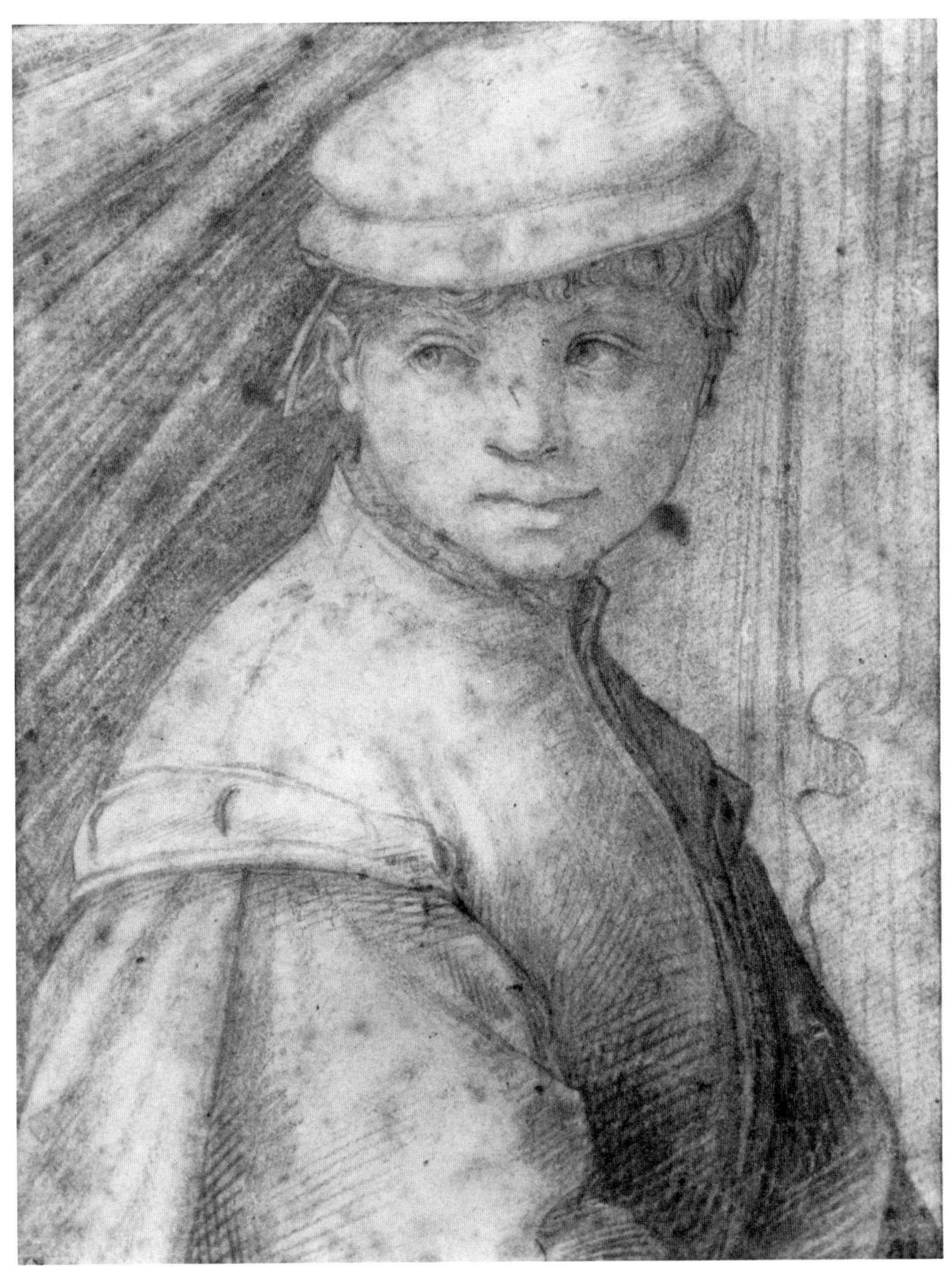

Francesco de'Rossi
called Francesco Salviati

Florence 1510 – 1563 Rome

11 *The Siege of Parma; Design for a Wall Decoration Flanked by Pilasters*

Pen and brown ink and wash, heightened with white (in places oxidized). 149 x 111 mm. Inscribed at left in pen and ink: *parma* and *piano*

Provenance: A Continental Collector (according to Christie's as follows); Christie's, London, 9 December 1982, lot 29.

This drawing and a related sheet (fig. 11a) which appeared with it at auction provide telling information about the fresco decorations in the *salotto dipinto* (Sala dei Fasti Farnesiani) in the Palazzo Farnese, Rome. The room, situated at the middle of the *piano nobile* on the front, with a balcony overlooking the square, functioned as an important reception room and its decorations were intended to glorify the Farnese family.[1] It is not known exactly when Francesco Salviati took on the commission, but the frescoes themselves must have been mostly done after the patron, Cardinal Ranuccio Farnese, returned to Rome in the summer of 1552, following a year's exile. Only the two side walls of the room were finished by Francesco Salviati; after his death in 1563, Taddeo Zuccaro took over the commission, but the deaths of Cardinal Ranuccio in 1565 and then of Taddeo Zuccaro in 1566 brought this campaign to an end. The room was finally completed by Taddeo's brother, Federico, under the patronage of Cardinal Alessandro Farnese.

The two side walls by Francesco Salviati are subdivided into five vertical sections, usually with allegorical subjects alternating with historical ones. The historical subjects, framed by simulated Corinthian piers, appear as views out imaginary openings in the wall. On the northwest wall (on the right-hand side, looking at the front of the palace) the subject matter concerns Farnese warriors who had served the church. In the middle of the wall appears the figure of the ideal Farnese warrior who, like a new Aeneas,[2] receives a lance and other armour from Venus, who is depicted above as on an unfurled tapestry. Immediately to the left of this is the historical episode of Pope Eugene IV giving the baton to Ranuccio the elder, and to the right, Pietro and Ranuccio Farnese leading the Florentine troops in victory over the Pisans in 1363. In all parts of this wall the light is painted

as if coming from the right, in accordance with the direction of the natural light itself.

The present drawing and its companion must be discarded ideas for the historical scenes of the wall just mentioned; they must also have been executed after the design for the wall as a whole had been largely worked out. In the drawings, the light again comes from the right, and the historical events are flanked by Corinthian piers similar to those of the fresco. Most telling of all, in both drawings the shadow of the feigned tapestry in the central part of the wall is shown on the pier at the upper right. This detail suggests that both drawings were alternate ideas for the same section – immediately to the left of the central warrior – a conclusion further supported by the fact that in both drawings not just the front but the side of the left pier is shown, as in the fresco. If either of these designs had been transferred to the wall, battle scenes would then have flanked the central seated warrior, whereas in the present solution a battle appears only to the right.

The exact event represented in each of the two drawings is difficult to identify precisely, but the standard in the one drawing can be assumed to belong to the Farnese, since it is emblazoned with their device, the *fleur-de-lys* (although only three instead of the customary six),[3] and the inscriptions on the other drawings indicate *Parma* and the *plain*. It is most likely then that both drawings represent the successful defence of Parma by Ottavio Farnese, with the support of the French king, Henry II, against the papal and imperial forces during 1551-52.[4] If this is indeed the subject, the drawings were ultimately rejected no doubt because scenes of the Farnese defending the Church, rather than in conflict with it, were understandably, much more desirable.

Both drawings are executed in the idiosyncratic and highly imaginative style of Francesco Salviati's full maturity.[5]

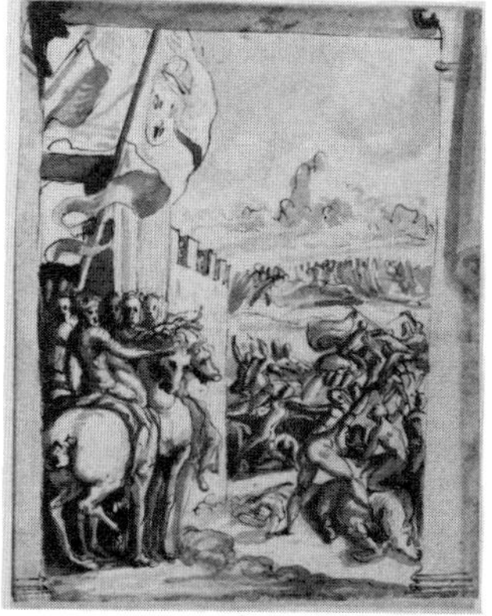

fig. 11a Francesco Salviati, *Siege of Parma*, pen and brown ink and wash, over traces of black chalk, private collection.

---

1 For a recent discussion of the room and its decorations, see I. Cheney, ''Les premières décorations: Daniele da Volterra, Salviati e les frères Zuccari,'' *Le Palais Farnèse,* Rome, 1981, pp. 243-67.

2 F. de Vavenne, *Rome, le Palais Farnèse et les Farnèse,* Paris, 1914, p. 598, cited in Cheney, *op.cit.,* p. 256.

3 For the Farnese heraldic devices see M. Pastoureau, ''L'emblématique Farnèse,'' *Le Palais Farnèse,* Rome, 1981, pp. 431-55.

4 For these events, see L. von Pastor, *The History of the Popes,* ed. R.F. Kerr, XIII, London, 1951, pp. 92ff, pp. 130ff.

5 Only four drawings have so far been discovered for Salviati's decorations as executed: I. Cheney, ''Catalogue of preparatory drawings related to the mid-sixteenth century decorations in Palazzo Farnese,'' *Mélanges de l'Ecole Française de Rome,* Moyen Age, Temps moderne, vol. XCIII, no. 2, 1981, pp. 793-96.

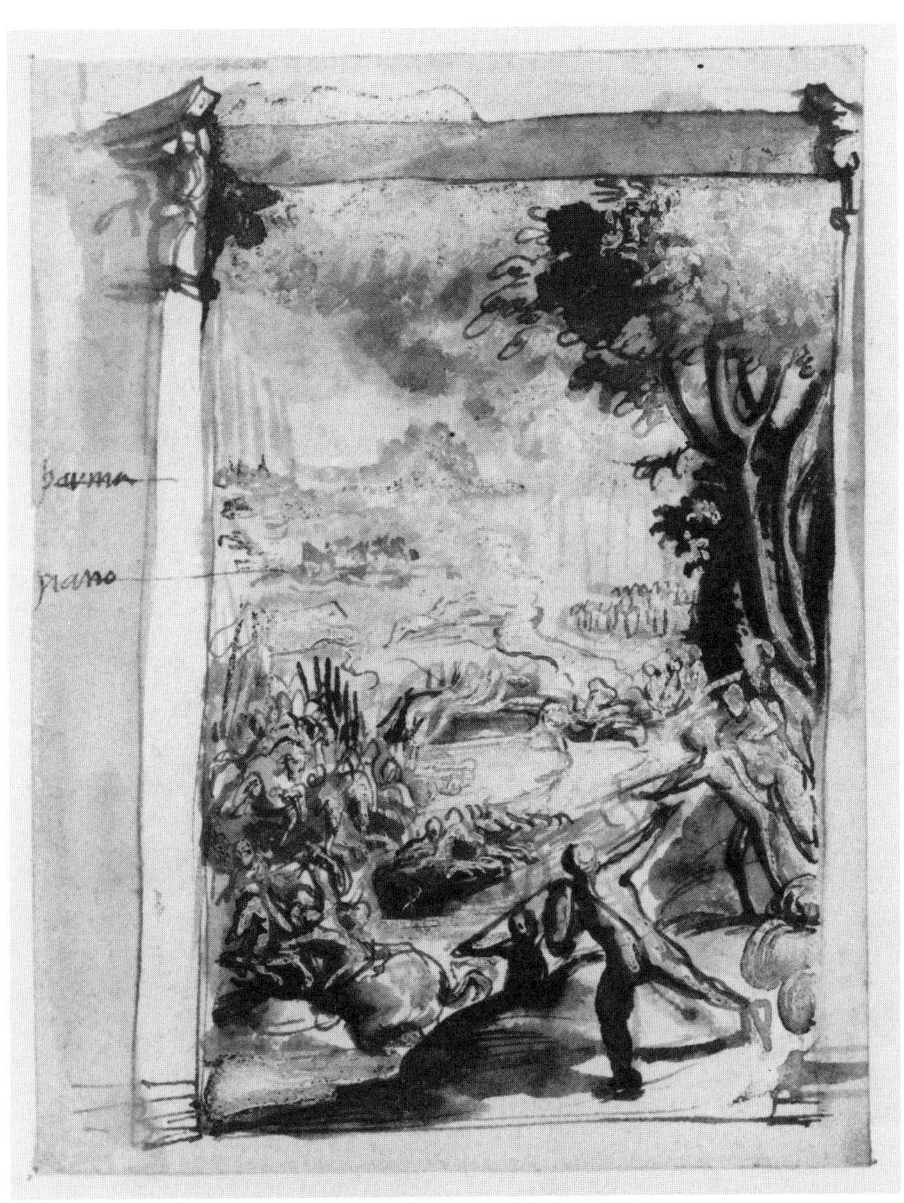

fiume
piano

Giorgio Vasari

Arezzo 1511 – 1574 Florence

12 *A Bearded Man Filling a Glass*
13 *A Running Youth*

Pen and brown ink and wash over traces of black chalk, heightened with white on blue paper. 448 x 197 mm maximum

Literature: L.C.J. Frerichs, *Italiaanse Tekeningen II de 15de en 16de Eeuw,* Rijksprentenkabinet, Rijksmuseum, Amsterdam, 1981 p. 72; P.L. de Castris, ''Napoli 1544: Vasari e Monteoliveto,'' *Bollettino d'Arte,* 12, 1981, p. 84, note 16, and fig. 5; C. Monbeig Goguel, ''Chronique vasarienne,'' *Revue de l'Art,* 56, 1982, p. 70 and fig. 8.

Provenance: Paul Sandby (Lugt 2112); Sotheby's, London, 9 July 1981, lot 7.

Until recently the two drawings were mounted together, joined along their vertical axis by a column which was drawn in at some later date. Identified independently by L.C.J. Frerichs, Catherine Monbeig Goguel, and the present author, the drawings are closely related to paintings Vasari executed in 1544-5 for the refectory of the monastery of Monteoliveto, Naples.[1] The drawings correspond to the side segments of the *Feast in the House of Simon,* a panel painting divided into three sections, which was inserted under the gothic vault at the head of the long room. The pointed side panels, representing a bearded man filling a glass on the left and two young men with a platter of meat on the right, are now preserved at Capodimonte, Naples, while the rectangular central panel is lost.[2] However, a large and highly finished drawing in the Rijksmuseum, Amsterdam (fig. 12a), has recently been identified as Vasari's solution for the central section of the painting.[3] Showing Mary Magdalen drying Christ's feet with her hair in front of a table thronged with agitated guests, the Amsterdam drawing includes Solomonic columns and a coffered ceiling similar to those in the Ferretti drawings. In addition, the orthogonals of the coffering and the floor tiles are directed to a vanishing point in the right-hand panel, in accordance with the present drawings.

For the arched space above the entrance door at the other end of the refectory Vasari painted the *Gathering of Manna,* similarly divided into three panels. Again the central panel is lost, but the side sections have recently been found in the Museo Arcivescovile, Palermo.[4] The entire composition is included in a less highly evolved drawing by Vasari in the Ecole des Beaux-Arts, Paris.[5]

As part of the same campaign, Vasari also undertook the fresco decoration of the vaulted ceiling of the refectory.[6] The decoration comprises stucco and grotesques surrounding large allegorical figures, the few surviving drawings for which are among Vasari's most imposing and elegant.[7] Such drawings for the vault as the *Prudence* in the Fondation Custodia, Paris, and the *Abundance* in the British Museum also display a remarkable technical refinement, not unrelated to that of the two drawings exhibited here.

The figures in the left-hand drawing reappear, with some modification, in Vasari's *Marriage of Esther and Ahasuerus,* in Arezzo of 1549, while the running youth at the right is a variation, in reverse, of a figure in Vasari's *Christ in the House of Mary and Martha,* S. Michele in Bosco, Bologna of 1539.

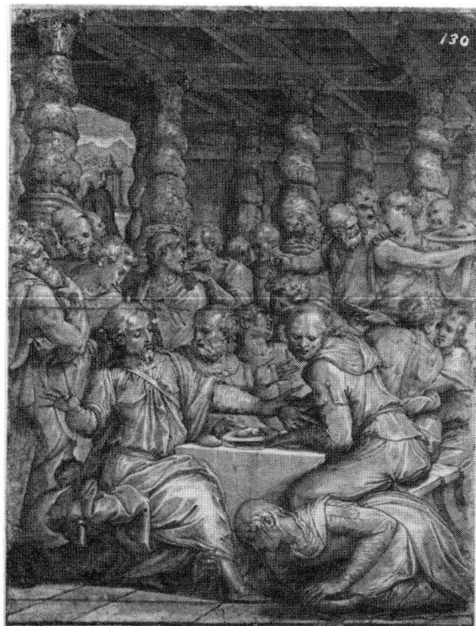

fig. 12a Giorgio Vasari, *Feast in the House of Simon*, pen and brown ink and wash, heightened with white on blue paper, Rijksmuseum, Amsterdam.

1 Frerichs, *op.cit.*; de Castris, *op.cit.* Monbeig Goguel, *op.cit.*

2 de Castris, *op.cit.*, p. 62 and figs. 3-4; Monbeig Goguel, *op.cit.*, p. 70, and figs. 6-7. Vasari himself described the paintings as follows: ''*Nella testata, che è a somma, è Cristo che desina in casa di Simone, e Maria Maddalena che con lagrime gli bagna i piedi e gli asciuga con i capelli, tutta mostrandosi pentita de' suoi peccati. La quale storia è partita in tre quadri: nel mezzo è la cena, a man ritta una bottigliera con una credenza piena di vasi in varie forme e stravaganti, ed a man sinistra uno scalco che conduce le vivande,*'' (Vasari, VII, p. 675).

3 1951:1; pen and brown ink and wash over black chalk, heightened with white on blue paper; 556 x 414 mm; Frerichs, *op.cit.*, p. 72, no. 155, repr.; de Castris, *op.cit.*, p. 62 and fig. 8.

4 de Castris, *op.cit.*, p. 62 and figs. 6-7.

5 Monbeig Goguel, *op.cit.*, p. 70 and fig. 5.

7 Vasari arrived in Naples in the autumn of 1544, had finished the panel paintings by March 1545, and then with the help of assistants completed the frescoes; de Castris, *op.cit.*, pp. 60, 63.

7 de Gastris, *op.cit.,* p. 70, fig. 21.

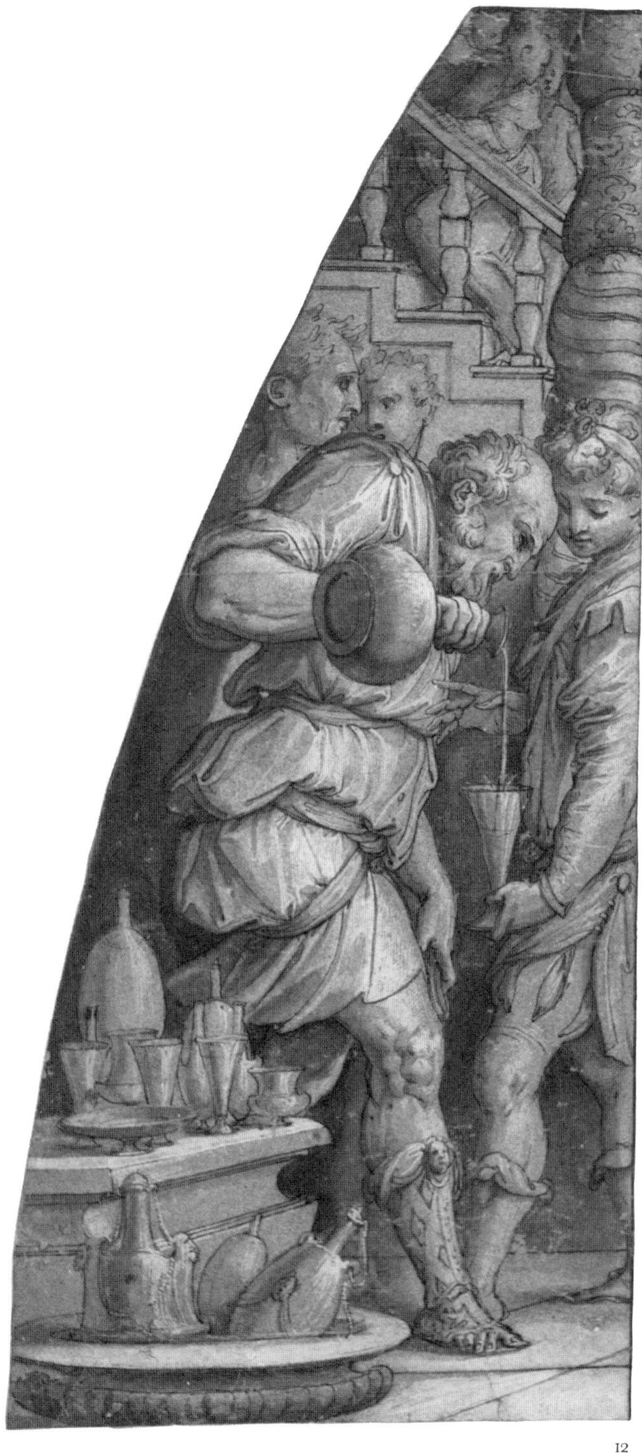
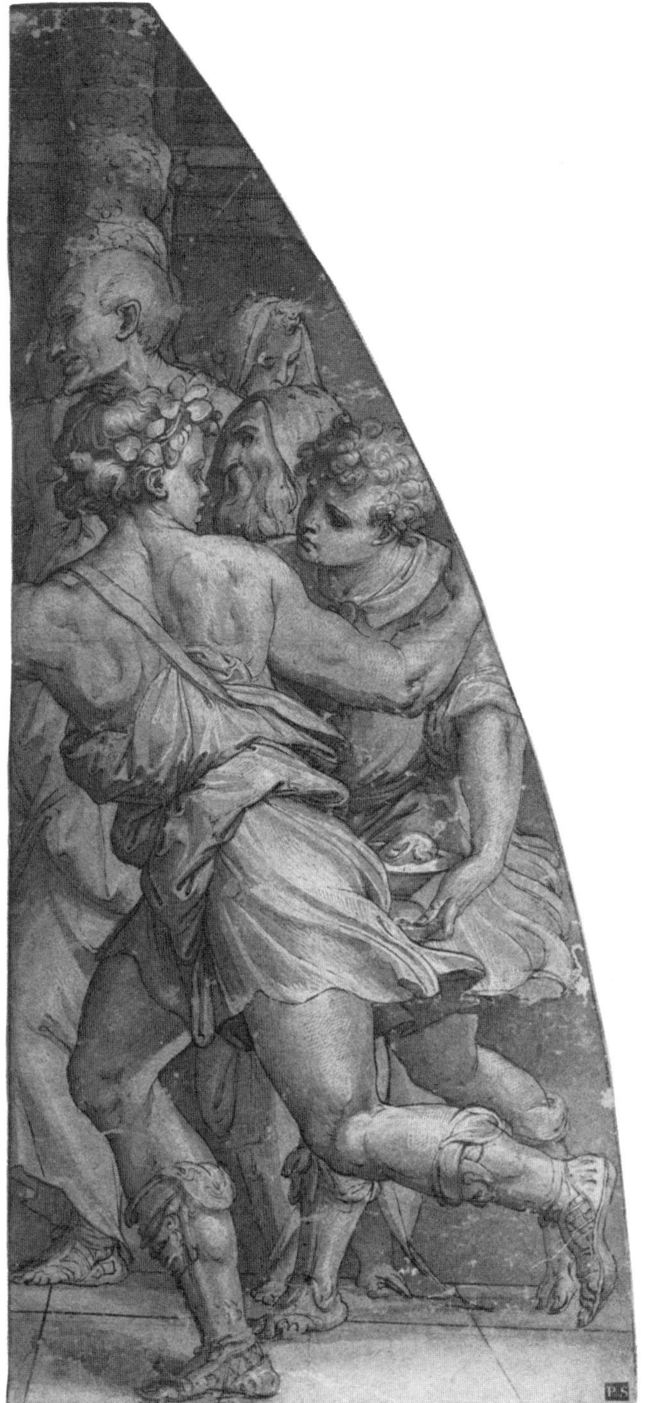

12 13

41

Luca Cambiaso

Moneglia 1527 – 1585 Genoa

14 *Martyrdom of St. Sebastian*

Pen and brown ink and wash. 745 x 430 mm (two sheets joined).

This large drawing has not been connected with any known painting by Luca Cambiaso. However, the long-haired youthful type and the contrapposto pose of St. Sebastian are generally analogous to the same saint in Cambiaso's *St. Roche between Saints Siro and Sebastian* (ca.1555) in the church of Santa Maria della Castagna, Quarto dei Mille, Genoa.[1] In addition, the setting with tall columns on plinths and various buildings *all'antica* finds parallels in a number of Roman subjects done by Cambiaso, often in collaboration with Giambattista Castello, il Bergamasco, in the 1550s and 1560s, such as the frescoes in the Palazzo Imperiale in Campetto (ca.1560).[2]

Mary Newcome Schleier points out that a related drawing attributed to Bergamasco is in the Bagnasco collection, Switzerland.[3]

1 B. Suida Manning and W. Suida, *Luca Cambiaso, la vite e le opere,* Milan, 1958, pp. 53-54, fig. 58.

2 *Ibid.*, pp. 87-89, figs. 49-50.

3 Private communication to the present owner.

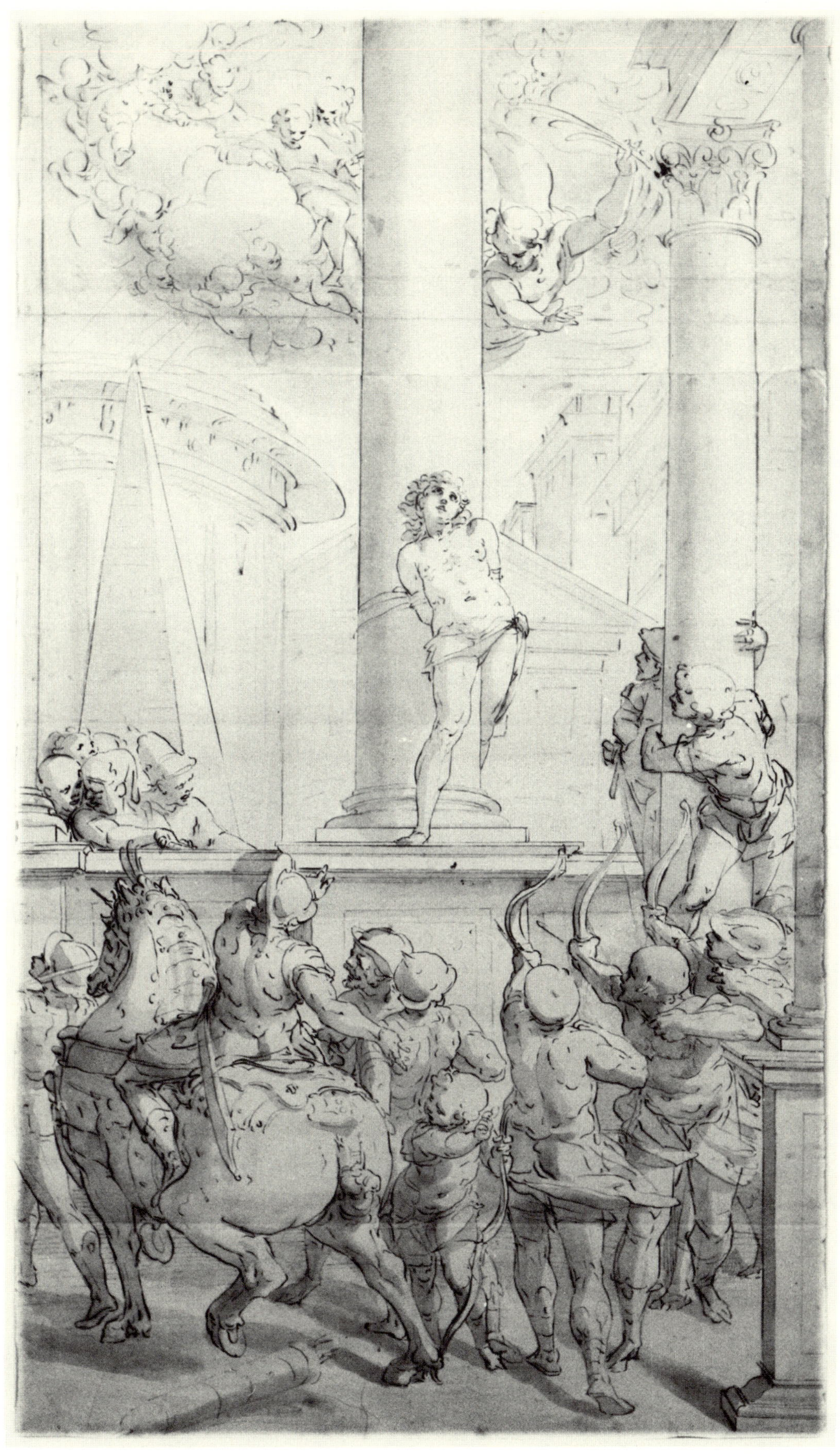

Giuseppe Porta
called Giuseppe Salviati

Castelnuovo di Garfagnana ca.1520 – ca.1575 Venice

15 *Christ, the Saviour, above Saint John the Baptist, St. Jerome, St. Catherine and St. Thomas*

Pen and brown ink and wash, over traces of black chalk, heightened with white, on blue paper. Above, an inscribed arch. 208 x 108 mm. Inscribed on the mount in an old hand: *Palma Vecchio*

Provenance: John Brophy; Sotheby's, London, 25 November 1971, lot 158 (as Palma il Giovane); Christie's, London, 15 April 1980, lot 2.

Although the drawing was ascribed to Palma Giovane when it was in the Brophy collection, there can be no doubt about its present attribution to Giuseppe Salviati. The same four saints in an arched frame appear in Salviati's altarpiece in the Bragadin chapel, immediately to the right of the main door of San Francesco della Vigna, Venice (fig. 15a).[1] In the altarpiece, Saints Jerome and Catherine have been moved to the front, but their poses show similarities to those of the foreground saints in the drawing. In both drawing and painting, St. Catherine looks diagonally upward, and places one hand at her breast, while her other hand holds the palm and wheel. The hovering Saviour of the drawing has been substituted in the painting with a crucifix, secured to a branch growing out of the hillock at the left.

Three of the four saints are shown with conspicuous attributes and are easily recognized; the fourth figure can be almost certainly identified by reference to the patron's immediate family.[2] On the floor of the chapel a tomb slab is inscribed with the names of Girolamo Bragadin, *Procurator de ultra* who died in 1545, his wife Caterina and son Tommaso. Another son, Giovanni, is named in Girolamo Bragadin's will. Since the three identifiable saints are the name saints of the donor, his wife and one son, it seems likely that the fourth saint is St. Thomas, the name of the second son. In the final painting it is also possible that the figures are portraits of the Bragadin family.[3]

The drawing's elongated figures, with animated but artificial gestures and in the case of the two anchorites a dishevelled Parmigianino-like mien, become in the painting more stocky and altogether more stolid. This transformation is not uncommon in the evolution of Giuseppe Salviati's compositions.

The relative looseness of the draughtsmanship and the lack of emphatic modelling suggest a reasonably advanced date in the artist's career, at least in the latter part of the 1550s.[4]

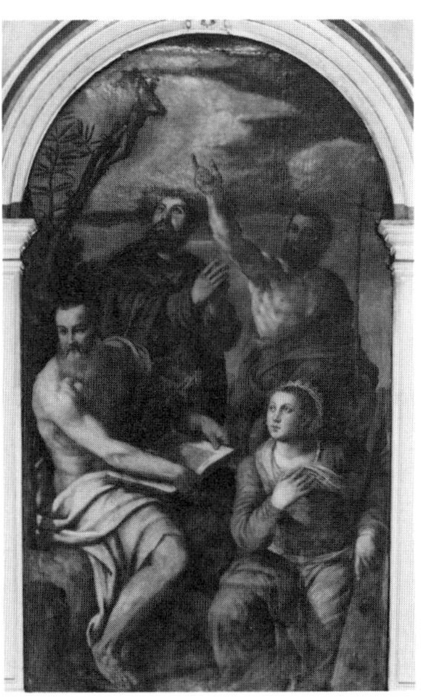

fig. 15a Giuseppe Salviati, *Sts. Jerome, Thomas, John the Baptist and Catherine*, oil on canvas, San Francesco della Vigna, Venice.

1 Repr. D. McTavish, *Giuseppe Porta called Giuseppe Salviati,* New York and London, 1981, fig. 192.

2 *Ibid.*, pp. 167-69, 289-93.

3 As occurs in Giuseppe Salviati's altarpiece in the Dandalo chapel in S. Francesco della Vigna, and probably also in Paolo Veronese's altarpiece (ca.1551) in the Giustiniani chapel of the same church. In the latter, Antonio Giustiniani is shown as St. Anthony Abbot and Lorenzo Giustiniani as St. Joseph.

4 The drawing may even be compared to Salviati's modello at Chatsworth (no. 17, repr. Tietzes, pl. XCVIII, 1) for the *Reconciliation of Alexander III and Frederick Barbarossa* of ca. 1562-64.

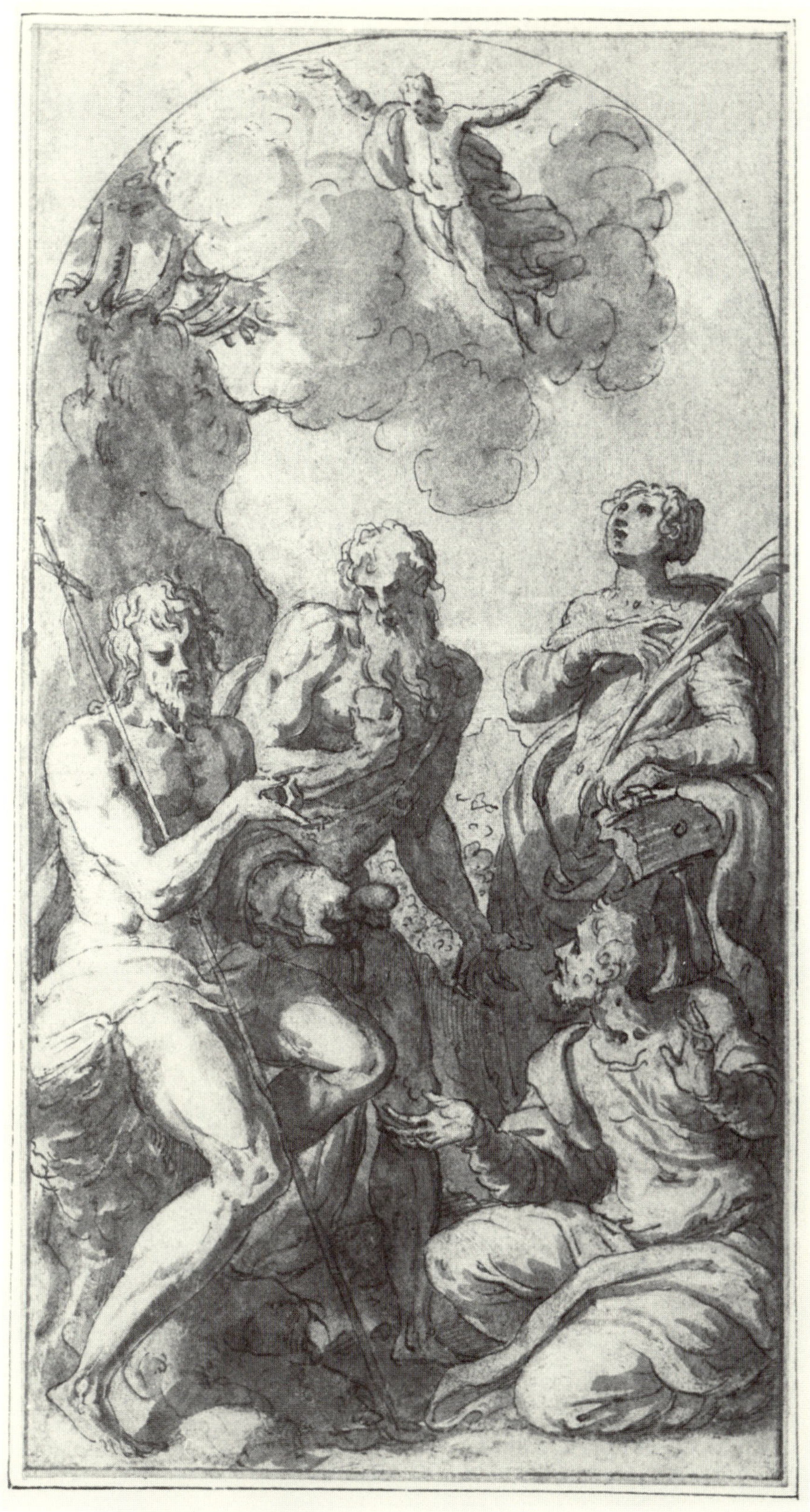

Paolo Caliari
called Paolo Veronese

Verona 1528 – 1588 Venice

16 *Studies of a Rape of Ganymede and a Last Supper*

Pen and brown ink and wash. Laid down. Additional studies on the *verso*. 288 x 192 mm. Inscribed in brown ink at the lower right: *Ganimede rapitto da Giove;* below that, in another hand: *di Paolo Veronese;* and on the backing *P. N° 46.*

Literature: R. Cocke, *Veronese's Drawings, A Catalogue Raisonné,* London, 1984, pp. 258-59, no. 110, repr.

Provenance: Unidentified collection (Lugt, Suppl. 2103a, sometimes identified as the Borghese collection; the inscription, however, only added in the second half of the eighteenth century; Sotheby's, London, 9 July 1981, under lot 132); H.M. Calmann; Christie's, London, 9 December 1982, lot 150.

The sequence in which Veronese studied the two unrelated subjects, one secular and one sacred, on this splendid sheet can be traced with uncommon assurance. Beginning at the upper left, Veronese set down the fully developed study of Ganymede and the eagle, and then proceeded to change the inclination of the head of each. Below in a quick pen sketch, without wash, he repeated the pose of Ganymede, alone, with the head in the corrected position. Veronese then undertook another full study, but with Ganymede seen from the side, and the eagle's pinions, which do not intersect the leg of the first Ganymede, flapping behind. Again the head of the eagle was studied in two positions. At the lower left Veronese reverted to the pose of the first study, but has now aligned the two heads and Ganymede's bent arm. Lastly, at the upper right Veronese drew the rectangular composition of a Last Supper which again does not impinge upon the forms of the first sketch. The sheet has probably been trimmed along the left side; the resulting *mise en page* is one of the drawing's most striking features.

No painting of Ganymede by Paolo Veronese is known, but the composition study of a Last Supper relates closely to a painting (fig. 16a) in the Cappella del Sacramento, to the left of the high altar in the church of San Giuliano (Zulian), Venice.[1] Although Ridolfi and other early writers ascribed the painting to the master, in this century most scholars have given it to a member of his studio, most likely his younger brother Benedetto Caliari.[2] Veronese may well have provided other, more detailed studies for the use of the workshop in completing the picture, but these have not been traced. The painting probably dates from about 1483 or shortly thereafter,[3] that is, from the last years of Veronese's life.

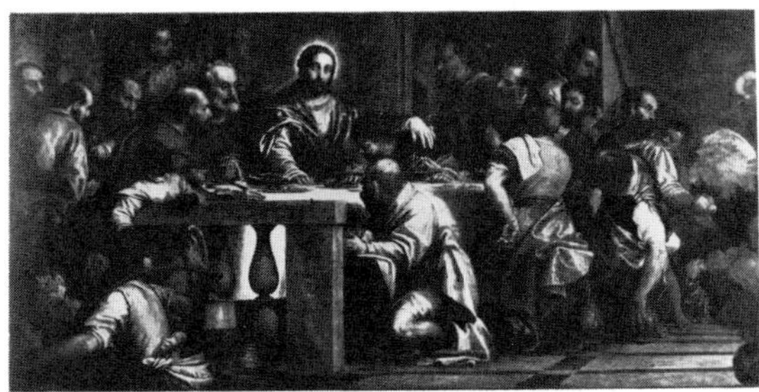

fig. 16a Workshop of Paolo Veronese, *Last Supper*, oil on canvas, San Giuliano, Venice.

1 An identification first made in *Important Old Master Drawings,* Christie's, London, 9 December 1982, lot 150. The association *(ibid.)* of the studies of Ganymede with Veronese's *Jupiter Crowning Germany,* formerly in the Kaiser Friedrich Museum, is not convincing.

2 Ridolfi, I, p. 325. Von Hadeln was the first to assign the picture to the studio (in his notes to Ridolfi, *ibid*). Also see T. Pignatti, *Veronese,* Venice, 1976, I, p. 215, A341.

3 S. Mason Rinaldi, ''La Cappella del SS. Sacramento in San Zulian,'' *Atti dell'Istituto Veneto di Scienze, Lettere ed Arti,* CXXXIV, 1975-76, p. 446, documenting that two outside windows, to be covered by paintings, were not filled in until 1583.

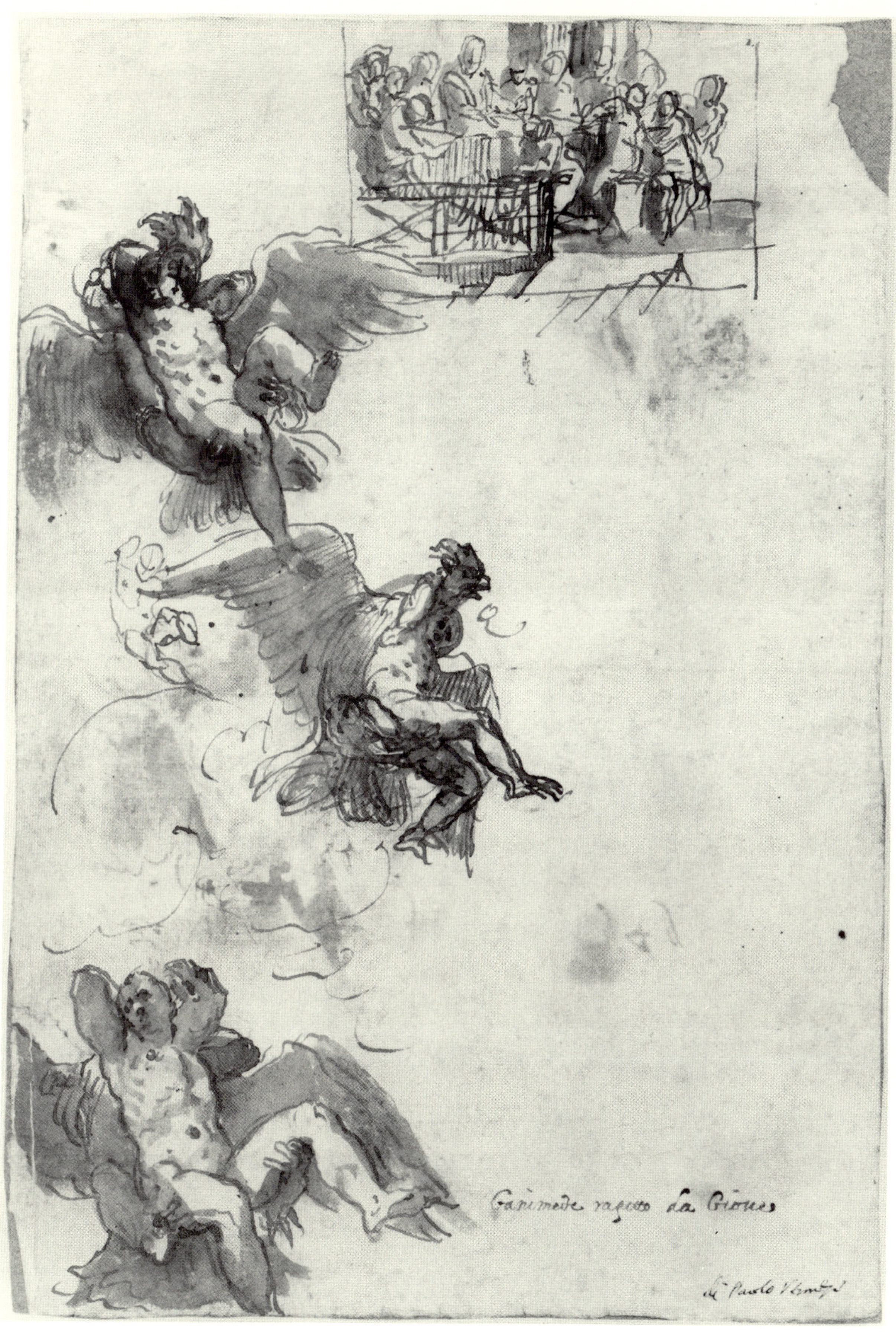

Ganimede rapito da Giove
di Paolo Veronese

Jacopo Palma
called Palma Giovane

Venice 1544 – 1628 Venice

17 *St. Christopher Bearing the Christ Child*

Pen and brown ink and wash, heightened with white (slightly oxidized) over black chalk on light brown paper. 265 x 194 mm

Provenance: Sir Peter Lely (Lugt 2092).

No known surviving painting relates to this drawing. The early written sources, however, refer to a painting of the subject by Palma Giovane in the church of Santa Maria dei Crociferi, which was replaced in the seventeenth century by the church of the Gesuiti.[1] The painting of St. Christopher is last mentioned in Marco Boschini's guide book to Venice of 1674.[2] Another drawing of St. Christopher, executed solely in pen and ink and showing the saint from the front, without a specific setting, has also been associated with the picture once belonging to the Crociferi,[3] but in the absence of further evidence this must also remain hypothetical. Both drawings represent Palma Giovane at his most monumental.

1 Ridolfi, II, p. 173; Sansovino-Martinioni, p. 169. Ridolfi implies that the painting was done early in Palma's career and was *'sotto il Coro.'* See also N. Ivanoff and P. Zampetti, *Giacomo Negretti detto Palma il Giovane,* I Pittori Bergamaschi, Il Cinquecento, vol. III, Bergamo, 1979, p. 610, no. 657; and S. Mason Rinaldi, *Palma il Giovane, l'opera completa,* Milan, 1984, p. 184.

2 M. Boschini, *Le ricche Minere della Pittura veneziana,* Venice, 1674, Cannaregio, p. 12.

3 S. Mason Rinaldi in *Fine Old Master Drawings,* Sotheby's, London, 9 April 1981, lot 70. The *verso* includes studies for a baptism and St. Catherine transported to heaven, both connected with paintings for Santa Caterina, Venice (1613). The figure of St. Christopher is closely repeated in a drawing in Budapest (inv. 2259), which, however, also includes brown wash; *Disegni veneti del Museo di Budapest,* catalogue by I. Fenyö, Fondazione Giorgio Cini, Venice, Vicenza, 1965, p. 36, no. 36, repr.

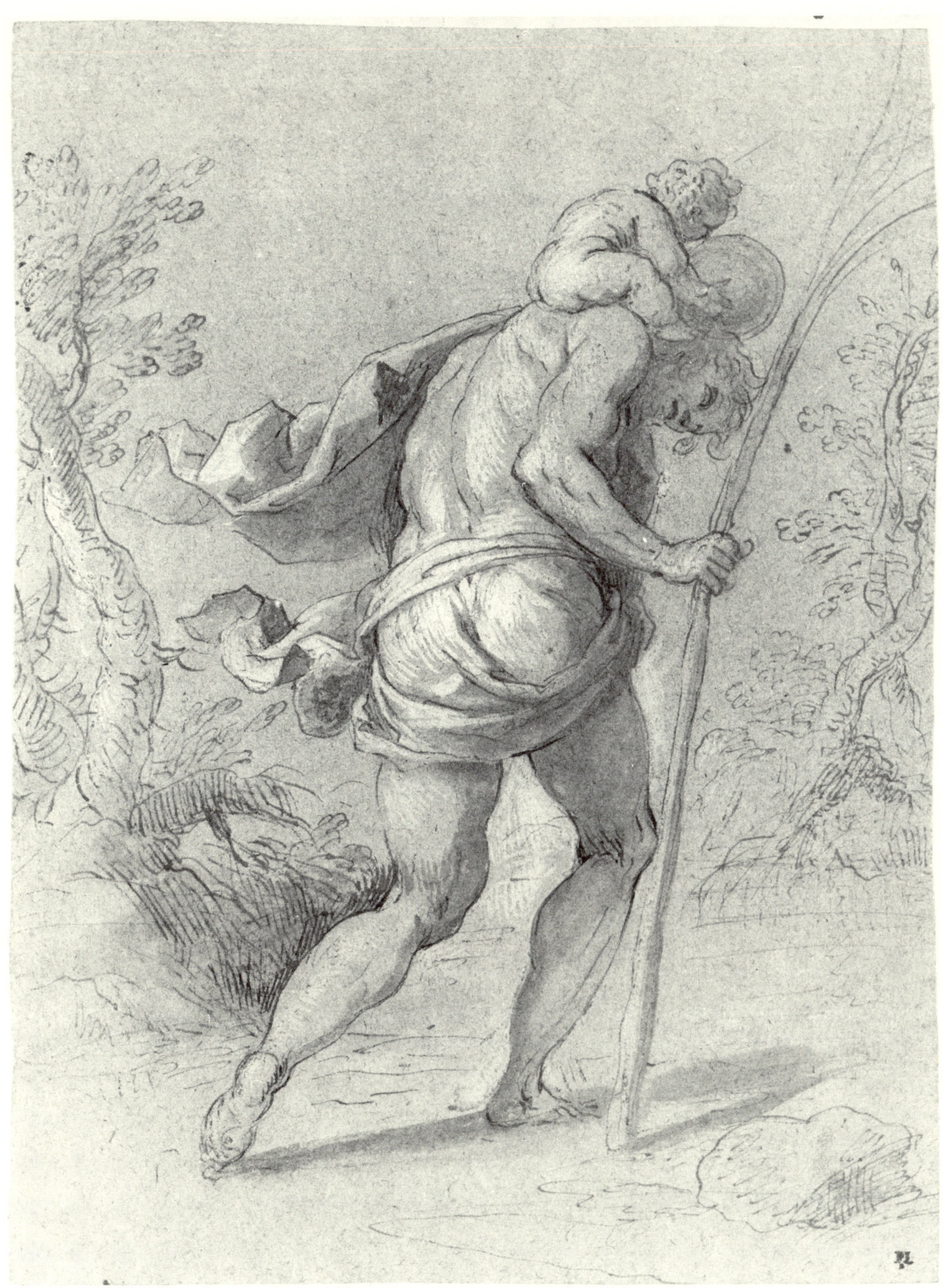

Jacopo Palma
called Palma Giovane

Venice 1544 – 1628 Venice

18 *Pentecost*

Oil on paper. Grisaille. 376 x 204 mm, arched top

Provenance: Sotheby's, London, 15 June 1983, lot 29.

This drawing was sold at auction as by Domenico Tintoretto, who made a specialty of doing monochromatic studies in oil on paper. Occasionally the technique was also used by Palma Giovane, and in fact, this drawing corresponds closely in most details to his altarpiece in the Duomo, Oderzo (Treviso).[1] The absence of the luminous dove of the Holy Spirit and the radiating tongues of fire in the drawing is the only major difference between the two. The painting must date from about 1605 when Monsignor Attilio Amalteo consecrated the altar, dedicated appropriately to the Holy Spirit. Palma Giovane completed at least two other paintings of the Pentecost (Omis, Yugoslavia and Agordo); all three reveal analogies with Titian's altarpiece of the Pentecost for Santo Spirito in Isola (now Santa Maria della Salute) and Jacopo Bassano's altarpiece for San Francesco, Bassano (now Museo Civico, Bassano).

Other drawings in a similar style by Palma Giovane include a sheet in Hartford for a painting in Sebenico and one in the Louvre for a painting in the church of San Geremia, Venice.[2]

1 For the painting see S. Mason Rinaldi, *Palma il Giovane, l'opera completa,* Milan, 1984, p. 97, no. 182, fig. 403. A squared drawing from the circle of Palma Giovane which relates in many details to both the present drawing and the altarpiece at Oderzo is in Budapest (inv. 2178); *Disegni veneti del Museo di Budapest,* catalogue by I. Fenyö, Fondazione Giorgio Cini, Venice, Vicenza, 1965, p. 39, no. 41, repr.

2 Tietzes, nos. 975 (then in the Cérenville collection, Lausanne) and 1108, figs. CLXXXI, 3-4.

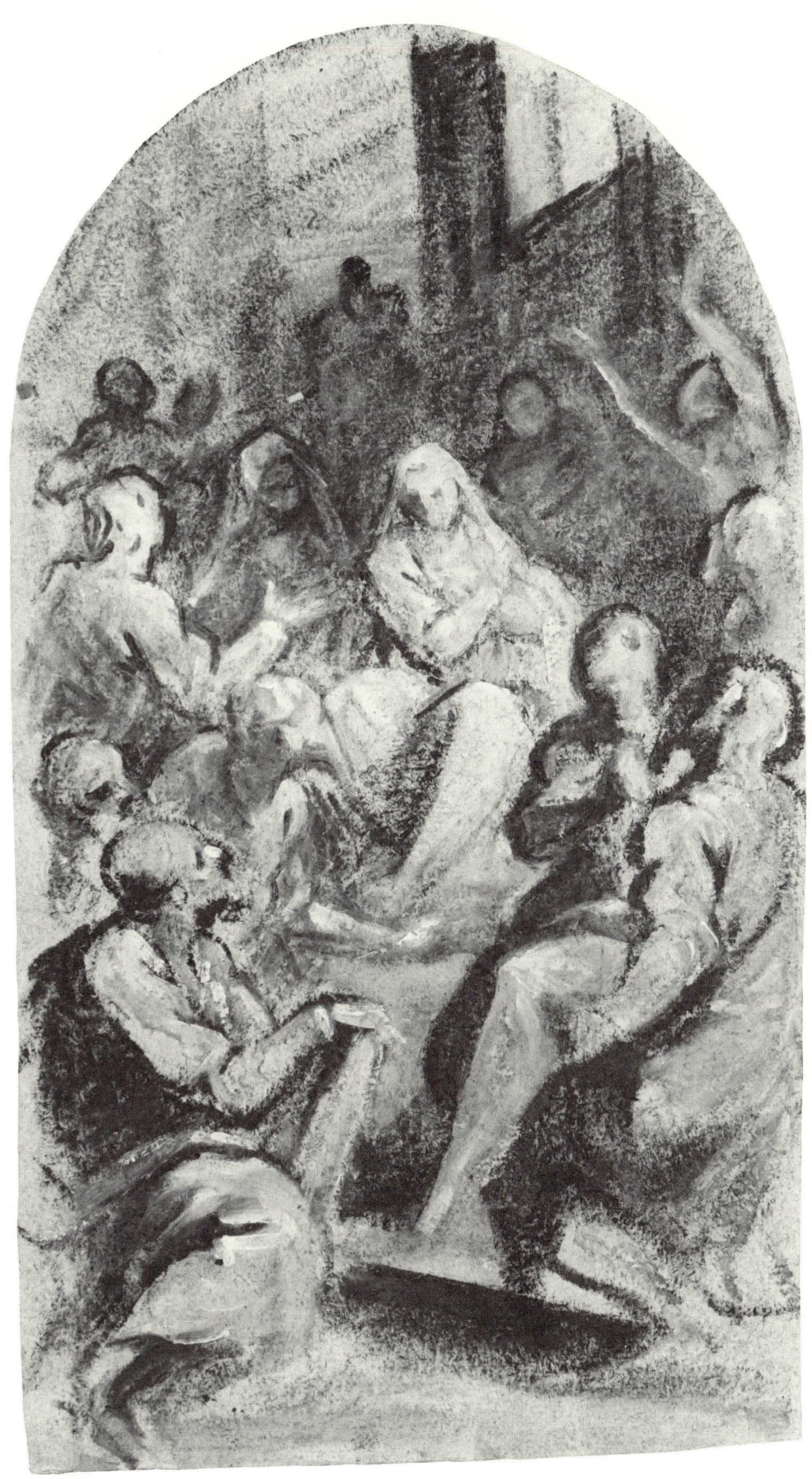

Pirro Ligorio

Naples 1513/14 – 1583 Ferrara

19 *Portrait Bust of An Unidentified Roman Matron*

Fol. 47 of a volume of sixty-one leaves, bound in sixteenth-century, gold-embossed red morocco. Pen and brown ink. 198 x 135 mm (folio); 202 x 140 mm (binding)

Literature: L. Dania, ''An Unpublished Manuscript by Pirro Ligorio,'' *Master Drawings,* XV, 1977, pp. 22-25, figs. 1-2, pls. 17a-20c.

Provenance: Giovanni Angelo Barbello; his brother Carlo Antonio Barbello, painter of Crema; Domenico Basso, 1660; Bernardino Sarsetti 1766 (all according to inscriptions in the book; *cf.* Dania, *op.cit.*, p. 22).

This small manuscript of sixty-one leaves is devoted entirely to Roman feminine hair styles.[1] It comprises both a hand-written, thirteen-page introduction to the subject and fifty-one bust-length portraits in pen and ink of prominent female figures from Roman antiquity. All but two (fol. 40-41) of the heads are in profile; the majority are identified, and many are accompanied by a short discussion of the hair style and/or its antique source, whether it be sculpted bust, funeral monument, or intaglio.

The introduction is signed *Pyrrho Ligorio Architetto di N.S./del Sacro Palazzo/Apostolico* (Pirro Ligorio, Architect to the Holy Father's Sacred Apostolic Palace),[2] and indeed Pirro Ligorio is well known as papal architect to Paul IV (1555-9) and Pius IV (1559-65). It is not, however, in Ligorio's capacity as architect, but rather as artist, and perhaps even more as antiquary, that the interest of the present volume lies. In the earlier part of his career, Ligorio had been especially active as a painter of frescoes on Roman façades, but these have all disappeared.[3] By 1553 he had also filled forty volumes of information about Roman antiquities, which he intended to publish; in 1568 he was recommended as the leading antiquary in Rome (*''un antiquario, il quale è il primo di Roma''*).[4] Executed in an engraver-like technique, the drawings in the present volume are typical of Ligorio's pen and ink illustrations and may be compared to other drawings by him after the antique, such as those in a volume now in the Biblioteca Nazionale, Naples.[5]

The present volume is dedicated to *Illustrissima e Eccellentissima signora donna Verginia,* whom Luigi Dania has identified as Donna Virginia della Rovere (1539-71), daughter of Duke Guidobaldo II and Giulia Varano.[6] She was married in 1560 to Federico Borromeo, nephew of Pius IV, Ligorio's patron. Dania dates the manuscript to about 1560.[7]

---

1 It has been discussed in detail by L. Dania, *op.cit.* Dania considers the drawings on fols. 25-30 to be by a later hand, but I see no reason for excluding them from Pirro Ligorio.

2 Repr. Dania, *op.cit.*, p. 23, fig. 2.

3 G. Baglione, *Le vite de'pittori, scultori et architetti…*(1642), ed. V. Mariani, Rome, 1935, pp. 9-12. The early drawings by Ligorio are discussed by J.A. Gere, ''Some Early Drawings by Pirro Ligorio,'' *Master Drawings,* IX, 1971, pp. 239-250.

4 By the Ferrarese ambassador to Rome; V. Pacifici, *Ippolito II d'Este, Cardinal di Ferrara,* Tivoli, 1920, p. 399, quoted in E. Mandowsky and C. Mitchell, *Pirro Ligorio's Roman Antiquities,* London, 1963, p. 5.

5 Published by Mandowsky and Mitchell, *op.cit.*

6 Dania, *op.cit.*, p. 22.

7 Dania, *op.cit.*, p. 25.

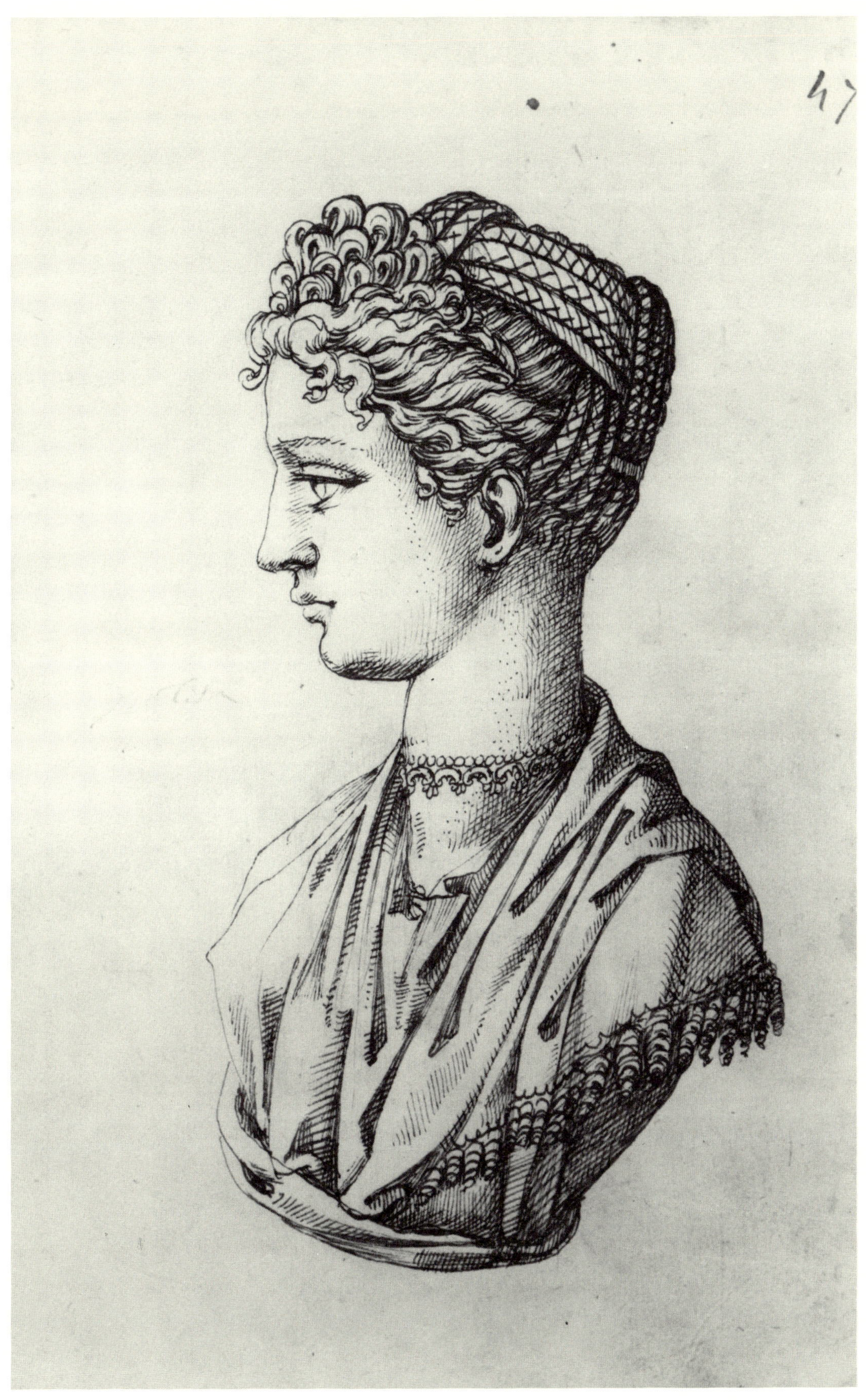

Federico Zuccaro

Sant'Angelo in Vado 1540/41 – 1609 Ancona

20 *A Group of Apostles (recto);*
The Virgin of the Assumption (verso)

Pen and brown ink and wash over black chalk, heightened
with white, incised with the stylus *(recto)*; black chalk *(verso)*.
Stains. 239 x 177 mm

Literature: J.A. Gere. ''Two of Taddeo Zuccaro's last
commissions, completed by Federico Zuccaro. I: The Pucci
Chapel in S. Trinità dei Monti,'' *Burlington Magazine,* CVIII,
1966, p. 293, fig. 18; *idem., Taddeo Zuccaro, His Development
Studied in His Drawings,* London, 1969, p. 147, under no. 52.

Provenance: Albert Wade; Christie's, London, II December
1979, lot 21.

John Gere has connected this double-sided sheet with the
Assumption of the Virgin on the lower part of the altar wall of the
Pucci Chapel, within the *clausura* of the north transept of Trinità
dei Monti, Rome.[1] Inadvertently, the frescoed decoration of the
chapel continued throughout most of the sixteenth century, with
an earlier campaign entrusted to Perino del Vaga and a later one
to Taddeo Zuccaro. The patronage of the chapel changed also:
after Cardinal Lorenzo Pucci died in 1531 his heirs evidently
made no attempt to finish the decorations and on 5 September
1562 the Archbishop of Corfu, Giacomo Caucho, acquired the
rights to the chapel. On 8 June 1563 Caucho commissioned
Taddeo Zuccaro to complete the decorations, but before that
could be accomplished the artist had died of a sudden illness on
2 September 1566. The chapel was only finished by Taddeo's
brother, Federico, in 1589.

The *Assumption of the Virgin* was one of the paintings begun by
the imaginative Taddeo and finished by the more pedantic
Federico. A number of surviving preliminary drawings both by
Taddeo and by Federico help to clarify the prolonged genesis of
the composition, and attest to the divergent artistic personalities
of the two brothers. The present drawing appears to mark a
transitional point between the contributions of the two. The
apostles on the *recto* of the sheet are clearly for the lower left of the
painting, yet none appears in exactly the same pose in the finished composition. The kneeling apostle in the foreground and
the one bending over the sarcophagus at the right closely repeat
the corresponding figures in a squared drawing by Taddeo Zuccaro in a private collection. (fig. 20a).[2] And the faint indications
in black chalk of two figures above them seem to bear a similar
relationship to Taddeo's squared drawing. In contrast, the figure of St. James the Greater, with his pilgrim's hat and staff, is a
new addition, perhaps inspired, as John Gere has suggested, by
the inclusion of the saint in the same place in Daniele da Volterra's *Assumption of the Virgin* in the della Rovere chapel of the
same church.[3] Whereas the introduction of the saint may well
be Federico's idea, the pose is not dissimilar to certain standing
figures by Taddeo.[4] In the fresco, St. James the Greater appears
second from the left with his left arm extended.

The downward glance and clasped hands of the Virgin on the
verso contrast even more decisively with the upturned head and
outstretched arms of the expansive Virgin of the fresco, generally agreed to be entirely due to Federico. The pose of the Virgin
in the drawing approximates Taddeo's solution in a drawing in
the Uffizi, which Gere has convincingly argued is by Federico
after a lost sheet or sheets by Taddeo.[5] This sort of pose also
appears in Taddeo's drawings executed contemporaneously for
the high altar of San Lorenzo in Damaso.[6] The drawing on the
verso, executed entirely in black chalk, resembles in a less vigorous fashion Taddeo's manner of modelling draped figures.[7]

In view of the number of close ties with Taddeo's work, the
present drawing is more likely to have been done shortly
after Taddeo's death than years later, when Federico finally
succeeded in bringing the pictorial decoration of the chapel to
an end.

1 ''Two of Taddeo Zuccaro's last commissions, completed by Federico
   Zuccaro I: The Pucci Chapel in S. Trinità dei Monti,'' *Burlington Magazine,*
   CVIII, 1966, p. 293.

2 J.A. Gere, *Taddeo Zuccaro, His Development Studied in His Drawings,* London,
   1969, p. 147, under no. 52.

3 Gere, *op.cit.* (footnote 1), p. 293.

4 *E.g.,* the drawing in the Louvre of an allegorical female figure for the Palazzo
   Farnese (repr. Gere, *op.cit.* (footnote 2), fig. 163).

5 Uffizi, 13629F.; Gere, *op.cit.,* (footnote 1), p. 290, fig. 12. Taddeo Zuccaro did
   investigate the pose of the Virgin with outstretched arms in a drawing now
   in the Louvre (RF1870-29242) repr. Gere, *op.cit.* (footnote 2), pl. 172. For a list
   of drawings by Federico Zuccaro for the Virgin with outstretched arms,
   see W. Vitzthum, *Italian Drawings from North American Collections,* Norman
   Mackenzie Art Gallery, Regina, 1970, p. 26, under no. 14.

6 Gere, *op.cit.* (footnote 2), figs. 174-75.

7 *E.g.,* Gere, *op.cit.* (footnote 2), fig. 59. For a chalk drawing by Taddeo
   Zuccaro for the Pucci Chapel, see the sheet of studies of three angels in the
   Uffizi (92139), *ibid.,* fig. 169.

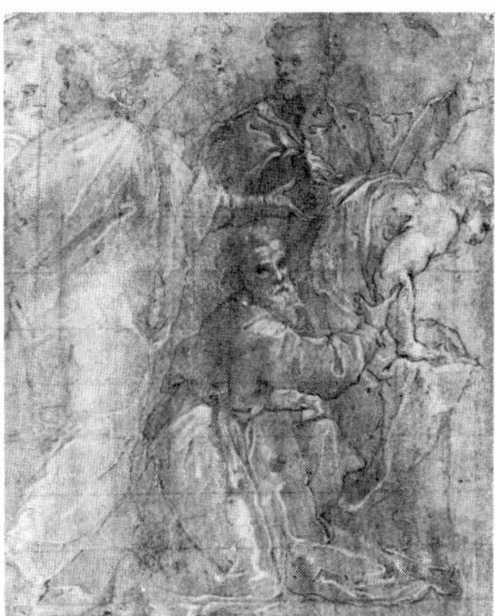

fig. 20a Taddeo Zuccaro, *A Group of Apostles,* pen and
brown ink and wash, heightened with white, squared
in black chalk, Rudolph S. Joseph collection.

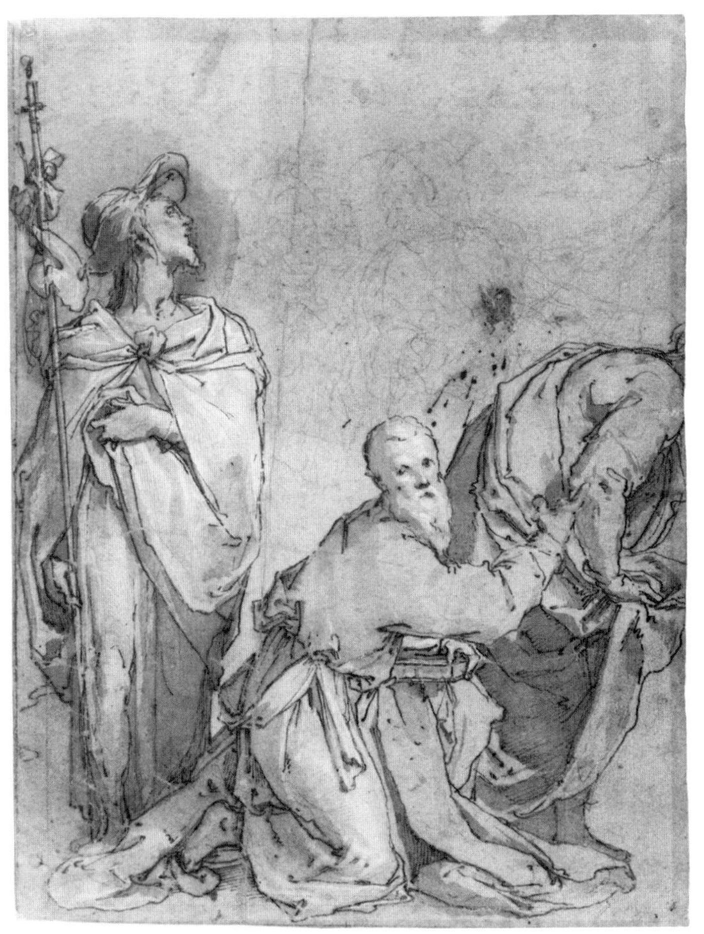

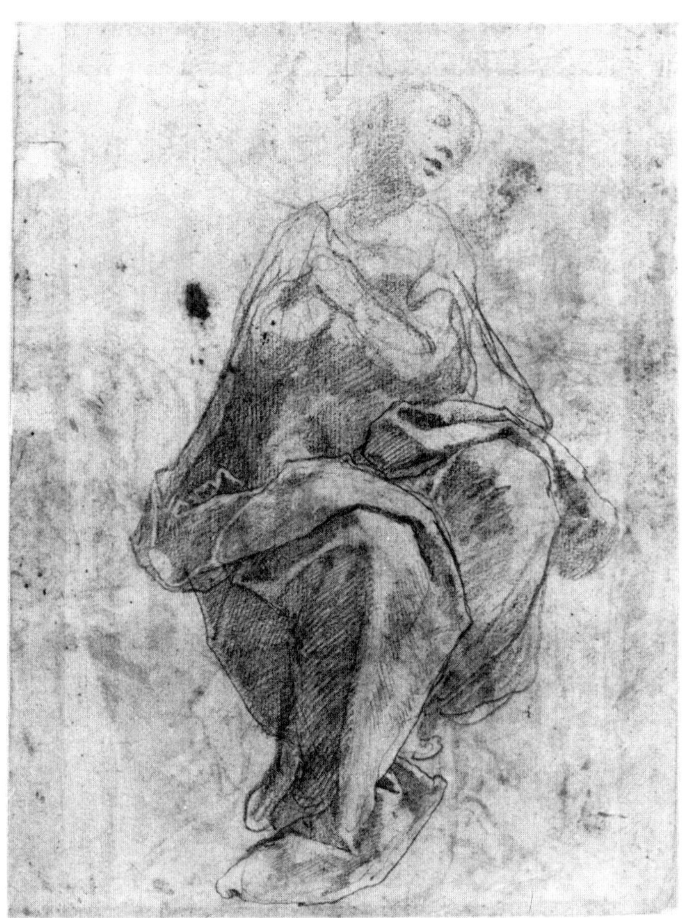

recto

verso

Federico Zuccaro

Sant'Angelo in Vado 1540/41 – 1609 Ancona

21 *David and Goliath (recto);*
Nude Female Figure with Geese (verso)

Pen and brown ink and wash over red chalk, the figure of
Goliath lightly squared in black chalk *(recto)*; red chalk *(verso)*.
Upper right stained. 304 x 252 mm. Inscribed in ink at lower
right: *Zuccari;* on the *verso*: *di Federigo Zuccaro*

Provenance: Unidentified collector's mark at lower left (not in
Lugt); Christie's, London, 29 November 1983, lot 16.

The purpose of this carefully composed drawing has not been
established, although because of the squaring it can be assumed
that the composition was intended for transfer to some other
surface.

Michelangelo, in one of the corner spandrels of the Sistine
Chapel, was the first to show David straddled above the fallen
body of the slain Philistine, "his face to the earth" (1 Samuel
17:49).[1] In Michelangelo's fresco, David clutches the hair of
Goliath's head with one hand, while with the other he is about to
decapitate the giant with his own sword. Federico Zuccaro's
drawing is a variation upon Michelangelo's composition, even
to the inclusion of the conical tent behind the protagonists, but
David is now shown leaping over the body of the already decapi-
tated Goliath. One hand holds high the giant's enormous sword
and the other thrusts forward the dripping head with the lethal
stone imbedded in its forehead. Another drawing by Federico
Zuccaro, in a horizontal format, represents the next moment in
the story: David (in more rustic garments) strides forward from
the body of Goliath, the enormous sword lowered and the head
of the giant held aloft.[2]

The red chalk drawing on the *verso* of a nude woman, accompanied by two geese and evidently pursued by two men, has not
been connected with any known work by Federico Zuccaro.

---

1 C. de Tolnay, *Michelangelo, II. The Sistine Ceiling,* Princeton, ed. 1969, p. 94.

2 Pen and ink and wash on blue paper, 225 x 290 mm. Present whereabouts
  unknown; in April 1953 it was with H.M. Calmann, cat. no. 13.

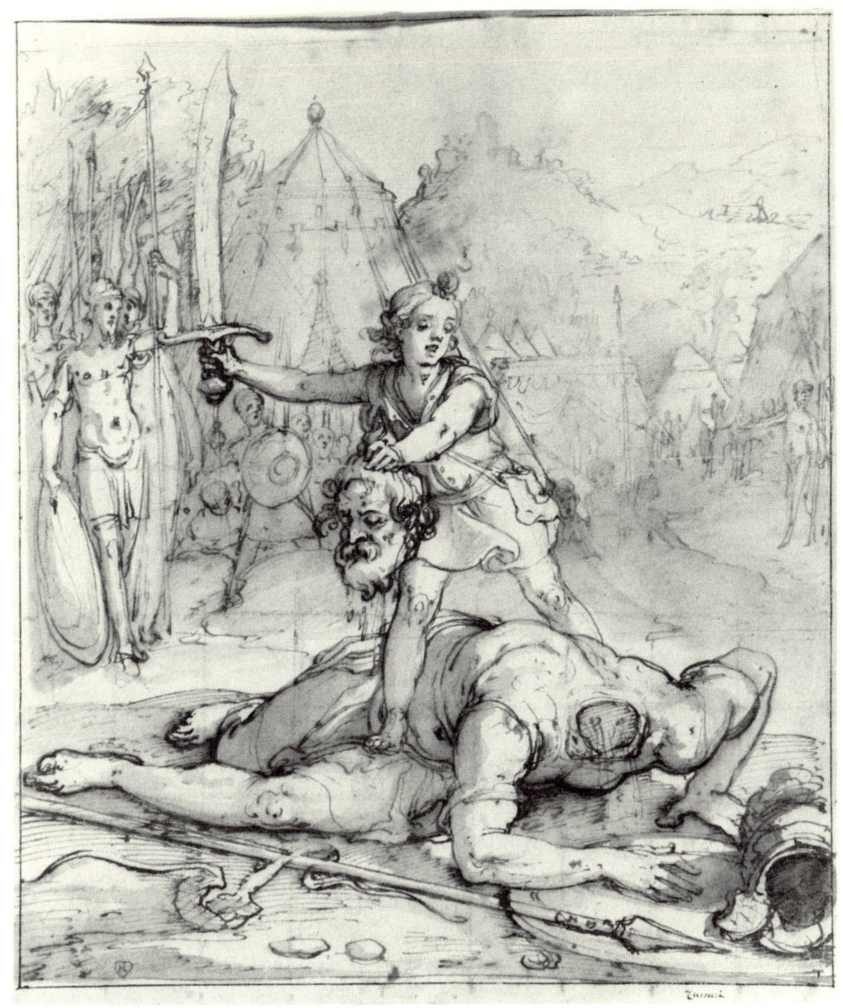

recto

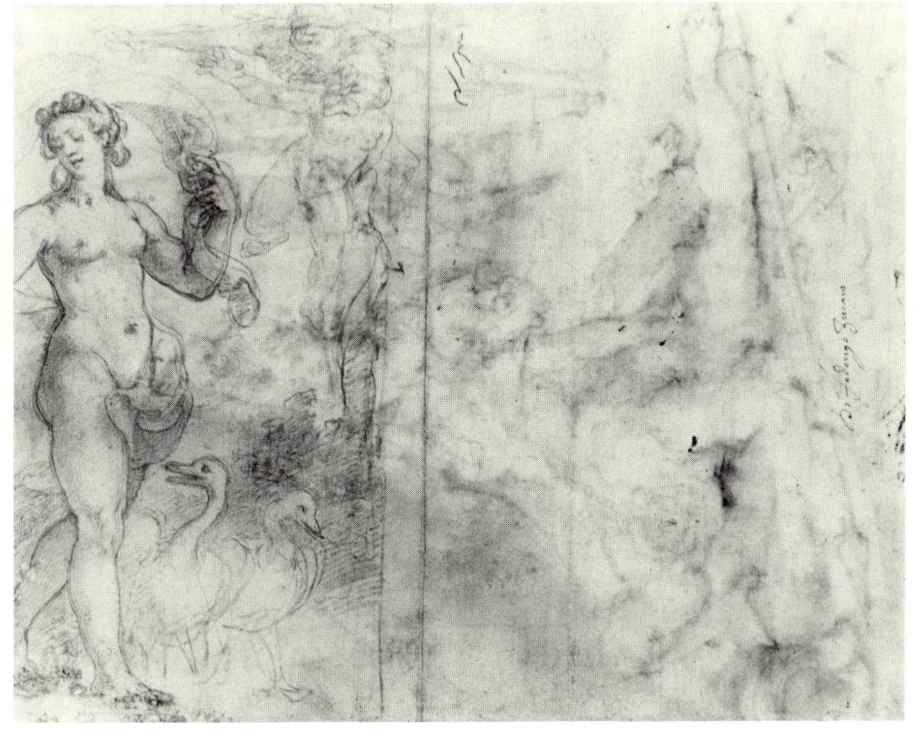

verso

Federico Barocci

Urbino ca.1535 – 1612 Urbino

22 *Aeneas with Anchises on His Shoulders*

Black chalk with some traces of white chalk; some lines incised with a stylus, in part squared in black chalk, squared with a stylus in the lower part, on light blue paper. 285 x 175 mm maximum

Provenance: Alessandro Maggiori.

See following entry.

23 *Head of a Boy*

Black, red, pink, and white chalk on blue paper. Laid down. Stains. 250 x 176 mm. Inscribed in ink at the upper left: *4*

Provenance: From a leather-bound album of drawings, mostly of heads, probably assembled in the seventeenth century (for which see Christie's sale catalogue as follows under no. 18), Christie's, London, 15 April 1980, lot 20.

Numbers 22 and 23 are connected with *Aeneas's Flight from Troy* (Virgil, *Aeneid*, II, lines 671-729), evidently Barocci's only non-religious painting apart from portraits. The picture was commissioned by Emperor Rudolf II in 1586 and was delivered to Prague in 1589, but is now lost. The composition was engraved by Agostino Carracci in 1595 and Barocci himself did a replica, dated 1598, for Monsignor Giuliano della Rovere, which is now in the Galleria Borghese, Rome (fig. 22a).[1]

As with the majority of Barocci's paintings, numerous preliminary drawings have been identified for *Aeneas's Flight from Troy.* No. 22, the nude figure study of Aeneas carrying his father Anchises, was preceded by a related nude study in the Uffizi, executed solely in black chalk and charcoal.[2] In no. 22 Barocci has gone further in his analysis of the musculature, such as

along the back of the father, and has begun to consider the drapery, including the kilt of Aeneas and the cloak billowing out from Anchises's waist. Barocci has also raised the position of Anchises's head, as can be seen in a *pentimento* at the upper left. In contrast, the artist has not yet begun to investigate such details as Aeneas's buskins and helmet; and the household gods held in Anchises's right hand are suggested only by a few circular lines. In Berlin there is a further study for the group in black, red, and white chalk, while at Windsor there is a detailed study in coloured chalks of Anchises's bearded head, as it appears in the finished painting.[3]

No figure study has yet been identified for Aeneas's son, Ascanius. His pose, however, is essentially worked out in the summary indications of the figures in a black chalk drawing in the Uffizi which is principally concerned with the architectural setting, and, which incidentally reveals that the relationship between the heads of Aeneas and Anchises was also at that moment taxing the artist considerably.[4] At Princeton there is a black and white chalk study of the arm and head of Ascanius, which closely resembles those details in the large cartoon recently rediscovered in the Louvre.[5] No. 23 represents a slimmer-faced, more youthful model, closer in type to a coloured chalk study of a head in Bayonne which has been connected with Ascanius by Edmund Pillsbury.[6] In all three drawings the figure is shown with straight hair, in contrast to the curly-headed boy of the painting. Lastly, there are detailed studies of the arm and hand of Ascanius in Berlin.[7]

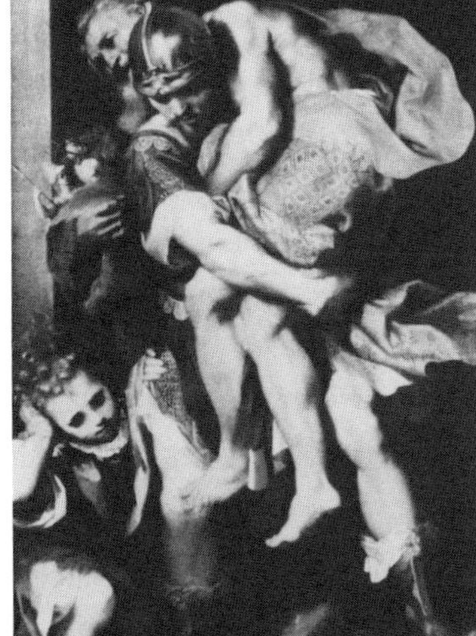

fig. 22a Federico Barocci, *Aeneas's Flight from Troy* (detail), oil on canvas, Galleria Borghese, Rome.

1 H. Olsen, *Federico Barocci,* Copenhagen, 1962, pp. 180-82, no. 39; A. Emiliani, *Mostra di Federico Barocci,* Museo Civico, Bologna, 1975, pp. 150-53.

2 n. 11642 F verso. The *recto* is a nude study for Creusa in the same painting. G.G. Bertelà, *Disegni di Federico Barocci,* Gabinetto Disegni e Stampe degli Uffizi, XLIII, Florence, 1975, p. 61, no. 56, fig. 64.

3 Berlin, KdZ 20294 (4417) (Olsen, *op.cit.*, p. 182). For the drawing at Windsor, see Emiliani, *op.cit.*, p. 150, no. 165 (repr.).

4 n.11296 F; Emiliani, *op.cit.* p. 150, no. 163 (repr.).

5 E. Pillsbury and L. Richards, *The Graphic Art of Federico Barocci,* The Cleveland Museum of Art, Cleveland, 1978, pp. 78-79, no. 55, repr.; for the cartoon see R. Bacou, *Cartons d'artistes du XVe au XIXe siècle,* Cabinet des Dessins, Musée du Louvre, Paris, 1974, p. 19, no. 14, pl. IX.

6 Pillsbury and Richards, *ibid.*; J. Bean, *Les dessins italiens de la Collection Bonnat,* Paris, 1960, no. 5 (repr.).

7 KdK 20220 (4232), 20293 (4240) and 20353 (4421), for which see Pillsbury and Richards, *ibid.*

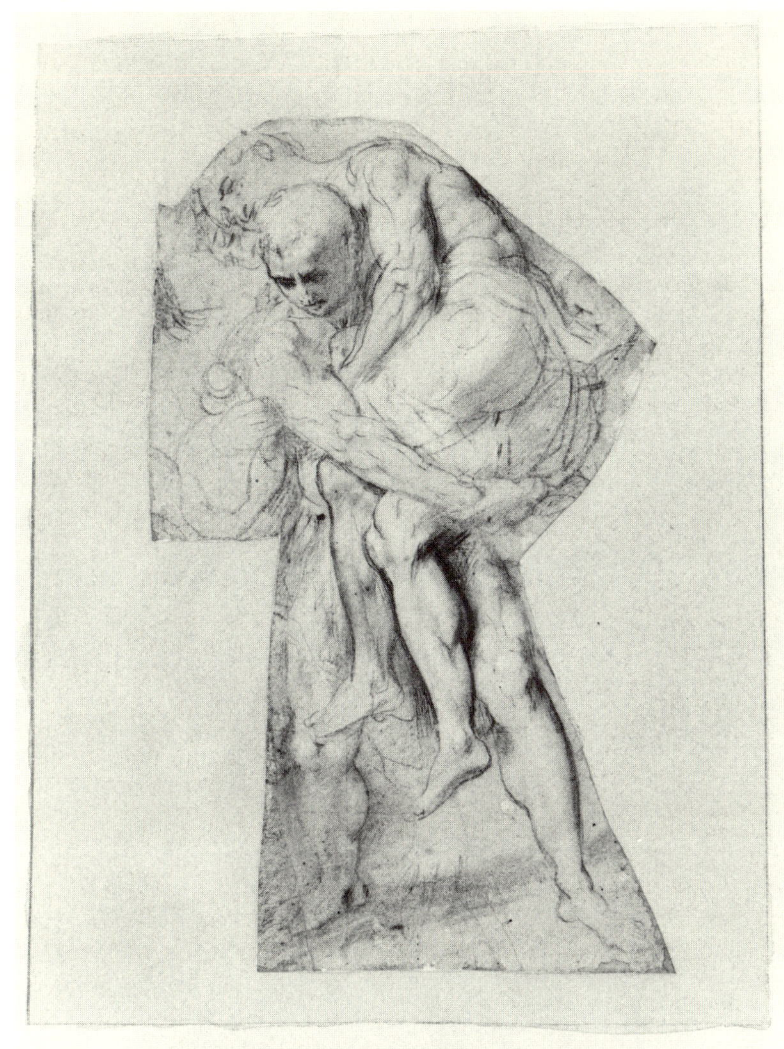

22

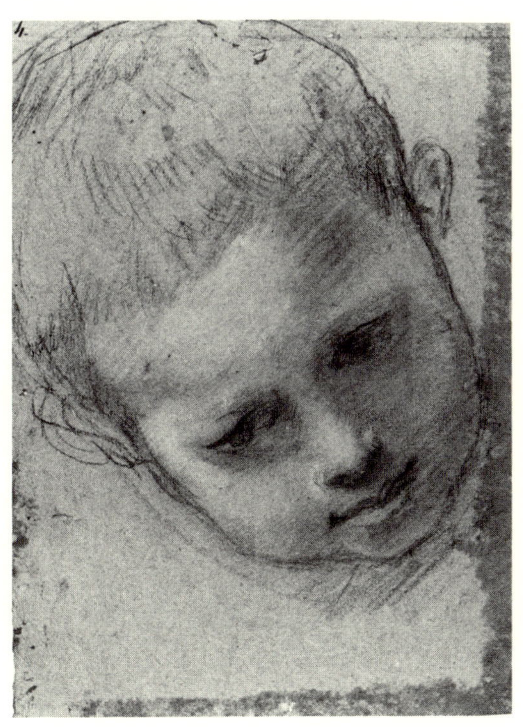

23

Cristofano Roncalli
called Pomarancio

Pomarance 1552 – 1626 Rome

24   *Two Studies of a Head with Eyes Closed*

Black and red chalk on blue paper. Some stains. Laid down.
217 x 353 mm. Inscribed lower left: *R*

Literature: Ileana Chiappini di Sorio, ''Due disegni del
Roncalli,'' *Notizie da Palazzo Albani,* X, no. 1, 1981, pp. 35-39.

Provenance: Paul Hatvany; Christie's, London, 24 June 1980,
lot 22.

Ileana Chiappini di Sorio has interpreted this drawing, already
attributed to Cristofano Roncalli, as alternative studies for the
emperor's head in the *Baptism of Constantine* (fig. 24a), one of the
large frescoes in the transept of San Giovanni in Laterano,
Rome.[1] Pomarancio's fresco was undertaken as part of a major
campaign, divided among eight artists with Cavaliere d'Arpino
as supervisor, to decorate the transept for the Jubilee of 1600.
The commission was given by Pope Clement VIII
(Aldobrandini), who together with his advisors also selected the
subject matter. Scenes from the life of the Emperor Constantine
were chosen in order to emphasize the origins and power of the
papacy. The frescoes were executed between May 1599 and
January 1601.[2]

In the *Baptism of Constantine* the emperor kneels in the foreground with his arms crossed at his breast and his head bowed to
the left. The position of the head at the left of the drawing
corresponds to the angle of the head in the fresco but, as Ileana
Chiappini has observed, the head at the right of the drawing in
other respects resembles the fresco more closely.[3] Thus the turn
of the head with the far cheek hidden, the juncture of the shoulder with the face at the chin, and the twist of the longer neck all
reappear in the fresco, but in reverse. Not present in either of
the heads depicted here are the moustache and slight beard of
the fresco.

In the Uffizi these are an early nude study for Constantine
and several head studies.[4] One head study (n.10145F) is based on
the *Apollo Belvedere* and supplies testimony to Pomarancio's keen
interest in classical sculpture as a source of artistic inspiration.
Many of his head studies are executed in a combination of red
and black chalk, as in the present example; as such these drawings combine the sculptural preoccupations of the Roman
school and the interest in light and *sfumato* of such Emilian
artists as Correggio.[5]

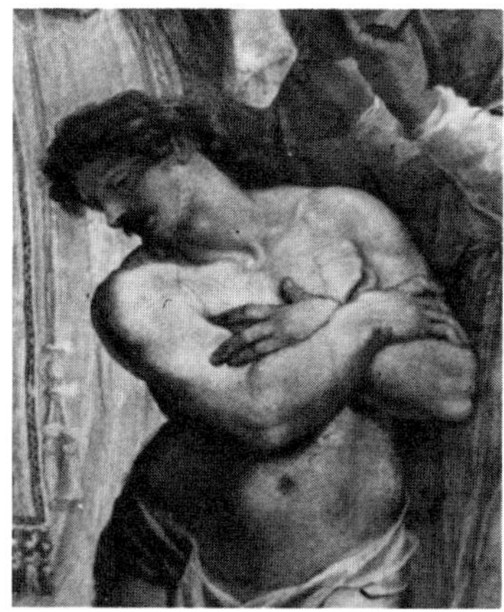

fig. 24a Pomarancio, *Baptism of Constantine* (detail),
fresco, S. Giovanni in Laterano.

---

1 Chiappini, *op. cit.*

2 W.C. Kirwin in *Disegni dei Toscani a Roma (1580-1620),* Gabinetto Disegni e
Stampe degli Uffizi, LIII, Florence, 1979, p. 37.

3 Chiappini, *op. cit.*, p. 36.

4 Uffizi, no. 10029F (Kirwin, *op. cit.*, pp. 36-38, no. 15, fig. 17) and nos. 10036F,
10145F-10147F, 10154F (Kirwin, *op. cit.*, p. 38); Uffizi 10145F is fig. 420 in
W.C. Kirwin, ''The Life and Drawing Style of Cristofano Roncalli,''
Paragone, XXIX, 335, 1978, and figs. 5 and 8 in Chiappini, *op. cit.*).

5 Cf. J.A. Gere, *Il Manierismo a Roma, I Disegni dei Maestri,* Milan, 1971, p. 21.

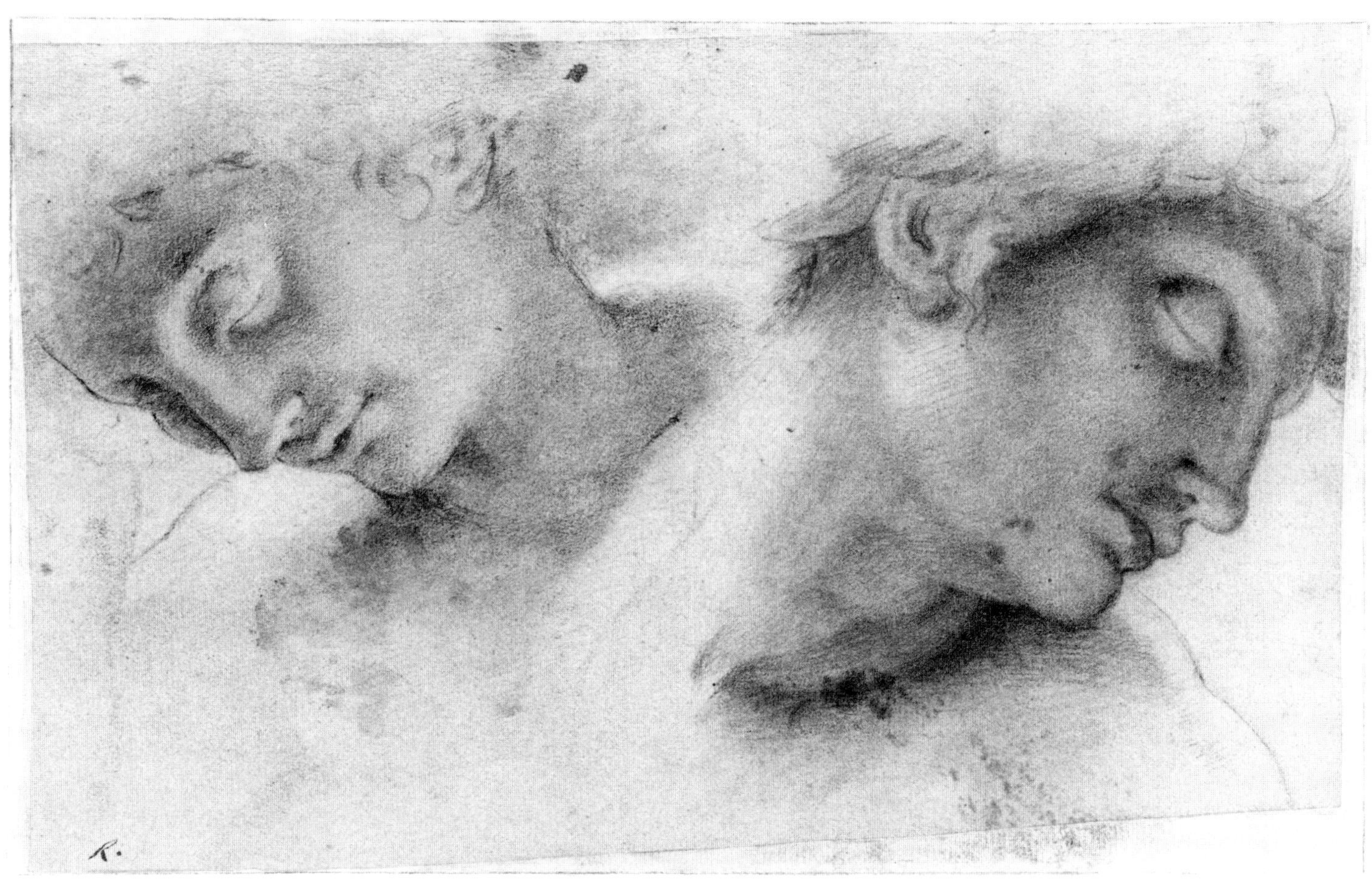

Belisario Corenzio

Naples ca.1560 – 1643 Naples

25 *The Flagellation*

Black chalk. Laid down. Some losses, repaired. 275 x 164 mm.
Inscribed on the mount: *Andrea Schiavoni*

Provenance: Sir Joshua Reynolds (Lugt 2364);
A.M. Champernowne (Lugt 153); Sotheby's, London,
27 April 1911; Christie's, London, 9 December 1980, lot 6.

The attribution on the mount to the Venetian Mannerist
Andrea Schiavone is irrelevant. Instead, the drawing allies itself
to a succession of depictions of the Flagellation, with brutish
scourgers seen both from the front and the back, done in Rome
during the sixteenth century. Especially relevant in this regard
are Federico Zuccaro's fresco in the Oratorio del Gonfalone of
1573 and a large engraving by G. Sadeler after Cavaliere
d'Arpino, dated 1593 (fig. 25a).[1] Because of the similarities
between the present drawing and the engraving it is tempting to
ascribe the drawing to the Cavaliere d'Arpino also. Yet the
figures in the drawing are less sharply articulated than
d'Arpino's and the draughtsmanship in general is lacking in his
characteristic crispness.

Herwarth Röttgen has suggested that the drawing should be
attributed to the Neapolitan artist, Belisario Corenzio, under
the influence of d'Arpino.[2] Beginning in 1589 the fashionable
Cavaliere had undertaken important frescoes on the vaults of
the choir and sacristy of the Certosa di San Martino, Naples,
and his influence on Corenzio was considerable. Corenzio's
own career was long and particularly productive: "he lived to
be almost one hundred and painted all Naples" quipped Padre
Resta.[3] Although numerous, and various, drawings have been
attributed to Corenzio,[4] the nature of his early drawings
remains ill-defined. In the absence of reliable comparative
material, then, the attribution of the present drawing should be
treated with some caution. Nevertheless, it may be noted that
the snub-nosed, almost caricature-like faces of some of the
figures in the drawing are a type frequently found in Corenzio's
work.

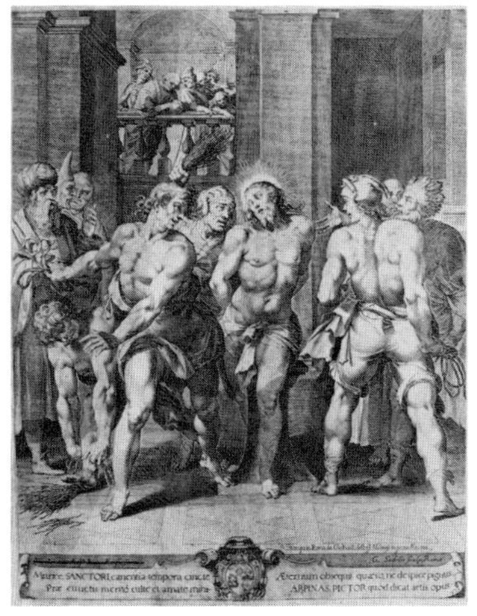

fig. 25a G. Sadeler after Cavaliere d'Arpino,
The Flagellation, engraving.

---

1 For the engraving see *Il Cavaliere d'Arpino*, catalogue by H. Röttgen, Palazzo
 Venezia, Rome, 1973, pp. 174-75, no. III.

2 *Important Old Master Drawings,* Christie's, London, 9 December 1980, lot 6.

3 *"visse poco meno di anni cento"* and *"ha dipinto…quasi tutta Napoli,"* with regard
 to a drawing by Corenzio in the Ambrosiana (n. 155), quoted by W. Vitzthum
 in *Cento Disegni Napoletani,* Gabinetto Disegni e Stampe degli Uffizi, XXVI,
 Florence, 1967, p. 14, under no. 2.

4 In particular by W. Vitzthum, *op.cit.*, pp. 14-17, nos. 2-5; *Disegni Napoletani
 dei Sei e del Settecento nel Museo di Capodimonte,* Naples, 1966, pp. 9-10, nos. 1-3;
 and *Le Dessin à Naples,* Cabinet des Dessins, Musée du Louvre, Paris, 1967,
 pp. 5-13, nos. 8-13.

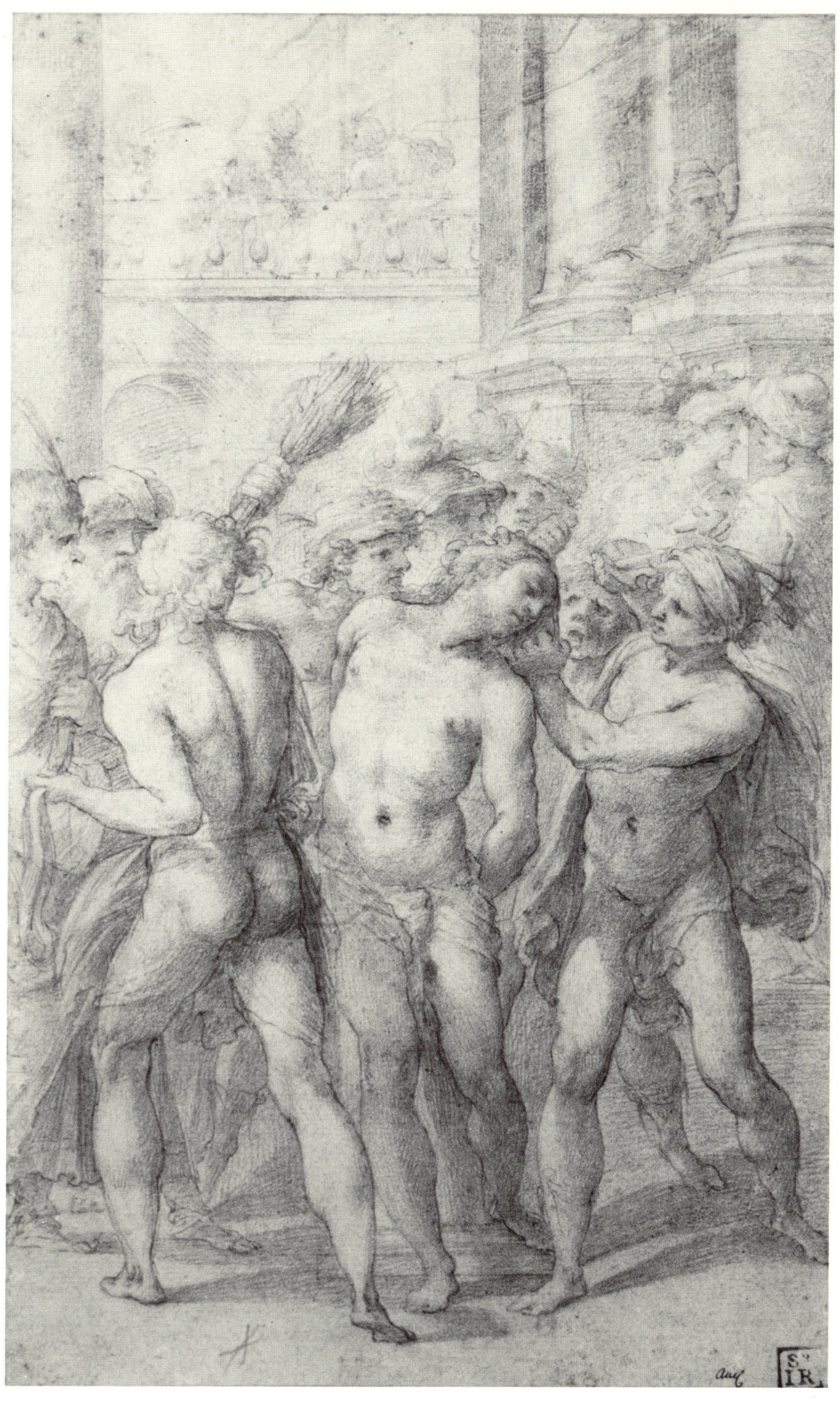

Anonymous

ca.1600(?)

26 *Head of a Young Man (recto);*
Head of a Man and Male Figure (verso)

Red and black chalk *(recto)*; red chalk *(Head of a Man)*, pen and brown ink *(Male Figure) (verso)*. Oil stains. 165 x 125 mm. Inscribed on the *recto* in pen and brown ink: *Bassano;* on the *verso* in red chalk and brown ink: *Jacopo Bassano;* lined with another sheet of paper inscribed: *Giacomo da Bassano* and *GG*(?) entwined in a monogram.

Literature: L. Grassi, "Cartella di Disegni inediti importanti," *Scritti in Onore di Ottavio Morisani,* Catania, 1982, pp. 236-39, figs. 124-26.

Provenance: Prof. Angelo De Gubernatis (according to Grassi, *op.cit.,* p. 237, n. 24).

Although attributed three times in old inscriptions to Bassano – twice specifically to Jacopo Bassano – this drawing is difficult to accept as being from the hand of Jacopo Bassano or of any other member of his family, at least as far as their drawings are now known. The sheet comes closest to a group of portrait drawings attributed either to Leandro Bassano or to Carletto Caliari, and indeed the Ferretti drawing has been published as "qualitatively the most significant of the entire group."[1] Yet the similarities with this group of drawings seem ultimately to be only generic. The drawings in the Leandro-Carletto group are executed in coloured chalks on blue or grey paper, whereas the present drawing is in red and black chalk on white paper. The differences between the two, however, are more fundamental than one of medium: the drawings of the Leandro-Carletto group present an emphatic and pictorial appearance with the chalk applied in a variety of touches, hatches, and smudges; in contrast, the Ferretti drawing possesses diagonal hatching which is softer and altogether more regular. In the use of *deux crayons* the Ferretti drawing may recall the portrait drawings of Federico Zuccaro, but its draughtsmanship is much less linear.[2] Less specific in the rendering of individual details than either the drawings in the Leandro-Carletto group or those by Federico Zuccaro, the sheet may well be by an artist who did not specialize in portraits.[3] That the artist is most likely to have come from the Veneto, however, is somewhat strengthened by the analogies of the small pen and ink sketch on the *verso* with Paolo Veronese's pen manner.

1 Grassi, *op.cit.,* p. 238, who accords the same distinction to the drawing of a head of a man in the Ashmolean Museum, Oxford (no. III). For a detailed discussion of these drawings and an argument in favour of the attribution to Carletto Caliari, see A. Ballarin, "Introduzione ad un catalogo dei disegni di Jacopo Bassano, II," *Studi di Storia dell'Arte in onore di Antonio Morassi,* Venice, 1971, pp. 144-49.

2 See D. Heikamp. "Federico Zuccaro a Firenze 1575-1579," *Paragone,* 205, 1967, pp. 55-56, pls. 36a-38.

3 It is worth noting certain similarities of the soft diagonal hatching with a drawing in Stockholm, bearing an old inscription to Alessandro Varotari (il Padovanino), after the fresco of *Diligence* formerly on the Palazzo Vendramin-Calergi; P. Bjurström, *Italian Drawings: Venice, Brescia, Parma, Milan, Genoa,* Stockholm, 1979, no. 149, repr.

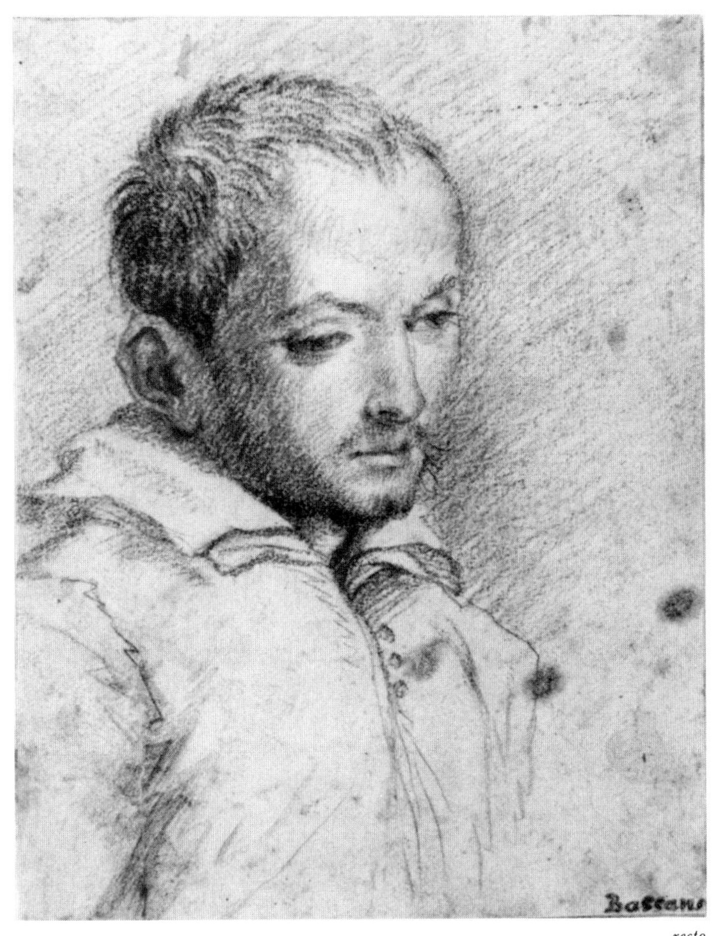

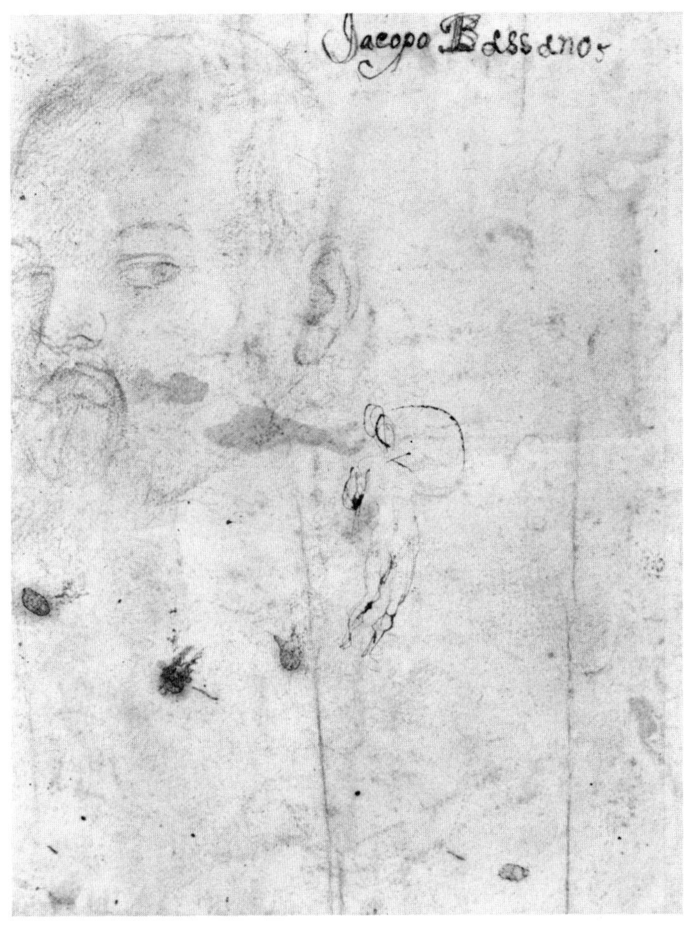

recto   verso

Ludovico Carracci

Bologna 1555 – 1619 Bologna

27 *The Flight into Egypt, with Angels*

Pen and brown ink and wash and grey wash over red chalk, heightened with white on light grey paper. 185 x 154 mm.

Exhibited: Mostra dei Carracci: Disegni, catalogue by D. Mahon, Palazzo dell'Archiginnasio, Bologna, 1956, ed. 1963, p. 41, no. 38, pl. 20.

Literature: H. Bodmer, *Lodovico Carracci,* Burg b. Main, 1939, p. 148, no. 11.

Provenance: Dukes of Devonshire, Chatsworth, no. 417; Christie's, London, 3 July 1984, lot 10.

This charming drawing, in which the red chalk underdrawing, the various densities of brown wash, and the tone of the paper all interact in a deft, pictorial way, has been dated reasonably late in Ludovico Carracci's career.[1] The drawing still retains some of the Mannerist gracefulness that characterizes Ludovico's work, even well after his younger cousin, Annibale Carracci, had helped create the Baroque style.

The purpose of this work is not known, but that the drawing was undertaken for a specific commission is suggested by the segments in the upper corners which have been deliberately left blank. No doubt the shape of the drawing had to conform to a predetermined frame, perhaps in stucco if the drawing was to be translated into fresco. Since the angels behind Mary are only partially seen, it is possible that the finished painting was to be located above eye level.

Many of the features of this drawing reappear in an engraving of the same subject by Francesco Brizio (1575-1623) after a design by Ludovico Carracci (fig. 27a); however, no detail is precisely the same in the two works.[2]

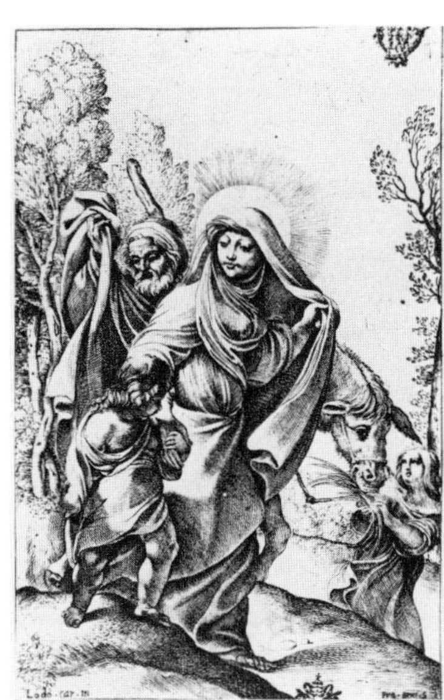

fig. 27a Francesco Brizio after Ludovico Carracci, *Flight into Egypt*, engraving, Pinacoteca Nazionale, Bologna.

1 R. Wittkower has dated the drawing to ca.1600-10 (in an annotation in the manuscript Chatsworth catalogue) and D. Mahon has suggested a date of ca.1610 (in the Bologna exhibition catalogue, *op. cit.,* p. 41, no. 38).

2 For the engraving (Bartsch, XVIII, p. 254, no. 2), see G. Gaeta Bertelà and S. Ferrara, *Incisori Bolognesi ed Emiliani del sec.* XVII, Bologna, 1973, no. 37, repr.; and *idem., Incisori Bolognesi ed Emiliani del sec.* XVI, Bologna, 1975, no. 743, repr.

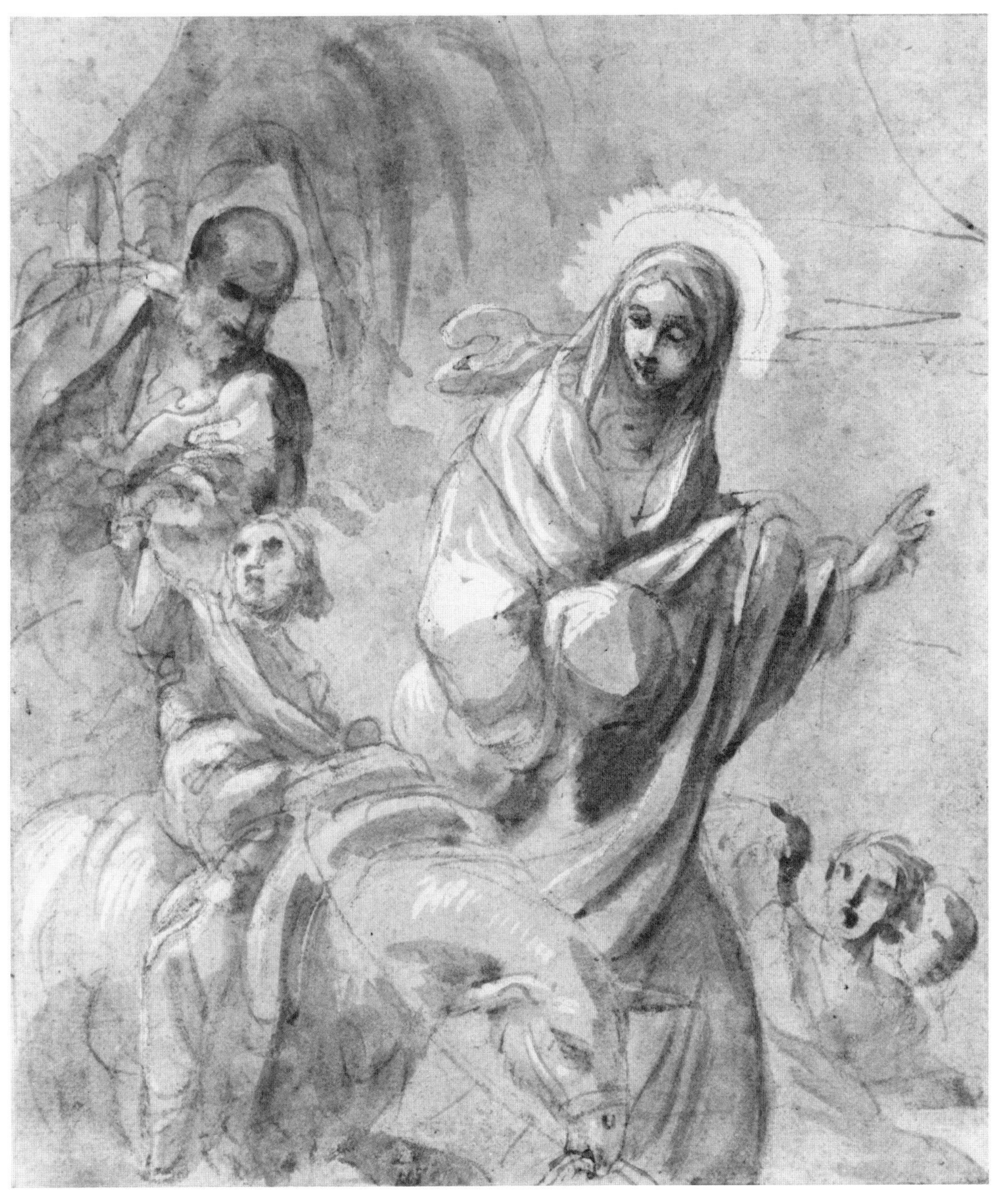

Guido Reni

Bologna 1575 – 1642 Bologna

28 *Study of a Woman's Head*

Black and red chalk on grey paper. 327 x 230 mm.

Literature: S. Pepper, ''Guido Reni at the Albertina,'' *Burlington Magazine,* CXXIII, 1981, p. 574.

Provenance: Earl Spencer (Lugt 1530); Sotheby's, London, 3 July 1980, lot 46.

The languorous pose and refined attitude of the figure are generally typical of Guido Reni.[1] Both the feathery delicacy and considerable economy of the draughtsmanship point to his maturity, and may be compared to such drawings as a sheet in the Teylers Stichting, Haarlem, of a sleeping child for the painting *Charity* in the Metropolitan Museum of Art, or a sheet in the Uffizi of the head of Mary for the *Immaculate Conception* in San Biagio, Forli.[2]

Catherine Johnston has suggested a connection between the present sheet and Reni's *Rape of Europa,* several versions of which are known. Malvasia mentions three paintings by Reni of the subject: one painted for Charles I, King of England; one for the Duke of Guastalla but destined for a Spanish collection; and one for Ladislaus IV, King of Poland, who thanked the artist for it in a letter dated 1640.[3] A canvas of Europa and the bull, now in a private collection in Switzerland, has recently been identified by Federico Zeri as the *Rape of Europa* commissioned by the Duke of Guastalla, and a related painting in the collection of Denis Mahon, London, may be the version once owned by the King of Poland.[4] The inclination of the head and the features of the face of Europa in these paintings are similar to the drawing, but the arrangement of the hair is different. Much closer to the drawing, with loops of hair at the top, is the head of Europa in a more extensive composition of the subject, including five handmaidens and a putto, at Sanssouci, Potsdam (fig. 28a). This painting has been considered by Otto Kurz to be a copy of a lost original by Reni, and by Stephen Pepper as a work by Reni's pupil, Francesco Gessi, which may reflect a composition by the master.[5] Since there is no reason to doubt the attribution of the present sheet, the drawing provides support for the supposition that the Potsdam composition relies on one by Reni himself.

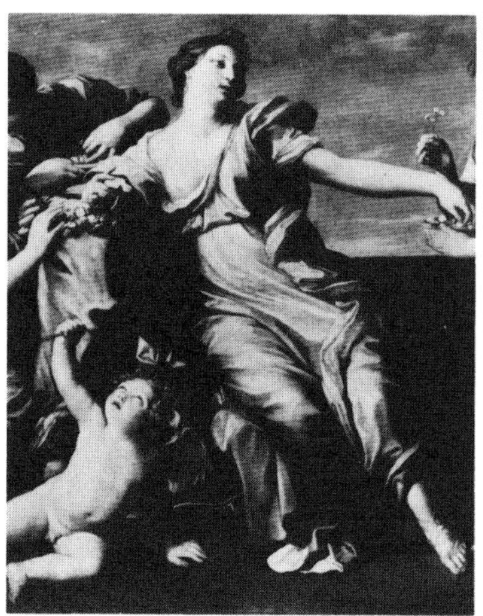

fig. 28a After Guido Reni, *The Rape of Europa* (detail), oil on canvas, Sanssouci, Potsdam.

1 *Cf.* the head of the angel at the left in the *Baptism of Christ,* Vienna, of ca. 1623 (repr. C. Gnudi and G.C. Cavalli, *Guido Reni,* Florence, 1955, pl. 109).

2 For the drawing in Haarlem, see C. Johnston, *Il Seicento e il Settecento a Bologna,* I Disegni dei Maestri, Milan, 1971, pl. XVI; and V. Birke, *Guido Reni, Zeichnungen,* Graphische Sammlung Albertina, Vienna, 1981, pp. 141-42, no. 99, repr. The painting has been dated to the second half of the 1620s. For the drawing in the Uffizi, see Birke, *op.cit.,* p. 143, no. 100, repr.

3 C.C. Malvasia, *Felsina Pittrice, vite de' Pittori Bolognesi,* Bologna, 1678, II, pp. 23, 31, 45.

4 S. Pepper, *Guido Reni,* Oxford, 1984, pp. 275-76, no. 164, pl. 191, and p. 285, no. 184, pl. 214.

5 *Ibid.,* p. 285, under no. 184, fig. 50. Pepper dates the picture to ca.1620.

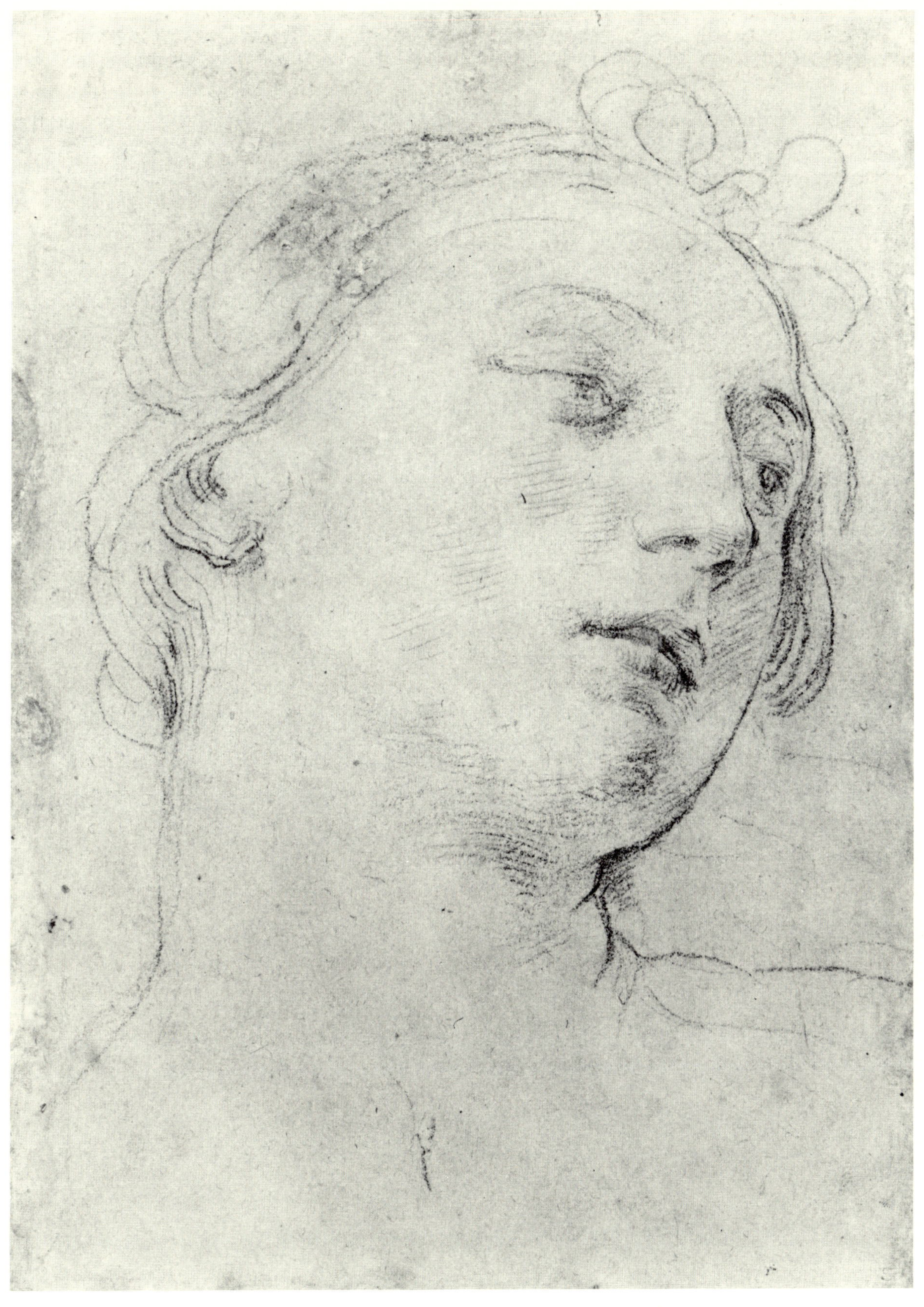

Giovanni Francesco Barbieri
called Guercino

Cento 1591 – 1666 Bologna

29 *The Risen Christ Appearing to His Mother (recto and verso)*

Pen and brown ink and wash *(recto)*; pen and brown ink *(verso)*.
Some restoration for ink corrosion. 374 x 245 mm. Inscribed
at the lower left of the recto: *Guercino*

Literature: J. Byam Shaw, *The Italian Drawings in the Frits Lugt
Collection,* Institut Néerlandais, Paris, 1983, p. 351.

Provenance: Sotheby's, London, 10 December 1979, lot 264.

The drawings on the *recto* and *verso* are connected with
Guercino's painting of the same subject, commissioned by the
Campagnia del Santissimo Nome di Dio for its oratory in
Cento, and now in the Pinacoteca Comunale, Cento. The
picture was finished in 1630, but was probably begun as early as
1628.[1] As Denis Mahon has remarked, the canvas with its clear
idealization and spatial simplification is perhaps the first to
reveal Guercino's acceptance of the tenets classicism.[2] The
preliminary drawings show the artist working toward that
solution.

A drawing in the Lugt collection, Paris, shows the two figures
in intimate proximity: Mary, kneeling, embraces Christ around
the waist and kisses His right hand.[3] Christ's left hand tenderly
wraps around her back. On the *recto* of the present drawing the
figures are somewhat less close: Mary's outstretched right arm
clasps Christ's shoulder and her left hand draws His right hand
to her face, but her body is now distinct from His. The same
pose – with Christ's arm extended diagonally across His torso –
reappears on the *verso,* but the two figures are further separated:
Mary has relinquished her grasp of Christ's shoulder and she
gazes up at Him rather than kissing His hand. Christ's right
arm is swung round to hold the banner free of His body at the
left. He is also draped from the waist down in an impressive
mantle, for which there is a red chalk drawing in the Koenig-
Fachsenfeld collection.[4]

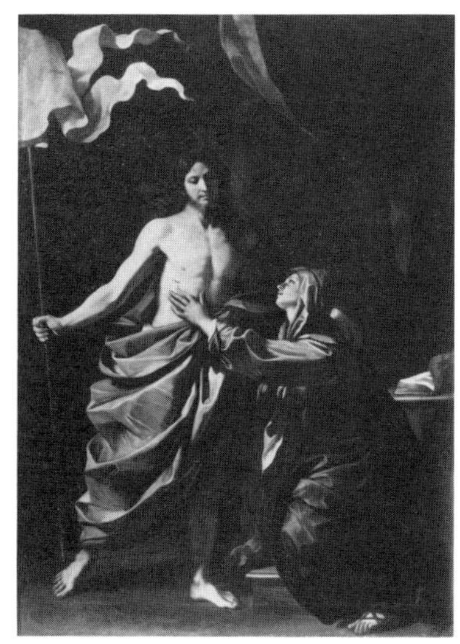

fig. 29a Guercino, *The Risen Christ Appearing to His Mother,*
oil on canvas, Pinacoteca Comunale, Cento.

1 D. Mahon, *Il Guercino, Dipinti,* Palazzo dell'Archiginnasio, Bologna, 1968,
pp. 153-54, no. 63, repr.

2 *Ibid.*, pp. 131, 154.

3 Byam Shaw, *op. cit.*, no. 350, pl. 399. In both the Lugt drawing and the *verso*
of the present sheet the hastily drawn outlines of what must be Mary's
prie-dieu appear at the lower right.

4 Mahon, *op. cit.*, p. 154; C. Thiem, ''Unpublished Chalk Drawings by
Guercino in the Collection of Schloss Fachsenfeld,'' *Master Drawings,* XVII,
1979, pp. 405, 415, no. 7, pl. 16. Mahon also mentions drawings for the
painting in the collection of Dr. Ernest Harms, New York (with the stamp of
H. C. Jennings) and in the Museo Civico at Pavia (the Virgin only).

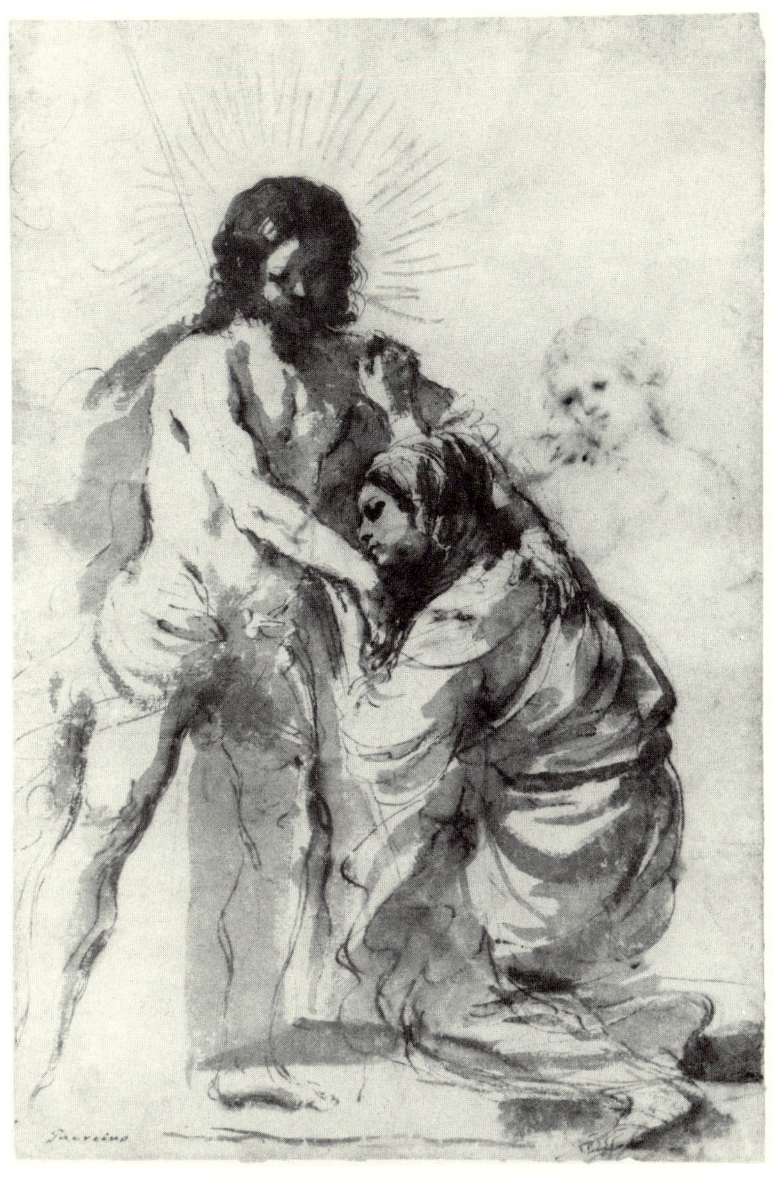

recto

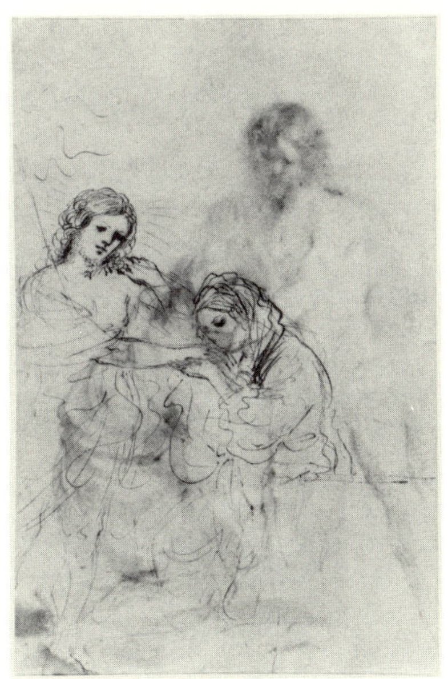

verso

Giovanni Francesco Barbieri
called Guercino

Cento 1591 – 1666 Bologna

30 *Study of a Boy in a Cap*

Black chalk. The four corners restored. 280 x 210 mm

Denis Mahon and Nicholas Turner have dated this drawing to about 1640.[1] Mahon suggests that the study, perhaps of a shepherd, was undertaken for a specific painting, most likely of a biblical subject. The suggestion is supported by the fact that the figure's left arm is not finished, probably because it was not to be shown in the finished picture; but to date the exact figure has not been discovered.

In facial type the drawing may be compared to a black chalk profile study of David in the Teylers Museum, Haarlem, for Guercino's *David and Abigail,* painted in 1636 for Cardinal Antonio Barberini, but destroyed in 1941.[2] Also similar in type and mood is Guercino's oval canvas of St. John the Baptist in the Pinacoteca Nazionale, Bologna.[3]

1 Orally to the owner.

2 No. H 33; D. Mahon, *Il Guercino, Disegni,* Palazzo dell' Archiginnasio, Bologna, 1968, pp. 134-35, no. 140, repr.

3 N. Grimaldi, *Il Guercino,* Bologna, 1957, pl. 113.

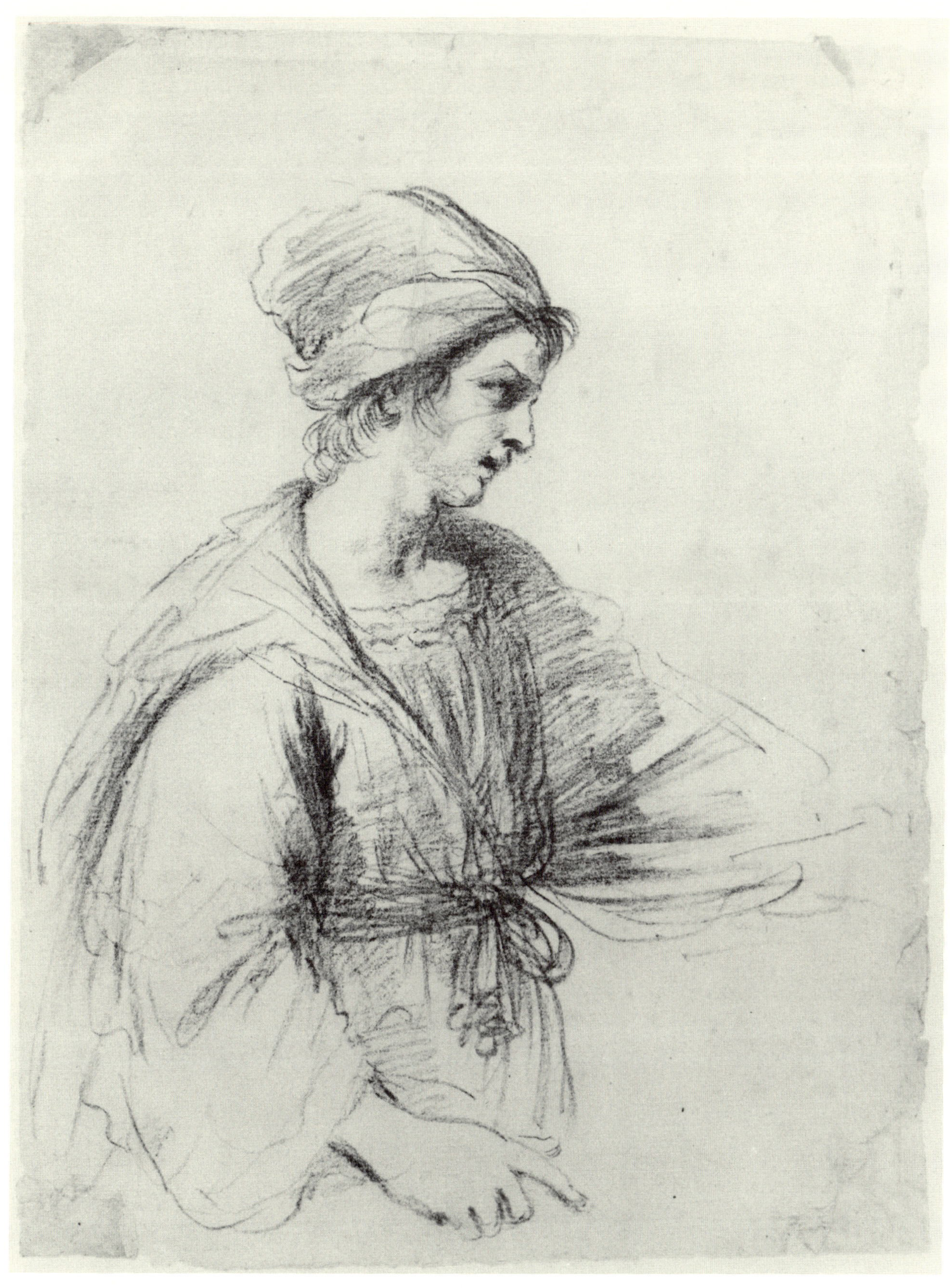

Pietro Berrettini
called Pietro da Cortona

Cortona 1596 – 1669 Rome

31 *Moses and the Israelites Building the Tabernacle*

Pen and brown ink and wash, with some red and grey wash, heightened with white over traces of black chalk on light-brown prepared paper. Rubbed, with losses, especially at the left. 273 x 424 mm

Literature: R. Ferretti, ''A Preparatory Drawing for One of the dal Pozzo Paintings of the Series of Moses' Life,'' *Burlington Magazine,* CXXVII, 1985, pp. 617-21.

Provenance: Christie's, London, 23 March 1982, lot 35.

The subject is from Exodus 35: 21-29 – at Moses's command the children of Israel bring offerings of fine jewels and precious metals, spun cloth and animal skins, shittim wood, oil and spices for the new tabernacle.

The drawing has been ascribed to Giovanni Francesco Romanelli,[1] but the variety of pictorial effects, in particular the subtlety of the white heightening as in the group at the centre left, seems instead to point to his master, Pietro da Cortona. This would be especially true of Cortona's work in his early maturity. Although the drawing does not relate to any surviving painting by Cortona, the rare subject can be connected with a painting once belonging to a series of four pictures, two by Cortona and two by Poussin, which was in the collection of Amadeo dal Pozzo, Marchese di Voghera (a cousin of Cassiano dal Pozzo) in Turin. While the paintings by Poussin were mentioned somewhat earlier, the canvases by Cortona were first alluded to in print by Luigi Pellegrino Scaramuccia in 1674.[2] Scaramuccia does not mention the subjects of the four paintings, but he does say that they showed scenes from Holy Scripture *(Historie della Sacra Scrittura)*. The two paintings by Poussin have always been identified with *The Passage of the Red Sea,* in Melbourne, and *The Adoration of the Golden Calf,* in the National Gallery, London. Both of these paintings show episodes from the life of Moses, and with the recent discovery of the manuscript inventories of the collections of the dal Pozzo family in Turin, it is possible to confirm that the other two paintings followed suit.[3]

In the earliest of these inventories, dated 1634, the other two paintings are listed as *Moses and the Gathering of the Manna (''Mosè fece raccogliere la manna'')* and *Moses and the Building of the Tabernacle (''Mosè fece costruire il Tabernacolo'')*. The former is given to Cortona, but the second to Romanino, surely meaning Romanelli. In later inventories the second painting is listed as by Pietro da Cortona and is more fully described as *The Women of Israel bringing their Ornaments to Moses for the Building of the Arc (''Le donne di Israele portano a Mosè i loro ornamenti per costruire l'Arca'')*.[4] The proximity between these descriptions and the present drawing lends support to the supposition that the drawing was indeed done for the dal Pozzo commission. It is highly unlikely that the young and little-known Romanelli (ca.1610-1662) would have been commissioned, on his own, to undertake a painting to hang with those by Poussin and Cortona; yet because Romanelli was an assistant to Cortona at this time, it is possible that he played some part in the execution, if not the invention, of at least one of the pictures.[5] This drawing may well, then, supply information about a major commission shared by Poussin and Cortona, as well as highlighting an important moment in the association of Cortona and his pupil Romanelli.

1 *Important Old Master Drawings,* Christie's, London, 23 March 1982, lot 35. The figure immediately to the left of Moses is repeated with some variations in a drawing in the Albertina, published as a Romanelli by B. Kerber, ''Kupferstiche nach Gianfrancesco Romanelli,'' *Giessener Beiträge zur Kunstgeschichte,* II, 1973, pp. 151ff, fig. 36.

2 *Le Finezze dei Pennelli Italiani,* Pavia, 1674, p. 157. The paintings by Poussin are mentioned in G. P. Bellori, *Le Vite de' Pittori, Scultori e Architetti Moderni,* Rome, 1672, p. 419. Also see J. Thuillier, ''Pour un «Corpus Pussinianum»,'' *Nicolas Poussin,* II, Paris, 1960, p. 119, for mention of the paintings by Poussin in the ms. journal of B. de Monconys, 28 June 1664.

3 Ferretti, *op.cit.*

4 In the nineteenth-century inventories, *ibid.* In like fashion the subject of the other painting given to Cortona is changed in the nineteenth-century inventories to *Moses Striking the Rock* from *The Gathering of Manna* in the seventeenth- and eighteenth-century inventories. *Moses Striking the Rock* is the subject of a painting given variously to Romanelli and Cortona in Oslo; for which also see Ferretti, *op.cit.*

5 Romanelli was paid for painting in the chapel of the Palazzo Barberini on 17 November 1631 (G. Briganti, *Pietro da Cortona,* Florence, 1962, pp. 139, 196).

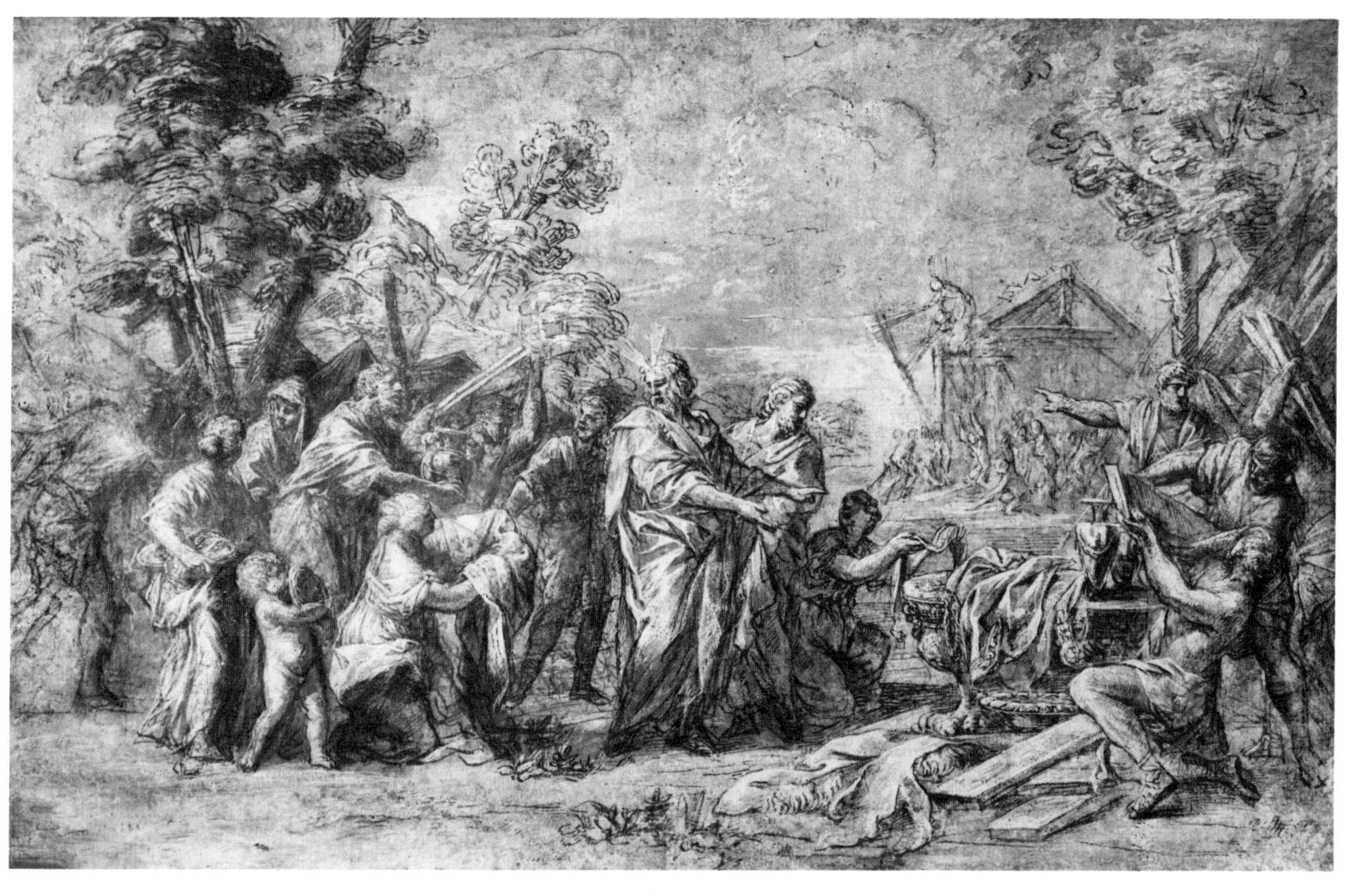

Pietro Berrettini
called Pietro da Cortona

Cortona 1596 – 1669 Rome

32 *Study of a Head*

Black chalk. Some stains and foxing. 190 x 168 mm. Inscribed
in pencil on the mount: *Pietro da Cortona*

Literature: F[rancis] R[ussell], ''Saleroom Discovery: A Study
by Pietro da Cortona,'' *Burlington Magazine,* CXXI, 1979, p. 405
and fig. 98.

Provenance: Christie's, London, 28 March 1979, lot 173A
(as Francesco Romanelli: the attribution changed to Pietro da
Cortona by the date of the sale).

Although listed at auction as by Giovanni Francesco Romanelli,
this sensitive head was recognized by Francis Russell as Pietro
da Cortona's study for the angel carrying the cross on the ceiling
of the sacristy of Santa Maria in Vallicella, Rome (fig. 32a).[1] It is
possible that the head was studied from life. In the fresco the
head is somewhat more idealized, and plumes, only vaguely
suggested in the drawing, fan out prominently from the back of
the helmet. A drawing for the entire figure was once with de
Boer, Amsterdam.[2]

The fresco, which shows the angel and putti carrying the
Instruments of the Passion, was Pietro da Cortona's earliest
commission for the Chiesa Nuova; probably the fresco dates
from 1633, as the ceiling is said to be finished in the record of
payment to the artist dated 12 January 1634.[3]

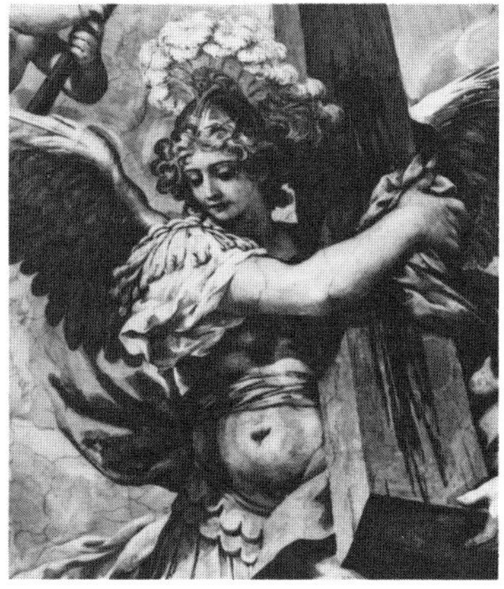

fig. 32a Pietro da Cortona, *Angels with Instruments
of the Passion* (detail), fresco, Sacristy, S. Maria in
Vallicella, Rome.

1 F[rancis] R[ussell], *op. cit.*

2 G. Briganti, *Pietro da Cortona,* Florence, 1962, p. 205.

3 *Ibid.*

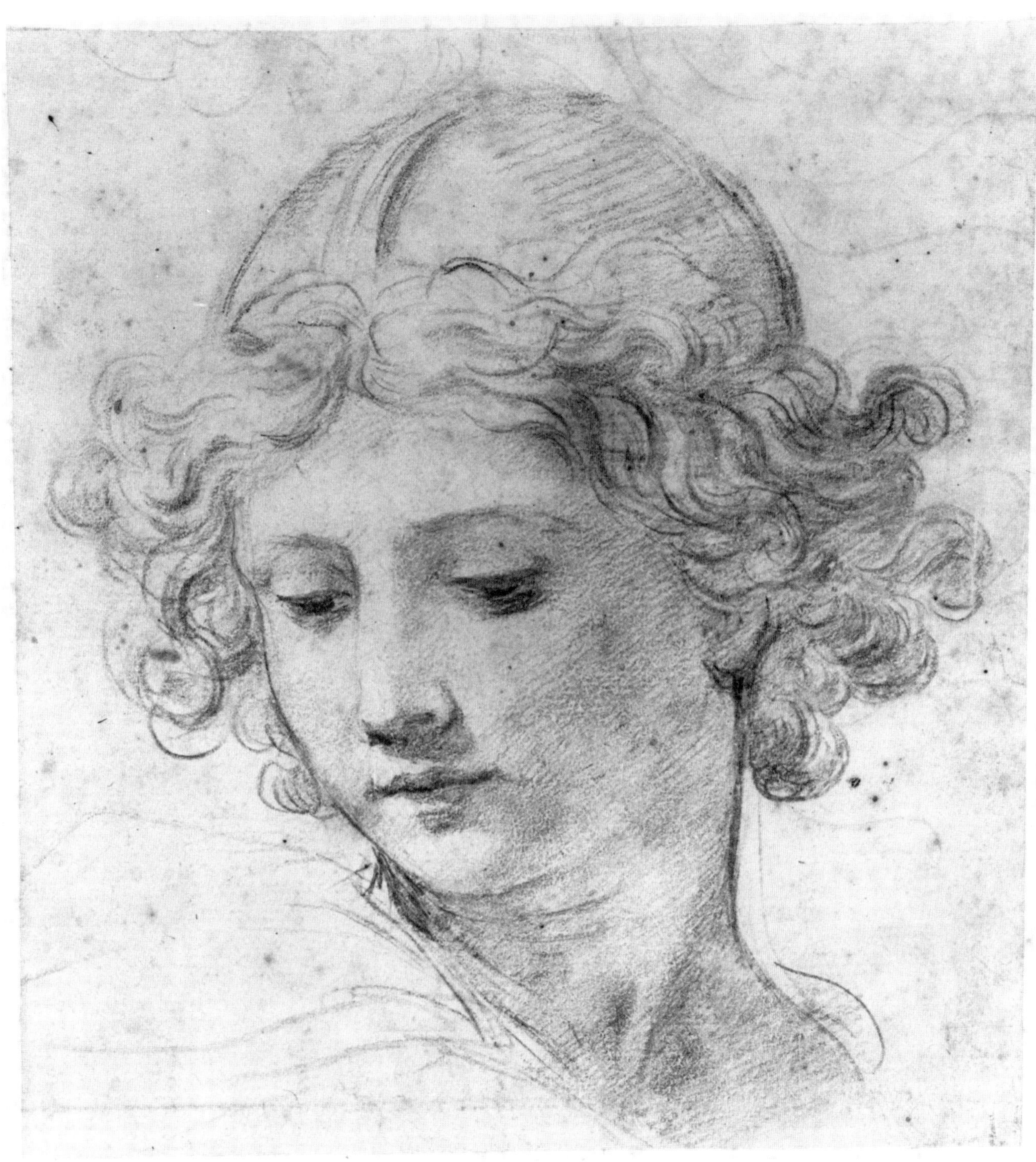

Pietro Berrettini
called Pietro da Cortona

Cortona 1596 – 1669 Rome

33   *Conversion of St. Paul*

Black chalk, squared for transfer. Some stains at top.
365 x 209 mm, arched top. Inscribed in pen at lower left:
Carle marate

Exhibited: Exhibition of Old Master Drawings, P. & D. Colnaghi,
London, June 1954, no. 75.

Literature: L. Mortari, *Il Museo capitolare della cattedrale di Velletri*,
Rome, 1959, pp. 32-3, under no. 11; G. Briganti, *Pietro da
Cortona,* Florence, 1962, pp. 271, 303, 330, pl. 288, no. 64;
W. Vitzthum, Review of Giuliano Briganti: *Pietro da Cortona e
della pittura barocca, Master Drawings,* I, no. 2, 1963, p. 50; *idem,*
"Inventar eines Sammelbandes des späten Seicento mit
Zeichnungen von Pietro da Cortona und Ciro Ferri," *Studies in
Renaissance and Baroque Art Presented to Anthony Blunt,* London,
1967, pp. 115-16; N. Turner, "Some Drawings by Lazzaro
Baldi," *Burlington Magazine, CXXI,* 1979, p. 153 and fig. 17;
A. Pampalone, *Disegni di Lazzaro Baldi nelle collezioni del
Gabinetto Nazionale delle Stampe,* Rome, 1979, p. 57; G. Briganti,
Pietro da Cortona, Florence, 2nd ed. 1982, pp. 289, 316, 402.

Provenance: Gwen, Lady Melchett; Colnaghi's, London, 1954;
Brian Thomas (according to Christie's as follows); Christie's,
London, 7 April 1981, lot 83.

Although the old inscription gives the drawing to Carlo
Maratta, the sheet was exhibited in London in 1954 and
published by Giuliano Briganti in 1962 as by Pietro da Cortona.[1]
Walter Vitzthum then recognized a summary sketch by
Cortona of the same composition in a book of drawings by
Cortona and Ciro Ferri in a private collection in New York.[2]

Briganti pointed out that the drawing is typical of Cortona's late
style and he connected the sheet with an arch-topped altarpiece,
formerly in the church of San Giovanni Battista and now in the
Museo Capitolare, Velletri (fig. 33a). The altarpiece was
traditionally ascribed to Cortona, but more recently has been
given to his school and now specifically to Lazzaro Baldi
(1624-1703), whose independent career began in the mid-1650s.[3]
In an inventory of paintings left unfinished at Cortona's death,
there is listed a canvas of the conversion of St. Paul, which was
sold a short time afterward; and it is possible that this is the
painting at Velletri, completed by Baldi.[4] Both an etching and a
closely related (reversed) drawing of the *Conversion of St. Paul* by
Baldi share a number of features with the altarpiece.[5] However,
the present drawing and the altarpiece are closely connected
only in the shape of the entire composition and in the positions,
but not the poses, of the major figures. A direct relationship
between the drawing and the Velletri painting should not,
therefore, be taken as necessarily proven.[6]

Another drawing by Pietro da Cortona of the same subject is
at Windsor.[7] Not connected with any known commission, the
Windsor drawing is executed in Cortona's highly evolved
earlier manner, in pen and wash and much heightening with
white and even blue and grey gouache, all of which contrasts
with the restricted use of black chalk in the present sheet, from
late in the artist's career.

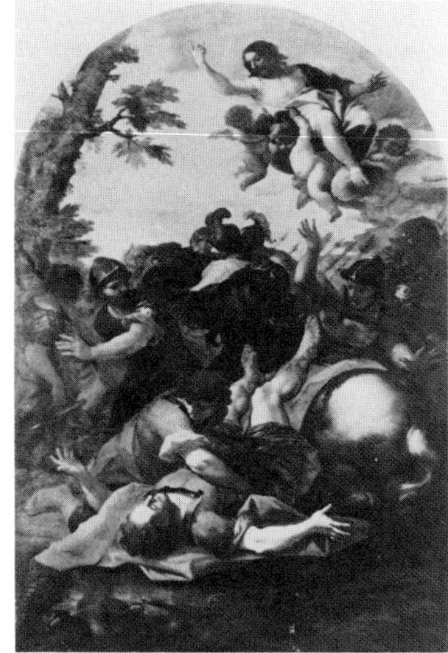

fig. 33a Attributed to Lazzaro Baldi, *Conversion of St. Paul,*
oil on canvas, Museo Capitolare, Velletri.

---

1   *Exhibition of Old Master Drawings,* P. & D. Colnaghi, London, June 1954,
no. 75 (as formerly in the collection of Gwen, Lady Melchett); G. Briganti,
Pietro da Cortona, Florence, 1962, pp. 271, 303, 330.

2   "Inventar eines Sammelbandes des späten Seicento mit Zeichnungen von
Pietro da Cortona und Ciro Ferri," *Studies in Renaissance and Baroque Art
Presented to Anthony Blunt,* London, 1967, pp. 115-16 (fol. 52).

3   Mortari, *op.cit.,* pp. 32-33 (as seventeenth-century follower of Pietro da
Cortona). The attribution to Baldi is found in *Mostra di Pietro da Cortona*
[Cortona], Rome, 1956, Addenda ed Errata Corrige, unpaginated, for p. 20,
no. 45; and in Briganti, *op.cit.,* pp. 271, 330 (under Windsor no. 4510).
Recently an attribution to Guglielmo Cortese, as collaborator of Baldi, has
also been put forward: Pampalone, *op.cit.,* pp. 56-57.

4   Pampalone, *op.cit.,* p. 57. The subject was also found in a painting by
Cortona, once in the Palazzo Ruffo, Naples (Briganti, *op.cit.,* ed. 1982,
p. 367).

5   N. Turner, "Some Drawings by Lazzaro Baldi," *Burlington Magazine, CXXI,*
1979, pp. 150-53, figs. 14-15. Pampalone, *op.cit.,* p. 58, no. 54, repr., adds
another drawing by Baldi with sketches of Paul and Christ, the latter in a pose
similar to the present drawing.

6   It is true that Briganti, *op.cit.,* p. 330, calls the drawing a *"primissima idea"* for
the altarpiece.

7   Windsor, no. 4510. Briganti, *op.cit.,* p. 330. A. Blunt and H. L. Cooke,
The Roman Drawings...at Windsor Castle, London, 1960, p. 80, no. 614, pl. 18.

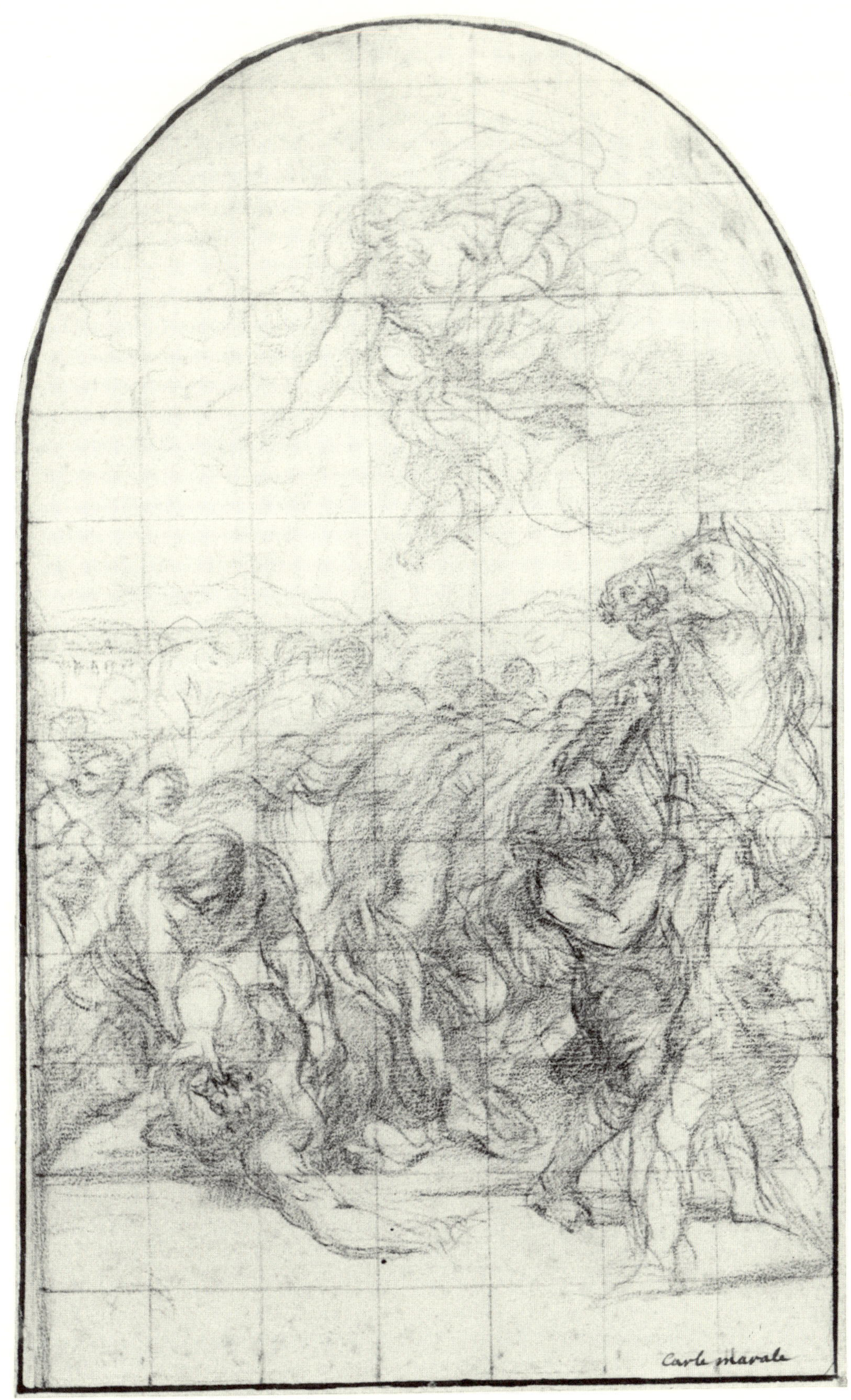

Carlo Maratta

Andrea Sacchi

Nettuna 1599 – 1661 Rome

34 *Sheet of Studies (recto);*
A Standing Ecclesiastical Figure (verso)

Red and white chalk *(recto)*; black and white chalk *(verso)*; on buff paper. Stains. 252 x 334 mm. Inscribed in ink along the lower edge *(recto)*: *à Barberini*

Provenance: Christie's, London, 12 April 1983, lot 65.

As the old inscription laconically intimates, these studies are connected with Sacchi's painting of the visit of the Barberini pope, Urban VIII, to the church of the Gesù on 2 October 1639, during the centennial celebrations of the Jesuit Order (fig. 34a). Executed in 1641, the large canvas was in the collection of Cardinal Antonio Barberini and is now in the Palazzo Barberini (Galleria Nazionale d'Arte Antica).[1] The painting shows an unencumbered view down the broad nave of the church, with the façade removed. In the foreground, horses and carriages wait on the street outside, while a short distance inside the church the pope and cardinals receive members of the Jesuit order.

The haughty youth at the left of the drawing is for the figure, probably Maffeo, son of Taddeo Barberini, at the top of the steps leading into the church; and the half-length figure to the right is for the black page, leaning out the window of the carriage in the left foreground. The hands at the upper right are for the pope himself, while the study of an arm immediately below is for the cardinal in front of the pontiff. This cardinal holds his biretta in his left hand exactly as in the drawing. The remaining study of an ecclesiastic who clasps a biretta to his chest seems not to be related to any figure in the painting; however, a rather similar ecclesiastic appears three times at the lower left of the *verso* of a sheet sold at auction along with the present drawing,[2] and these studies seem to be for the foremost of the kneeling Jesuits.

According to an inventory of 1671 Andrea Sacchi was only responsible for the execution of the principal figures in the painting, while Filippi Gagliardi did the architecture and Jan Miel the other parts.[3] It has been reasonably argued that Miel painted the genre figures and the horses and carriages in the foreground,[4] but with the evidence of the present drawing the

extent of Sacchi's contribution, at least in the preliminary stages, will have to be increased.

A drawing related to the pope, his entourage, and the kneeling Jesuits is in a private collection in New York; it is mainly executed with the tip of the brush and wash, a rare medium among the surviving drawings by Sacchi.[5]

The purpose of the drawing of a cleric looking upward to the left with outstretched arms on the *verso* has not been discovered.

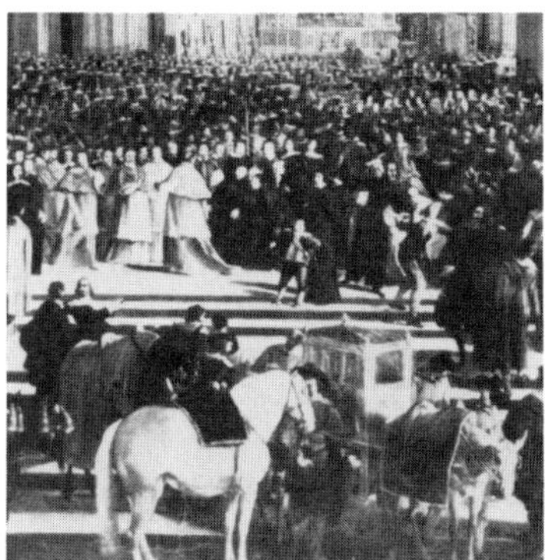

fig. 34a Andrea Sacchi, *Urban VIII visiting the Gesù* (detail), oil on canvas, Galleria Nazionale d'Arte Antica (Palazzo Barberini), Rome.

1 A. Sutherland Harris, *Andrea Sacchi,* Oxford, 1977, pp. 90-91, no. 63, pls. 130-31.

2 *Important Old Master Drawings,* Christie's, London, 12 April 1983, lot 64, repr., and Yvonne Tan Bunzl, *Old Master Drawings,* London, 1984, no. 30, repr. Nicholas Turner has identified a running youth on the same side *(verso)* of the sheet as a study for the figure descending the steps to the right of Maffeo (?) Barberini.

3 A. Sutherland Harris, *op.cit.*, p. 90, n.1.

4 C. Refice, G. Briganti and Sutherland Harris, *op.cit.*, pp. 90-91, n.5. Also A. Sutherland Harris, ''Drawings by Andrea Sacchi: *Addenda*,'' *Burlington Magazine,* CXX, 1978, p. 601.

5 A. Sutherland Harris, 1978, pp. 601-02, fig. 81.

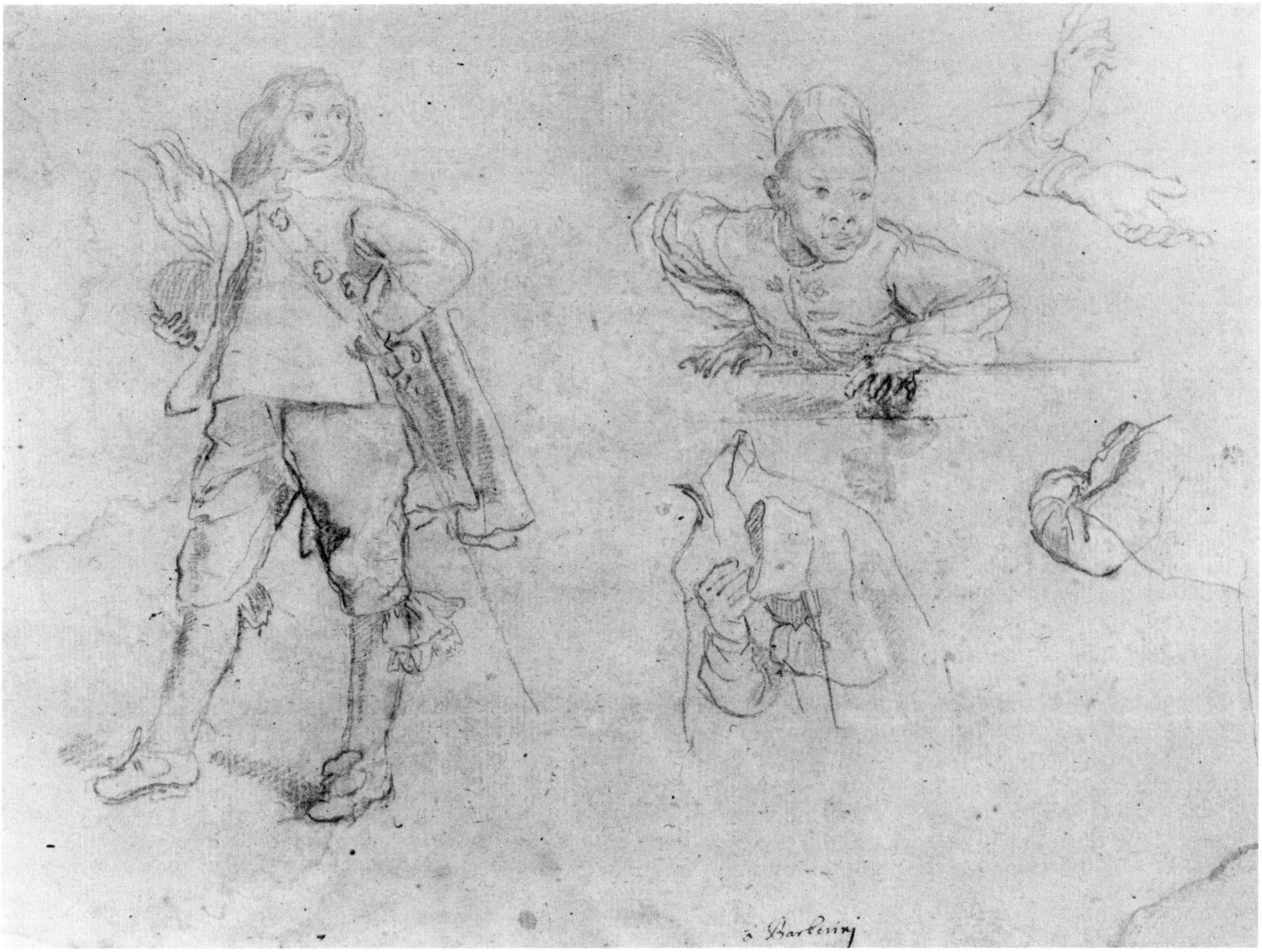

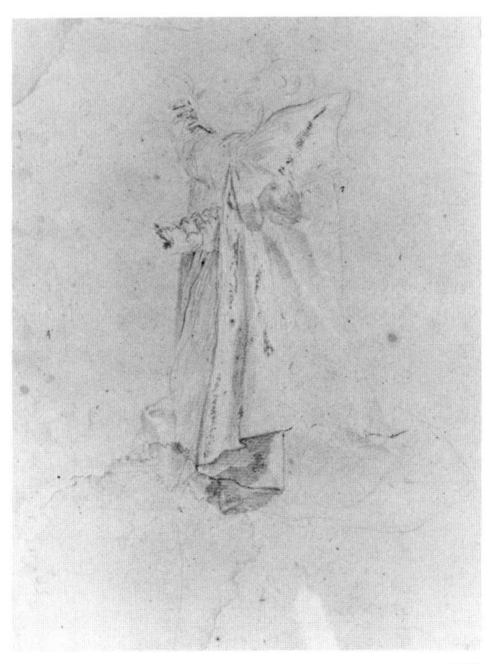

recto

verso

Alessandro Algardi

Bologna 1598 – 1654 Rome

35 *The Holy Family with Two Angels*

Black chalk. 260 x 200 mm

Exhibited: Bolognese Drawings in North American Collections: 1500-1800, National Gallery of Canada, Ottawa, 1981, not in catalogue.

Literature: D. McTavish, ''Bolognese Drawings at the National Gallery,'' *RACAR,* X, 1983, p. 84, and fig. 1.

Provenance: Sotheby's, London, 9 July 1981, lot 32.

Although the majority of known drawings by Algardi are in pen and ink, a small number in chalk have also survived. This fine example was first recognized by Nicholas Turner, and the attribution has been supported by Jennifer Montagu.[1]

Several other drawings by Algardi showing the Holy Family are known; it is possible, although by no means certain, that they were all undertaken for the same project. Of these drawings, two are in red chalk: one in the Uffizi showing at the lower left the baby John the Baptist presenting an unidentifiable object to the Christ Child; the other, discovered in Düsseldorf by Catherine Johnston, showing the Virgin suckling the Christ Child.[2] Two other sheets, likewise attributed to Algardi by Catherine Johnston, are in pen and wash: one in Lisbon with the child seated in the Virgin's lap, embracing the baby John the Baptist; and another at Windsor with the Virgin covering the sleeping Christ Child.[3] The latter is clearly a *Rest on the Flight into Egypt.* The precise purpose of these drawings is not known, although they may well have served as preparatory studies for a terracotta or bronze relief. Various casts of a composition representing this subject have been attributed to Algardi, but although the composition corresponds to some features of the drawings mentioned, the reliefs do not repeat the exact details of any of the drawings.[4]

The popularity in the mid-seventeenth century Rome of this sort of lyrical subject is attested by a number of paintings by Pier Francesco Mola, among others, likewise showing the rest on the flight with attendant angels.[5]

1 *Fine Old Master Drawings,* Sotheby's, London, 9 July 1981, under lot 32. Dr. Montagu has since published the drawing in *Alessandro Algardi,* New Haven and London, 1985, II, p. 439, no. 16.

2 C. Johnston, *Disegni Bolognesi dal XVI al XVIII Secolo,* Gabinetto Disegni e Stampe degli Uffizi, XL, Florence, 1973, pp. 85-86, no. 95, fig. 62. The drawing in Düsseldorf will be published shortly.

3 E. Schilling and A. Blunt, *German Drawings at Windsor Castle and Supplements to the Catalogue of the Italian and French Drawings,* London, 1971, p. 47, no. 4, pl. 35. The drawing in Lisbon is in the Museo Nacional de Arte Antiga (inv. 1168, formerly as Berettini).

4 See Montagu, *op.cit.,* II, pp. 307-09, no. 4.

5 Paintings in the Palazzo Doria, Rome, and the Hermitage, Leningrad: R. Cooke, *Pier Francesco Mola,* Oxford, 1972, pls. 85 and 114; Mola also did an engraving after F. Albani's *Rest on the Flight* which is especially relevant in the present context *(ibid.,* fig. 81).

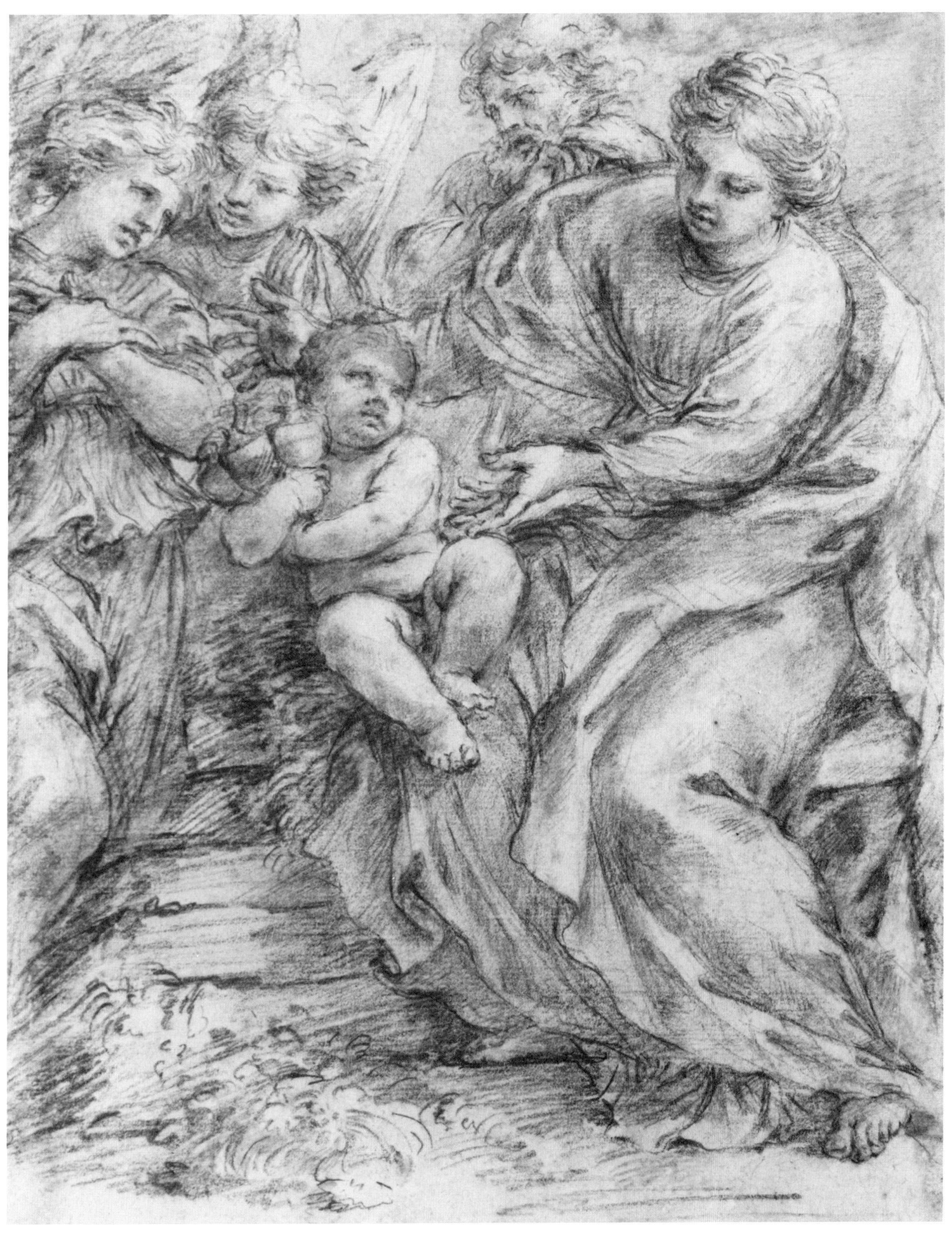

Giacinto Gimignani

Pistoia 1606 – 1681 Rome

36 *Rinaldo in the Enchanted Forest*

Pen and brown ink and wash, heightened with white, over black chalk and a touch of red chalk; squared for transfer in black chalk. Laid down. 270 x 250 mm

Provenance: L. Grassi Junior (mark at lower right, not in Lugt).

This composition drawing is closely related to a painting by Giacinto Gimignani, signed and dated 1640, in the Musée Historique, Bouxwiller, Alsace (fig. 36a).[1] The subject of the painting has been identified by Ursula Verena Fischer-Pace as Rinaldo encountering Armida in the enchanted forest, from Canto 18 of Torquato Tasso's *Gerusalemme liberata.* In addition, Dr. Fischer-Pace has discovered two other canvases in the same museum with subjects from Tasso's epic poem.[2] No doubt the three paintings were commissioned together as part of a larger series of scenes from *Gerusalemme liberata.*[3]

The three surviving canvases at Bouxwiller are horizontal in format, in contrast to the upright shape of the present drawing. Otherwise the drawing and painting are strikingly similar, except that in the picture an additional maiden holding up a tambourine has been inserted between Armida and the right edge. The drawing is highly typical of Giacinto Gimignani, who had been associated with Pietro da Cortona in the 1630s, but whose classicizing style owes much to Domenichino and Poussin. This is evident in the frieze-like band of classically attired figures and in the crisp definition of all the parts. The drawing may be compared to a recently discovered composition study, now in the British Museum, for Gimignani's *Triumph of David* in the Israel Museum, Jerusalem.[4]

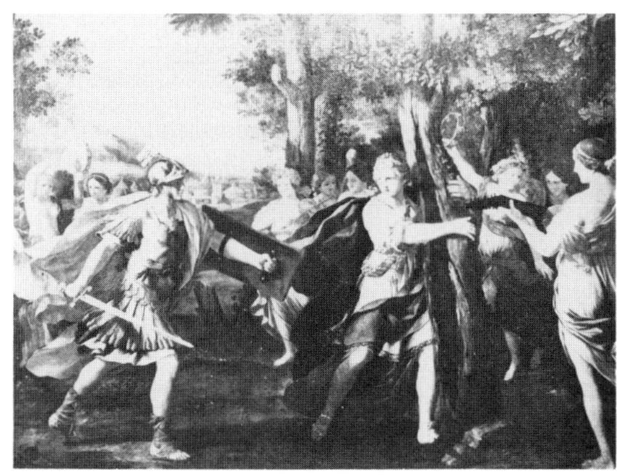

fig. 36a Giacinto Gimignani, *Rinaldo in the Enchanted Forest*, oil on canvas, Musée historique, Bouxwiller.

1 Signed *Hyacinthus gimignanus pistoriensis pinx A.D. 1640,* the painting was published by U. V. Fischer-Pace, ''Les oeuvres de Giacinto Gimagnani dans les collections publiques françaises,'' *Revue du Louvre*, XXVIII, 1978, pp. 343ff, fig. 1.

2 The other paintings have been identified by Fischer-Pace *(ibid.)* as *Rinaldo leaving Armida* (*Gerusalemme liberata* XVI, 62) and the *Miraculous Healing of Goffredo* (*Gerusalemme liberta* XI, 71-75).

3 Fischer-Pace *(op.cit.,* pp. 348-49 and n. 31) associates the pictures, whose provenance is not known, with a contract dated 20 May 1639, for sixteen paintings on subjects from *Gerusalemme liberata,* to be executed within six months by Giacinto Gimignani, François Perrier, Pierre Mignard, Pierre Lemaire, and Charles Errard.

4 For the drawing (1979-4-7-2) see N. Turner, *Italian Baroque Drawings,* British Museum Prints and Drawings Series, London, 1980, pp. 62-63, no. 22, repr. The painting in Jerusalem is associated stylistically with the *Rinaldo in the Enchanted Forest* in Bouxwiller by Fischer-Pace *(op.cit.,* p. 345), but she does not discuss the equally comparable preparatory drawings.

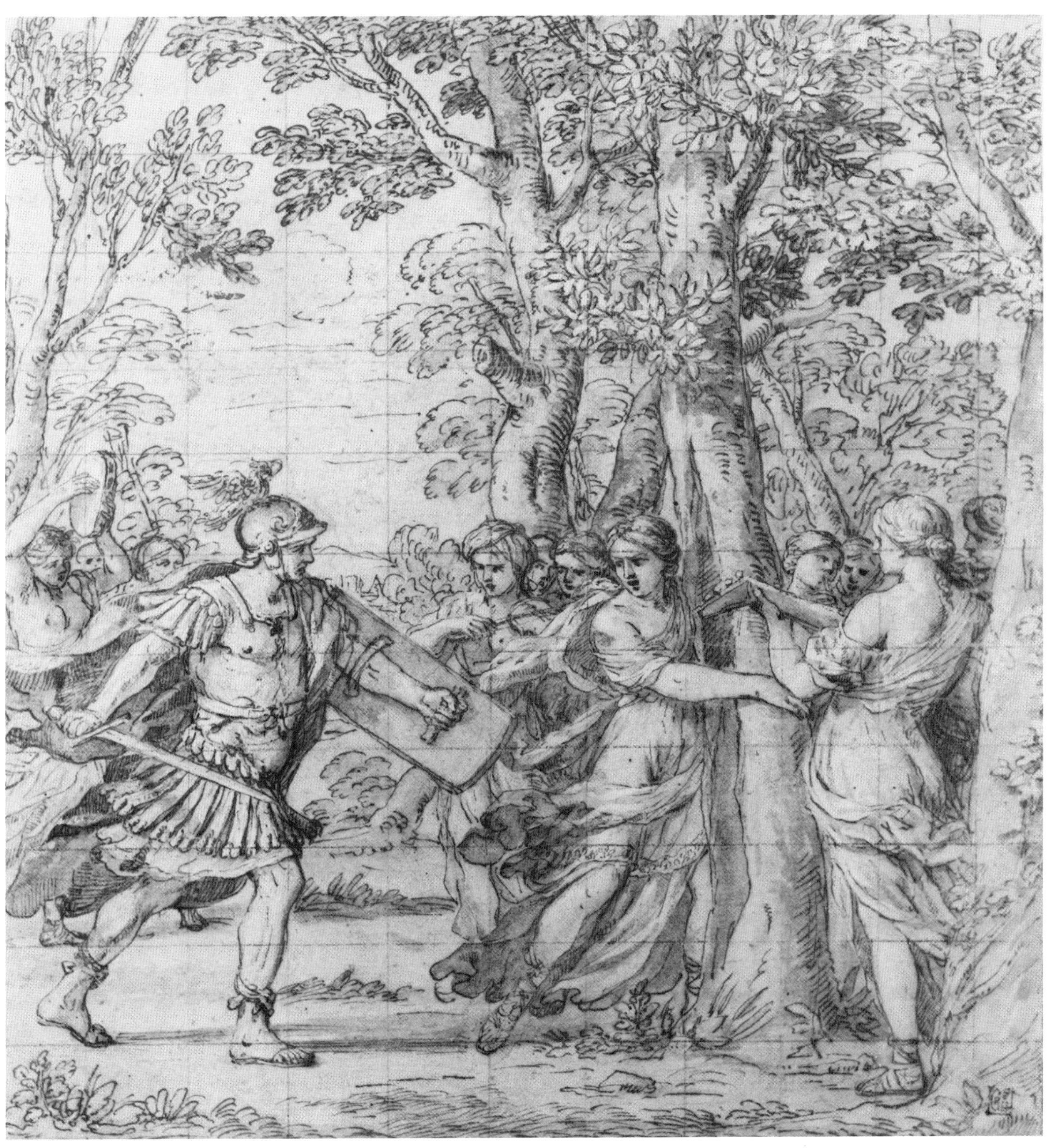

Pietro Novelli
called Il Monrealese

Monreale 1603 – 1647 Palermo

37   *The Coronation of the Virgin*

Pen and brown ink and wash over black chalk. Vertical and
horizontal folds. Laid down. 192 mm diameter. Inscribed at
lower centre: *P⁰ Novelli* and on the mount at upper right: *57*

Exhibited: Civiltà del Seicento a Napoli, Museo di Capodimonte,
Naples, 1984, II, p. 108, no. 3.53, repr. (catalogue entry by
J. Stock).

Provenance: Christie's, London, 12 December 1978, lot 41.

This quick study carries an old inscription, possibly a signature,
to Pietro Novelli, the only native Sicilian of note to paint during
the seventeenth century. His draughtsmanship is shown here in
a particularly fluid fashion.

Roberto Ferretti has pointed out that the drawing appears to
be an early idea for Novelli's ceiling, datable about 1630, in the
Oratorio del Rosario di San Domenico in Palermo (fig. 37a).
The ceiling represents the Coronation of the Virgin, but in an
oval shape, and the components of the drawing have had to be
rearranged to fit the different format. God the Father has been
moved to a location above the dove of the Holy Spirit and His
place has been taken by an angel with a harp. Numerous putti
have been added throughout. Christ at the left and Mary in the
centre remain relatively unchanged, except that Christ proffers
the crown with His right hand alone, and in His left hand He
holds a staff.

Another drawing by Novelli of a celestial coronation – the
Virgin crowning Santa Chiara, for a wall fresco in the Badia
Nuova, Palermo – is in the Ratjen collection, Vaduz.[1]

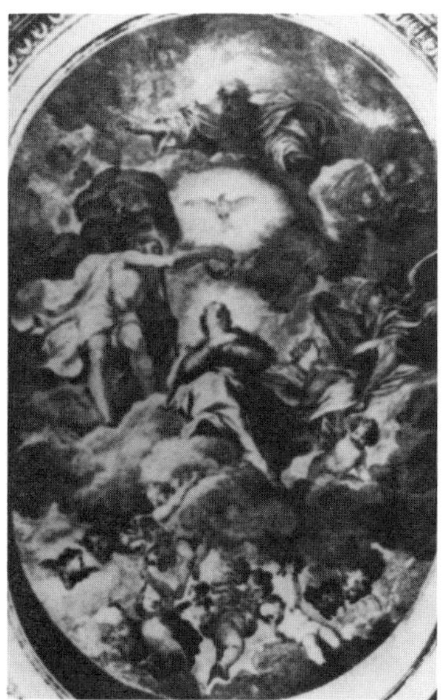

fig. 37a Pietro Novelli, *The Coronation of the Virgin,*
fresco, Oratorio del Rosario di San Domenico,
Palermo.

---

1 *Stiftung Ratjen: Italienische Zeichnungen des 16. – 18. Jahrhunderts,* Munich, 1977,
pp. 138-39, no. 63, repr.

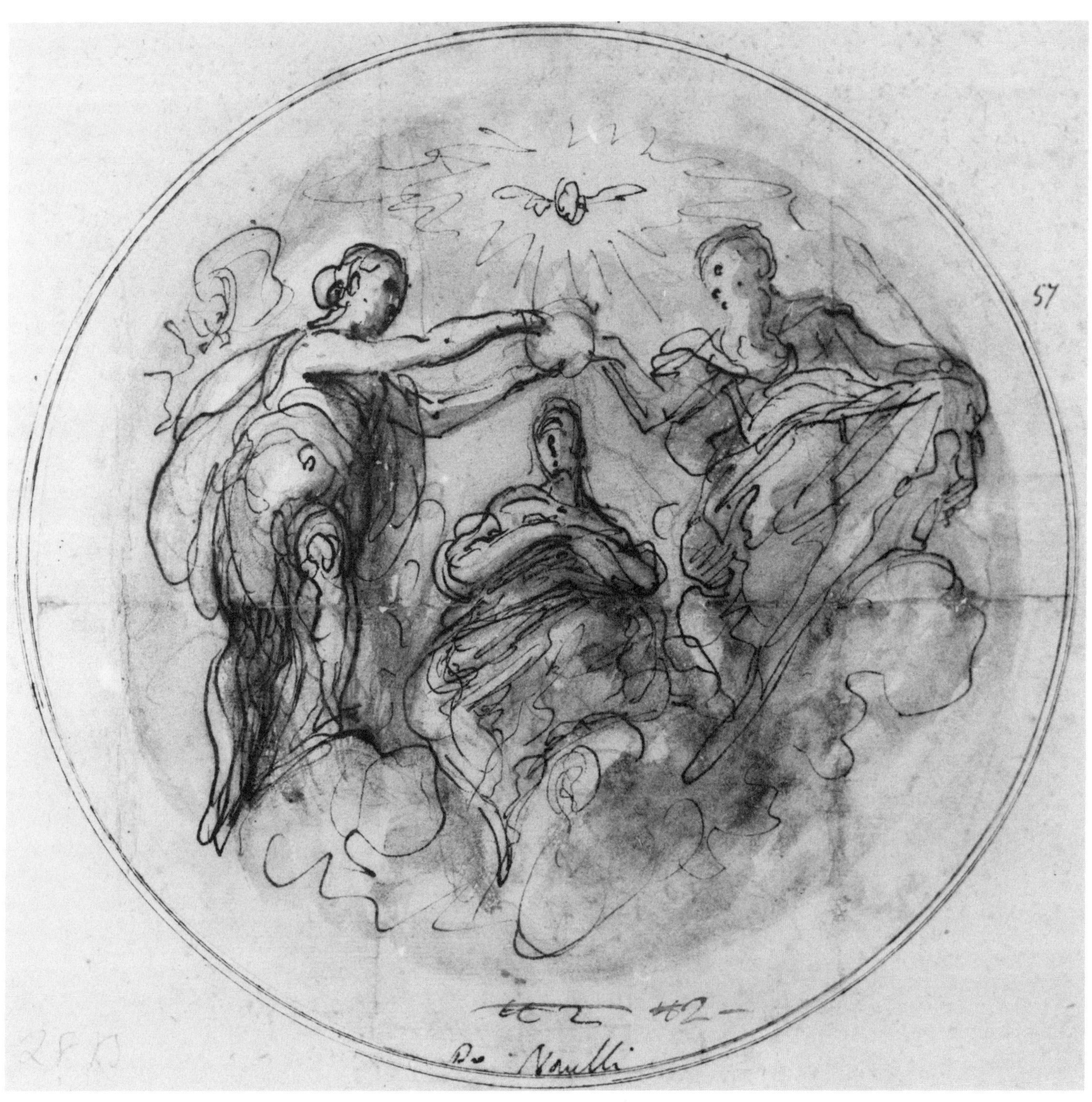

Salvator Rosa

Naples 1615 – 1673 Rome

38 *A Port with the Philosopher Crates Casting Money into the Sea (recto and verso)*

Pen and brown ink. Watermark: the Medici arms. Some repair at left of *recto*. 188 x 268 mm. Inscribed on *verso* in Rosa's hand: *Amico Caris. mo*

Provenance: ? Hon. Edward Bouverie (according to Christie's, as follows, p. 36); The Earl of Gainsborough; Christie's, London, 7 July 1981, lot 78.

Executed in Rosa's rapid pen manner, the studies on both sides of this sheet are connected with a painting, now in a British private collection, of a harbour with ships.[1] According to Filippo Baldinucci, the painting was undertaken for Marchese Carlo Gerini of Florence and it hung with a *pendant*, of Diogenes in an extensive landscape – *The Philosopher's Grove* – now in the Palazzo Pitti.[2] Both canvases have been dated to the first half of the 1640s, when Rosa was residing in Florence.[3] The Pitti *Philosopher's Grove* shows Diogenes, the Cynic philosopher, about to throw his bowl away, while in the *pendant* his disciple, Crates, casts his money into the sea.[4] Rosa was much attracted to the Cynic philosophy of the ancients and featured Crates in his ode *Delle Ricchezze.*

Rosa evidently started to use this sheet of paper as a letter: at the upper right of the *verso* there is the salutation 'Very dear friend' *(Amico carissimo)*. The drawing on the *verso* shows Crates on a small promontory at the left, whereas on the *recto* he is placed in the middle of the composition. In both cases a frantic crowd scrambles for Crates' disposed riches.

1 For the painting see H. Langdon in *Salvator Rosa,* Hayward Gallery, London, 1973, p. 23, under no. 12; and L. Salerno, *L'Opera completa di Salvator Rosa,* Milan, 1975, no. 86. The drawings bear comparison with Rosa's painting, *St. Anthony Preaching to the Fish,* at Althorp House (repr. Salerno, *op.cit.,* pl. XXXI).

2 *Baldinucci,* V, pp. 456-57.

3 Langdon, *op.cit.*; M. Mahoney, *The Drawings of Salvator Rosa,* New York and London, 1977, I, p. 316, opts for a date during the second half of the 1640s.

4 The lives of both Diogenes and Crates are told by Diogenes Laertius, *Lives of Eminent Philosophers,* VI, Ch. 2 and Ch. 5. However, Rosa may have been inspired by an apocryphal letter from Diogenes to Crates (M. Mahoney, *op.cit.,* p. 319, n.6.)

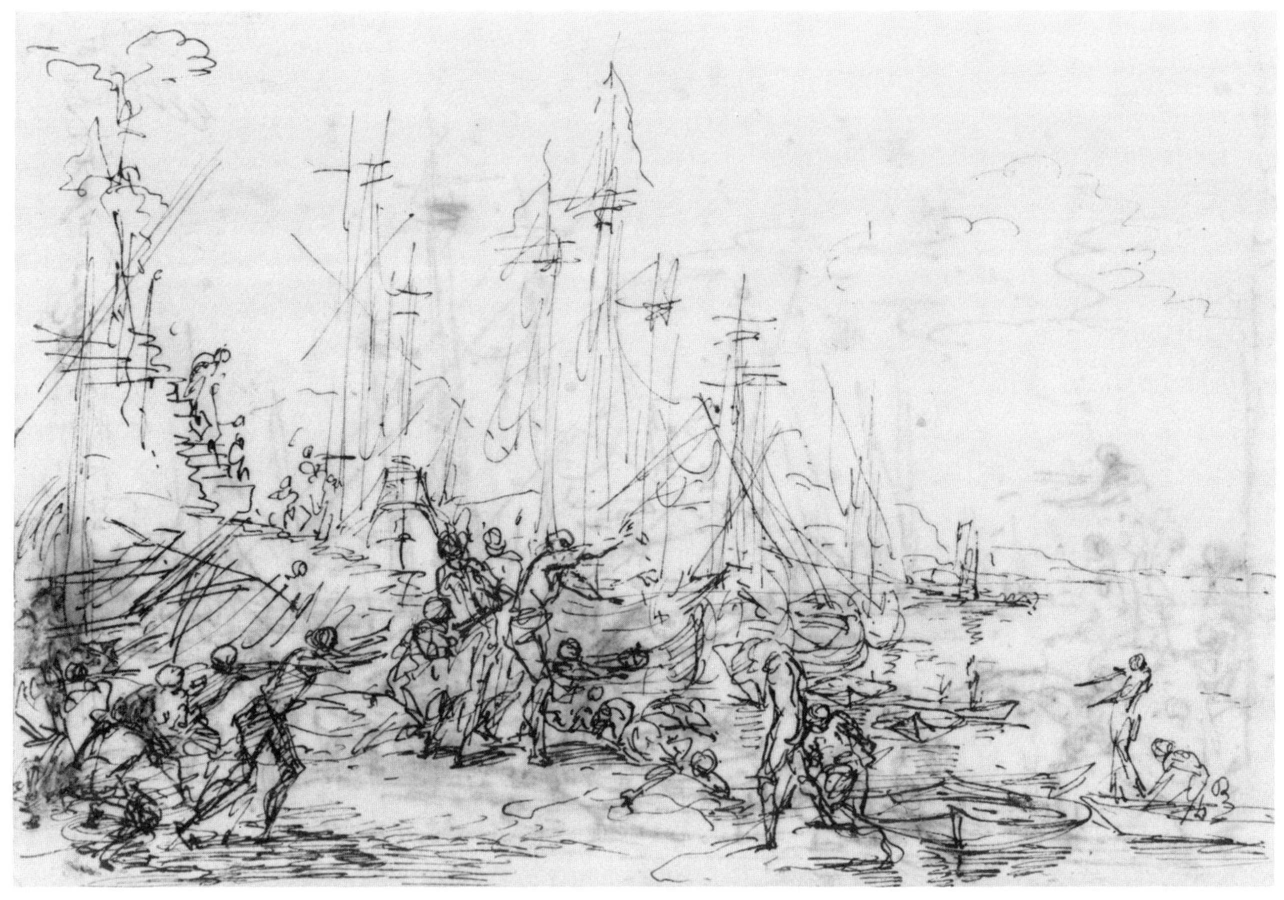

recto

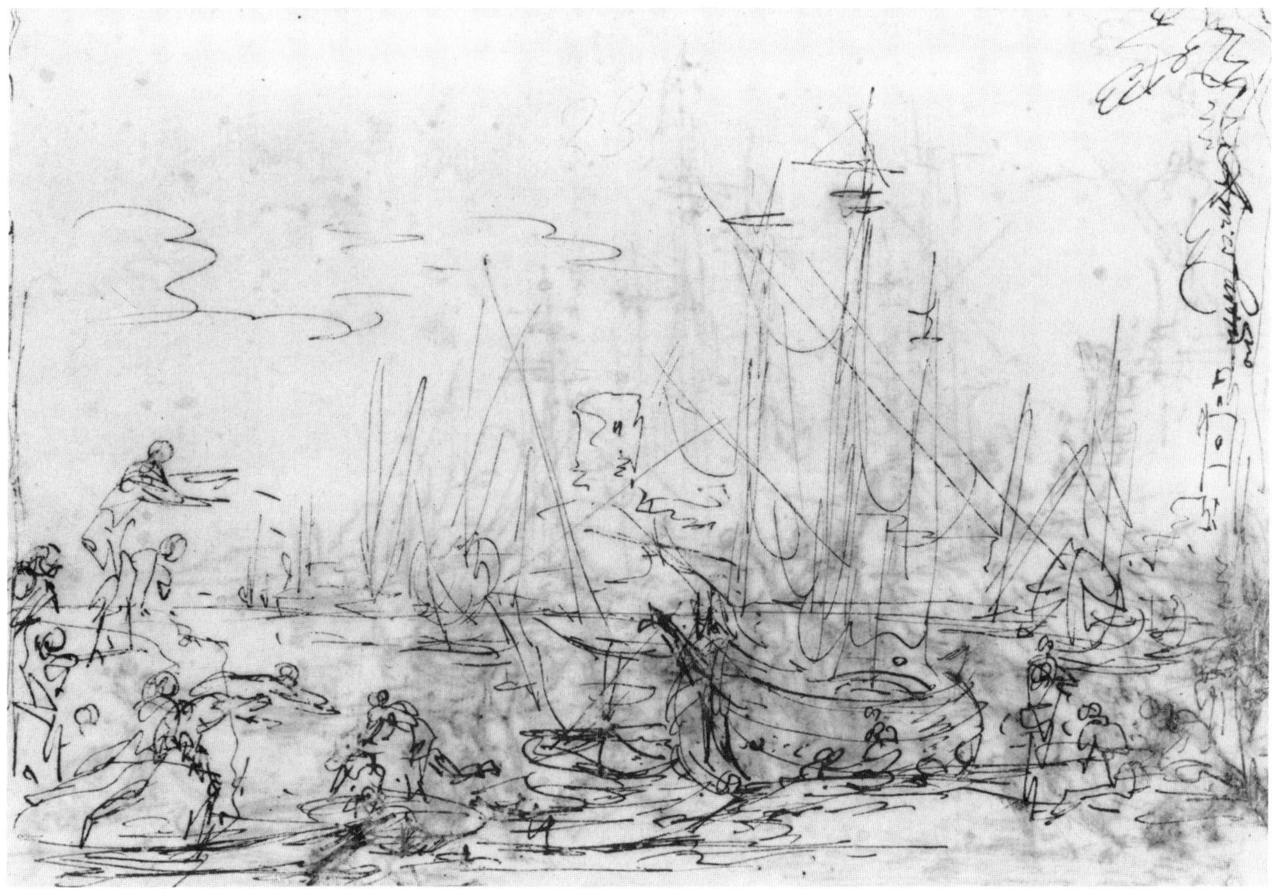

verso

Salvator Rosa

Naples 1615 – 1673 Rome

39 *A Young Man with Outstretched Arm in a Landscape*

Pen and brown ink, brown and red wash. 424 x 334 mm, oval. Signed on the stone at the right: *S. Rosa*

See following entry.

40 *A Philosopher Meditating in a Landscape*

Pen and brown ink and wash over black and red chalk. 436 x 330 mm, oval. Signed above the philosopher's feet: *Rosa*

Exhibited: Civiltà del Seicento a Napoli, Museo di Capodimonte, Naples, 1984, II, p. 122, no. 3.71 a-b, repr. (catalogue entries by J. Stock).

Literature: H.M. Hake, ''Pond's and Knapton's Imitations of Drawings,'' *The Print Collector's Quarterly,* IX, 1922, pp. 345-46.

Provenance: J. Richardson, Sen. (Lugt 2184), by 1735; J. Richardson, Jun. (Lugt 2170); Christie's, London, 7 July 1981, lots 94 and 95.

Single figures in various attitudes of meditation, especially in landscape settings, are common in Rosa's *oeuvre,* but drawings as carefully composed and finished as these are relatively rare.[1] The exact identity of the two figures is difficult to determine, although the inclusion of the bowl in the foreground of no. 40 may indicate that the philosopher is Diogenes. Whether or not they were originally intended as *pendants,* the two figures present a number of obvious contrasts: the bare-headed youth with outstretched arm of the one drawing opposing the older man with cap and contained gesture of the other.[2] Similarly, the lush landscape of the former contrasts with the sparser setting of no. 40. However, both landscapes possess those characteristic elements that Rosa had made his own: the precipitous banks and mounds, the striated rocks, the crossed tree trunks, and the leafy boughs juxtaposed with blasted branches.

Both sheets are signed, a practice Rosa evidently followed when forced to part with his drawings.[3] It is fitting, in view of the popularity of Rosa's work in eighteenth-century England, that from at least 1735 onwards these drawings were in the collections of the prominent connoisseurs Jonathan Richardson Senior and Junior. In 1735 the drawings were engraved by Arthur Pond as ovals in octagons. At probably about the same time the drawings were cut into an oval shape and were then mounted in contemporary English frames which have come down with the drawings.

[1] Such drawings are discussed by M. Mahoney, *The Drawings of Salvator Rosa,* New York and London, 1977, I, pp. 383-85, group 36. Mahoney dates this group to the first half of the 1650s.

[2] Another pair of signed drawings by Rosa that feature single male figures in contrasting attitudes in a landscape are in the British Museum; Mahoney, *op.cit.,* I, pp. 281-83, nos. 23.1-23.2, II, repr.

[3] For the signatures, most of which seem to date before 1649, see Mahoney, *op.cit.,* I, pp. 11-14.

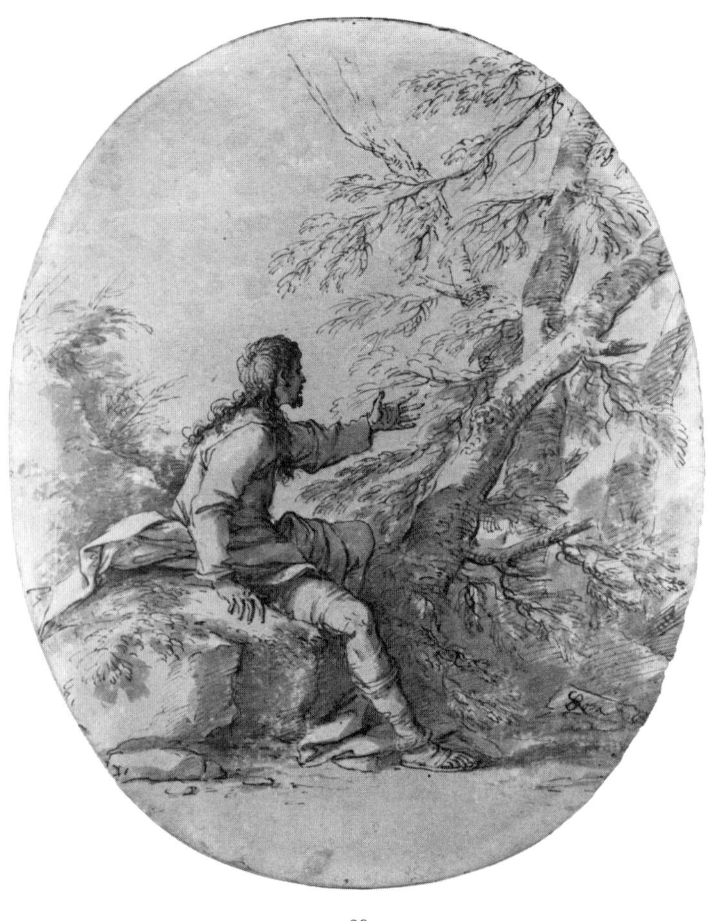

39

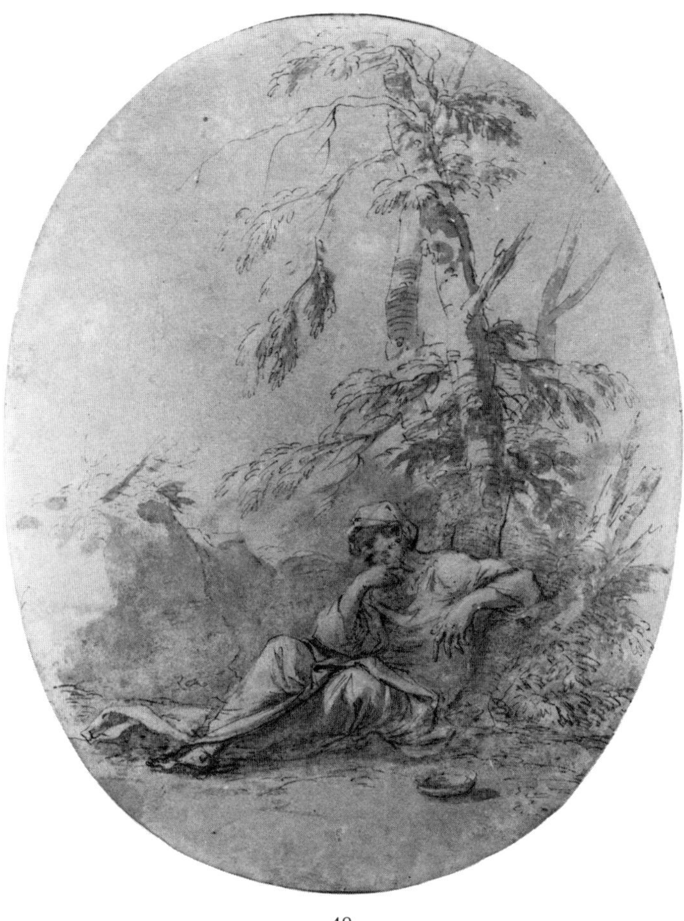

40

Baldassare Franceschini
called Il Volterrano

Volterra 1611 – 1689 Florence

41 *Half-length Study of a Male Nude, and Two Details of Legs and Feet*

Black chalk heightened with white on grey paper. Stains. 252 x 406 mm

Provenance: Sotheby's, London, 3 July 1980, lot 17.

Charles McCorquodale has connected this sheet of studies with the figure of Christ in the upper part of Volterrano's *St. Martin Dividing His Cloak with the Beggar,* a fresco executed about 1650 for the heirs of Senator Tommaso Guadagni in the Palazzo Duca di San Clemente, Florence.[1] Christ appears *di sotto in sù* with his arms outstretched, awaiting the transport of St. Martin's mantle by putti. In the drawing Volterrano has followed a time-honoured Florentine tradition and has studied the figure from a posed, nude model. In a second sheet of studies he has gone on to explore the figure clothed and to undertake detailed drapery studies.[2]

Other drawings for the fresco include an early study in the Albertina for the entire composition and a study for St. Martin, his rearing horse, and the beggar, recently on the art market in Italy.[3]

The elegant gestures and long pointed fingers of the present drawing are hallmarks of Volterrano's refined style.

1 *An Important Group of Drawings by Baldassare Franceschini, called Il Volterrano,* Sotheby's, London, 3 July 1980, p. 19, no. 17. Also see Baldinucci, v, p. 164. (The palace now houses the Faculty of Architecture of Florence University).

2 *Ibid.,* no. 18.

3 A. Stix, "Barockstudien", *Belvedere,* July-December, 1930, figs. 124-25; and E. Cortona and M. Jona, *Disegni Italiani dal XVI al XVIII Secolo,* Milan, 1980, no. 20, repr. Yet other related drawings are in the Uffizi (A.M. Petrioli Tofani, *Maestri del Sei e Settecento Toscano,* Biblioteca di Disegni, Florence, 1977, p. 37, no 26) and C. McCorquodale, *An Important Group of Drawings by Baldassare Franceschini, called Il Volterrano,* Sotheby's, London, 3 July 1980, pp. 19-20, nos. 18-20b.

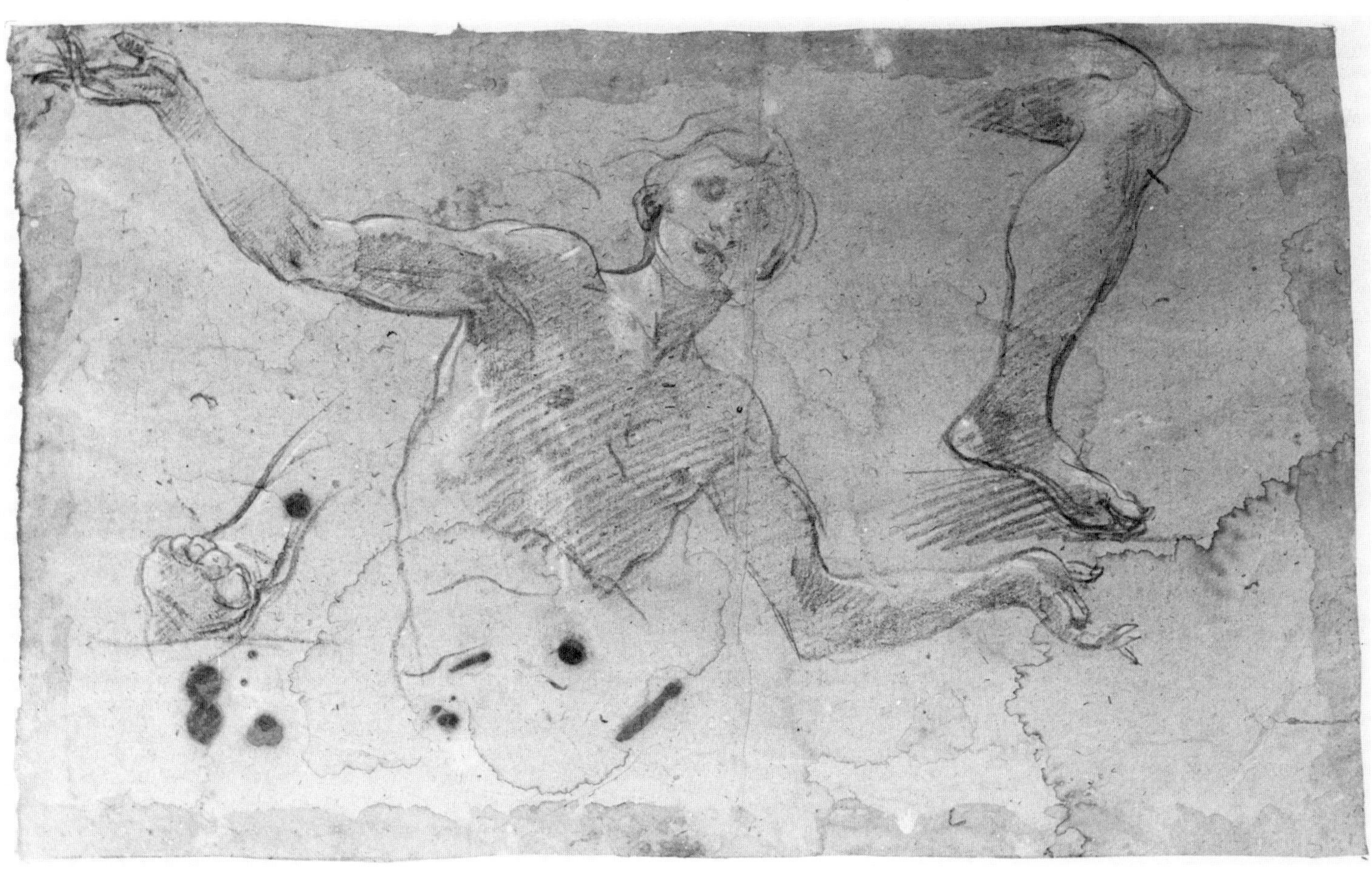

Baldassare Franceschini
called Il Volterrano

Volterra 1611 – 1689 Florence

42 *Studies for a Coronation of the Virgin
and Judith with the Head of Holofernes*

Red chalk, partly reinforced with pen and brown ink. Two flaps of paper, one on top of the other, glued onto the sheet at the upper right. Stains. 271 x 395 mm. Inscribed in red chalk in Volterrano's hand, upper left: *iudit,* and at upper middle, a partly illegible inscription and in brown ink at lower right: *64* and *4*

Provenance: Sotheby's, London, 3 July 1980, lot 24.

These six studies for all or parts of a Coronation of the Virgin have been related by Charles McCorquodale to Volterrano's frescoes in the vault of the Niccolini Chapel in the church of Santa Croce, Florence.[1] The sketch of Judith at the upper left is also for the same decoration. The frescoes were commissioned about 1652 by Marchese Filippo Niccolini, in whose palace (now the Palazzo Bouterline) Volterrano had just completed frescoes on the ground floor. But before work was begun on the chapel, Niccolini arranged for Volterrano to go to Parma to study afresh the works of Correggio, and also to visit Rome for the first time.[2] Accordingly, both the influence of Correggio and that of his seventeenth-century heir, Giovanni Lanfranco, have been remarked in Volterrano's decorations at Santa Croce.[3] In view of such a drawing as this, where the figures have been realized with an extremely fluid configuration of rippling lines and some diagonal hatching in red chalk, with reworking in ink, it is tempting to speculate that Volterrano had studied not only Correggio's paintings but also his drawings.

The present drawing is exceptionally revealing of Volterrano's exhaustive preparatory work for a painting. Not only has he worked and reworked the manifold possibilities of the subject on all parts of the sheet, but at the upper right – in the sketch which is most fully defined by the addition of ink – he has glued onto the sheet two flaps of paper with yet more variations of the motif. On the *verso* of the top flap there is a red chalk sketch of a frame for an altarpiece.

Late in his life Volterrano again painted the *Coronation of the Virgin,* in the cupola of the tribune of Santissima Annunziata, Florence; and drawings for that commission are easily confused with drawings for the Niccolini chapel. Additional sheets in the Albertina and at auction for the Niccolini chapel have, however, been convincingly identified by McCorquodale.[4]

1 C. McCorquodale, *An Important Group of Drawings by Baldassare Franceschini, called Il Volterrano,* Sotheby's, London, 3 July 1980, p. 23, no. 24.

2 Baldinucci, V, pp. 165-67.

3 McCorquodale, *op. cit.,* also citing L. Lanzi, *Storia Pittorica della Italia,* Florence, 1822, I, p. 203.

4 A. Stix and L. Fröhlich-Bum, *Beschreibender Katalog der Handzeichnungen in der Graphischen Sammlung Albertina, III: Die Zeichnungen der Toskanischen Umbrischen und Römischen Schulen,* Vienna, 1932, nos. 663-665r, 668-670, repr.; McCorquodale, *op. cit.,* pp. 23-24, nos. 25-27b. Further studies for the Sibyls in the pendentives of the chapel are in the Uffizi (34065, 15381 and 15383 F.) and in the Albertina, Stix and Fröhlich-Bum, *op. cit.,* no. 666.

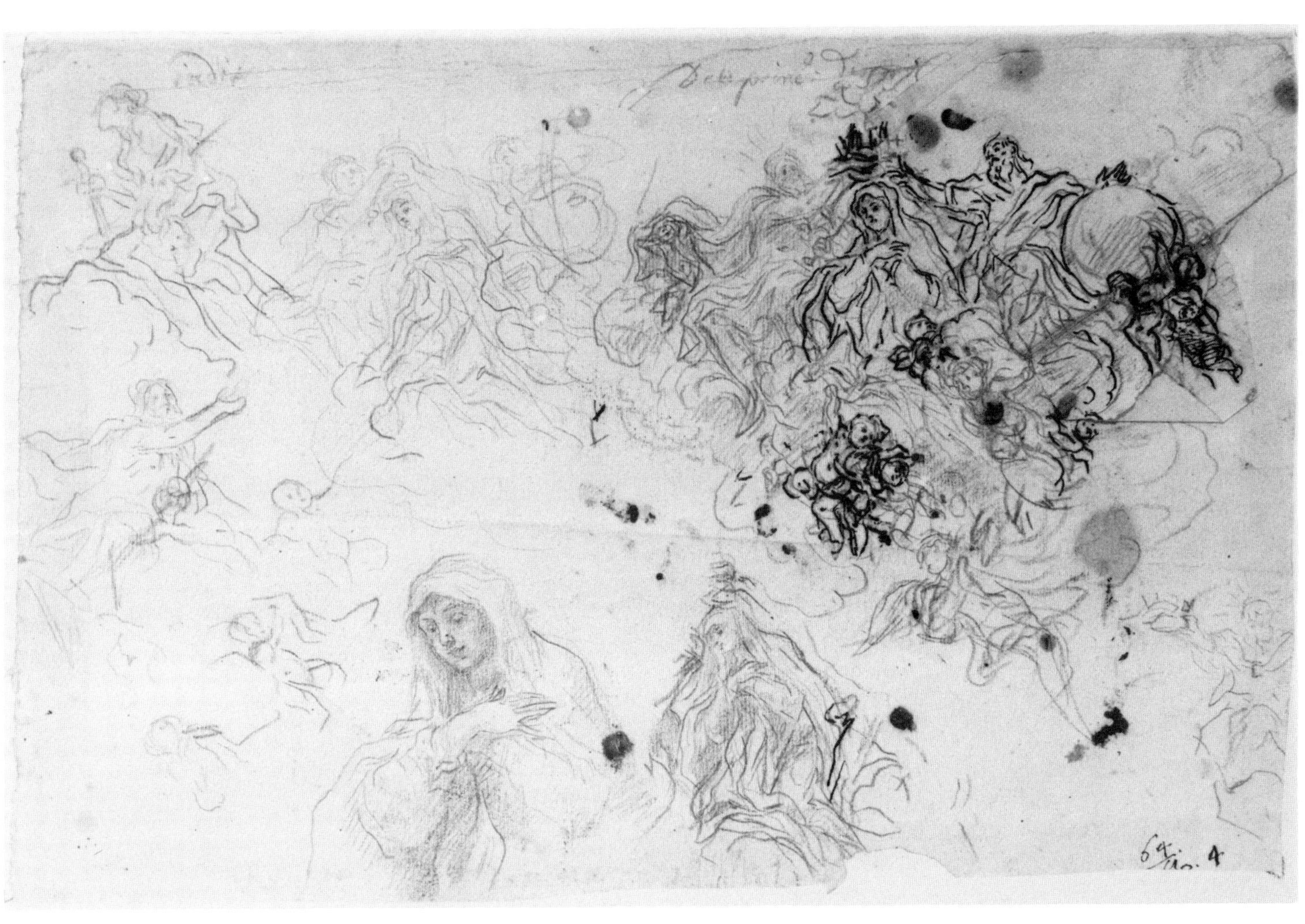

Baldassare Franceschini
called Il Volterrano

Volterra 1611 – 1689 Florence

43   *The Rest on the Flight into Egypt*

Black chalk. Oil stains. 292 x 214 mm. Inscribed in ink at upper right: *69*

Provenance: Sotheby's, London, 3 July 1980, lot 49.

Since only a small number of composition drawings by Volterrano have survived, it has been suggested that the artist may have troubled to make such studies only for major commissions.[1] This drawing is connected with such a commission, *The Rest on the Flight into Egypt* (fig. 43a). Baldinucci states that the painting was begun for Cardinal Gian Carlo de' Medici (1611-1663), but it was later in the possession of the Marchese Carlo Gerini, who then commissioned Volterrano to paint a pendant, *The Way to Calvary*.[2] Both canvases still belong to the Gerini family in Florence. There are supposed *modelli* for both paintings in the Corsini Gallery, Florence.[3]

The finished painting closely resembles the drawing, except that the Virgin's right leg has been moved away from her body to point downward toward the lower left corner (a direction also accentuated by the new direction of the staff), the angel with the bunch of flowers has acquired greater prominence and an altered pose, and another angel with a platter of fruit has been added at the upper right. Taken together, these changes produce a thrust to the upper right that is absent in the drawing.

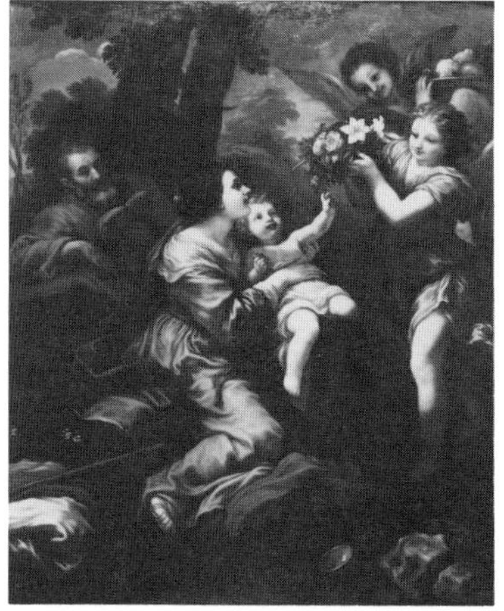

fig. 43a Volterrano, *The Rest on the Flight into Egypt*, oil on canvas, Marchesi Gerini, Florence.

1   C. McCorquodale, *Catalogue of Drawings by Baldassare Franceschini, called Il Volterrano,* Sotheby's, London, 3 July 1980, Introduction, unpaginated.

2   Baldinucci, V, p. 174.

3   G. Ewald in *The Twilight of the Medici,* The Detroit Institute of Arts, Detroit/Palazzo Pitti, Florence, 1974, p. 318.

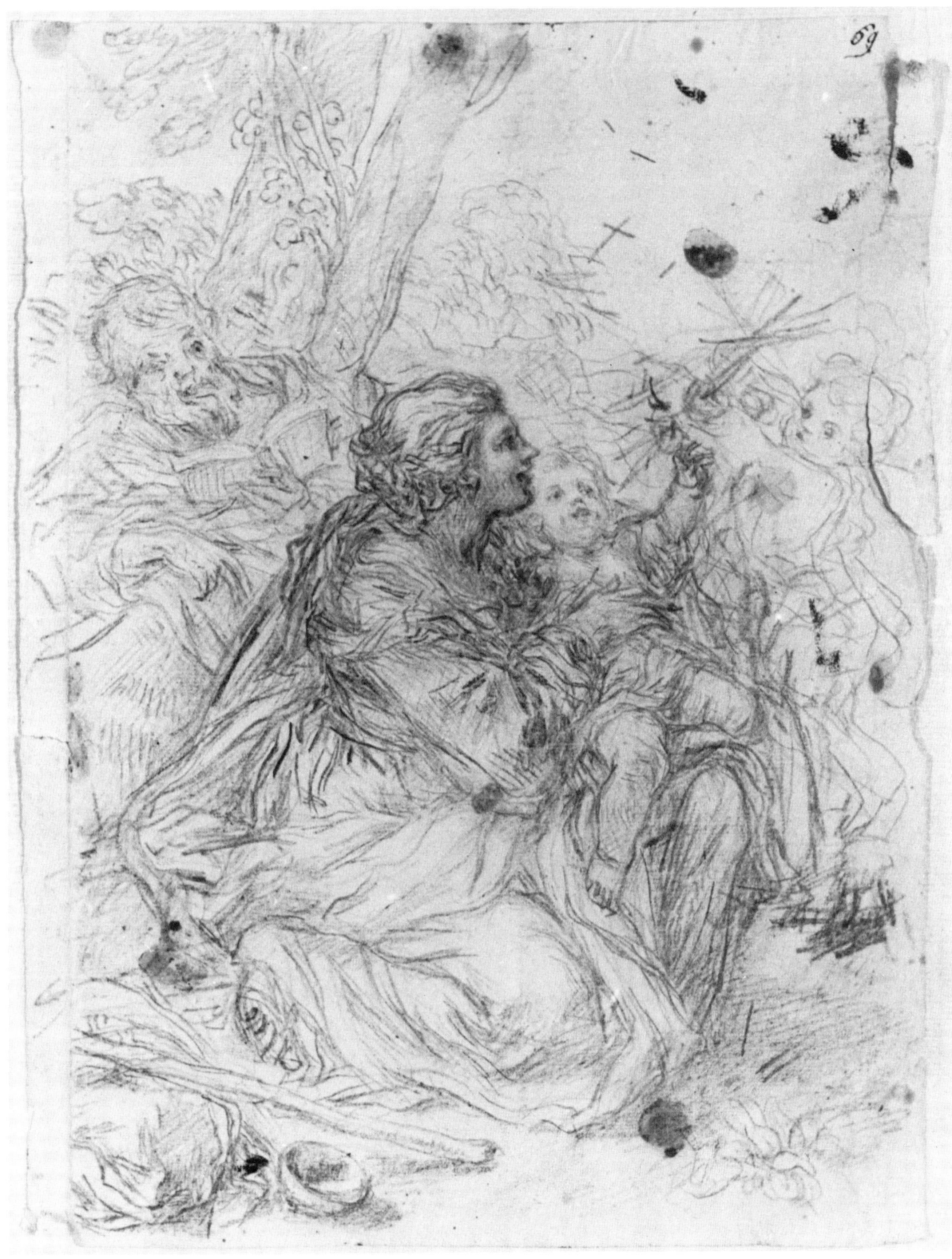

Pier Francesco Mola

Coldrerio 1612 – 1666 Rome

44 *Studies of the Virgin Immaculate and Male Heads (recto); Four Figure Studies, Including St. Michael and Diana (?) (verso)*

Pen and brown ink, and wash and red chalk *(recto)*; pen and brown ink, and red chalk *(verso)*. Upper right corner cut. 186 x 160 mm.

Provenance: Sotheby's, London, 9 July 1981, lot 27.

The most fully realized feature of this typical sheet of studies – the Virgin standing on a crescent moon and less distinct indications of small supporting angels – must have been undertaken with an Immaculate Conception in mind. The only mention of this subject among Mola's finished works is a large standard commissioned by Prince Camillo Pamphili about 1657, but even in this case, the exact subject is not certain.[1] Although now lost, the standard is mentioned by a number of witnesses in a court case brought by Mola against Prince Camillo Pamphili over a commission in the Palazzo Pamphili at Valmontone. In the testimony the standard is variously called an Assumption and an Immaculate Conception. Because of the inclusion of the crescent moon, there can be no doubt that the present drawing represents the *Immacolata,* but whether or not the study is connected with the Pamphili standard remains an open question.

A more fully developed composition drawing of the Immaculate Conception in the Steiner collection, New York, has also been associated with the Pamphili standard.[2] A considerable distance separates the pose of the Virgin in the two drawings; yet it was not unusual for Mola to produce widely differing preliminary drawings for a single picture, and it is possible that both the Steiner and Ferretti drawings were indeed executed for the same commission.

The other studies on this sheet have not been directly related to any known commission, although the male figure with slight indications of wings, on the *verso* at the left, may be an early idea for the archangel in *St. Michael Confounding Lucifer,* in the church of San Marco, Rome.[3] The male heads on the *recto* are analagous to those found in such frescoes as *Joseph Greeting his Brothers,* in the Palazzo del Quirinale, Rome, documented 1656-1657, and *St. Peter Baptizing in Prison,* in the Gesù, Rome, of about the same date.[4] Since all of these paintings date from approximately the same time as the Pamphili standard, there may be some additional reason for thinking that the study of the Immacolata was destined for that work.

1   L. Montalto, ''Gli Affreschi del Palazzo Pamphilj in Valmontone,'' *Commentari,* VI, 1955, pp. 294-97, documents XIX-XXI. R. Cocke, *Pier Francesco Mola,* Oxford, 1972, pp. 4, 56-57, 72 (L.3).

2   *Renaissance and Baroque Drawings from the Collection of John and Alice Steiner,* ed. K. Oberhuber, Fogg Art Museum, Cambridge, Massachusetts, 1977, pp. 72-74, no. 24 (catalogue entry by A.J. Adams).

3   Cocke, *op. cit.,* pp. 4, 32-33, 61 (no. 59), dates the painting 1655-59. The figure is similar, in reverse, to the youth in the Carracci's *Ludi Lupercali,* which is above the fireplace in the Palazzo Magnani, Bologna, while the figure of Diana(?) to the right of the *verso* resembles, in reverse, the female figure at the left of the same painting.

4   For the paintings see Cocke, *op. cit.,* pp. 26-29, 58 (no. 49), 59 (no. 53).

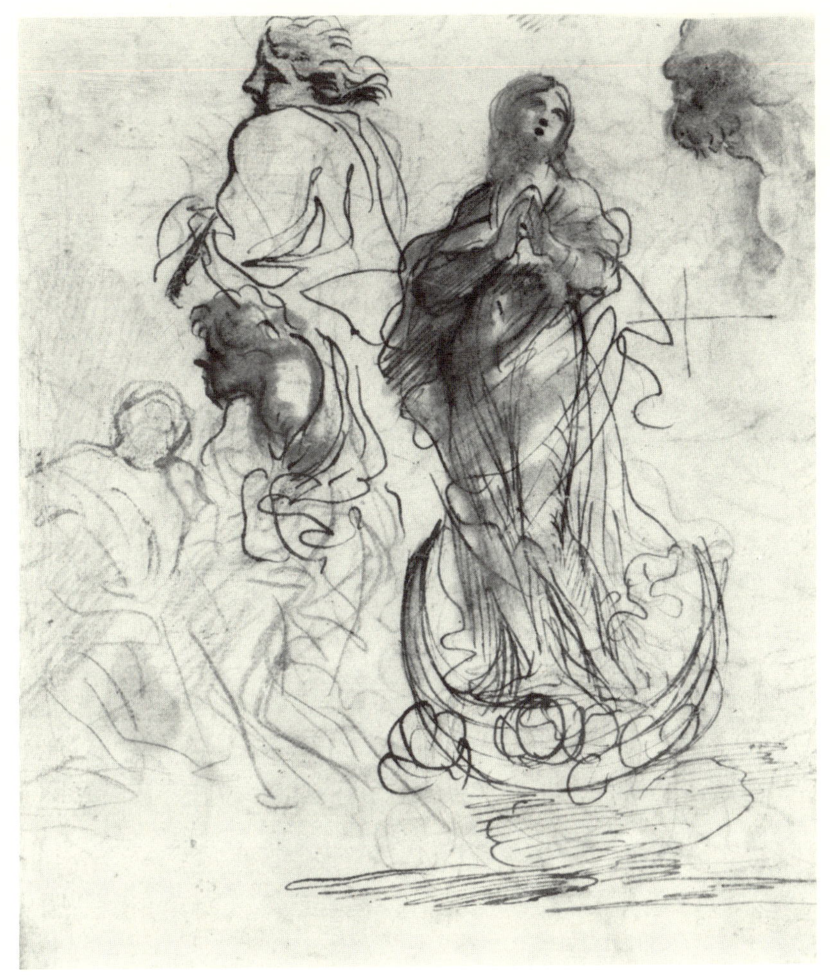

recto

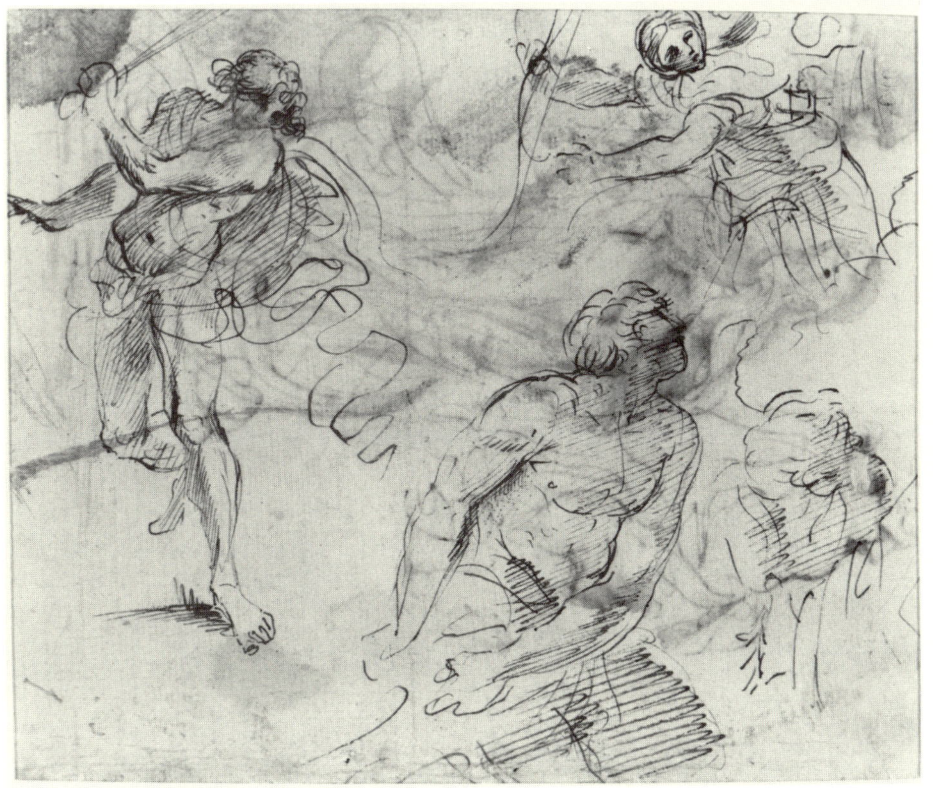

verso

99

Mattia Preti

Taverna 1613 – 1699 La Valletta

45 *A Female Figure in a Chariot Pulled by Two Horses*

Red chalk and red wash. Laid down.
Watermark: encircled fleur-de-lys on a three mountain symbol
below the letter M(?). 158 x 168 mm. Inscribed on the old
mount: *Il Calabrese.*

Exhibited: Civiltà del Seicento a Napoli, Museo di Capodimonte,
Naples, 1984, II, p. 113, no. 3.59, repr. (catalogue entry by
J. Stock).

Provenance: ?Cavaliere Francesco Maria Niccolo Gabburri
(1675-1742) (according to Christie's catalogue, as follows,
p. 5); Christie's, London, 7 April 1981, lot 18.

The correct attribution of this drawing is provided by the old
inscription, *Il Calabrese,* which refers to Preti's title *il Cavalier
Calabrese* and his birthplace in Calabria in southern Italy. Nicholas Turner has identified the sheet as a preliminary study for
Preti's frescoed ceiling in the Sala dell'Aria in the Palazzo Pamphili at Valmontone, near Rome. Between 1657 and 1661 the
palace was decorated by a number of prominent artists, including Pier Francesco Mola, Guglielmo Cortese, and Gaspard
Dughet.

Preti's ceiling, which was commissioned on 17 March 1661 by
Donna Olimpia Aldobrandini, Princess of Rossano, has been
called a watershed between High and Late Baroque fresco decoration.[1] The drawing is of Aurora in her chariot, who together
with Fortune, occupies one of the short sides of the ceiling (fig.
45a). In the fresco the horses are shown in a more horizontal
position, the putto with a torch is moved to the right, and
Aurora extends her right arm behind her in a pose closer to
Guercino's *Aurora* (1621), on the ceiling of the Casino Ludovisi,
Rome.

The combination of red chalk and red wash is rather unusual,
yet seems to have been congenial to Preti. He employed it again
in a double-sided drawing in the Metropolitan Museum for
decorations in the church of San Biago, Modena, and in a group
of drawings in the Uffizi which may relate to his frescoes in the
apse of Sant'Andrea della Valle, Rome.[2] On other occasions,
Preti supplemented the red colour with charcoal and a greyish
wash.

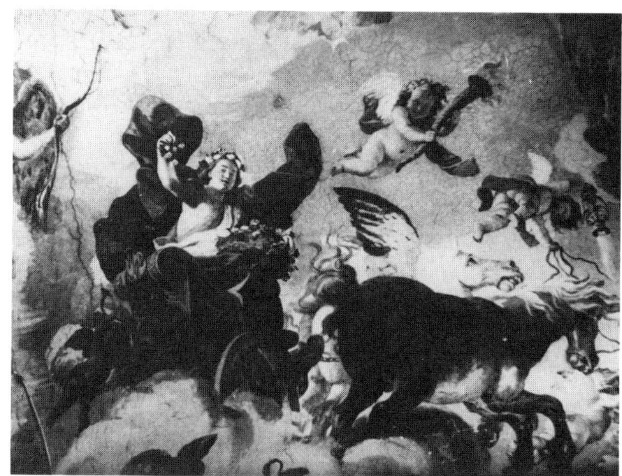

fig. 45a Mattia Preti, *Aurora,* fresco, detail of vault of the
Sala dell'Aria, Palazzo Pamphili, Valmontone.

1 N. Pevsner, "Die Wandlung um 1650 in der italienischen Malerei," *Wiener
Jahrbuch für Kunstgeschichte,* VIII, 1932, p. 69 (reprinted as "The Crisis of 1650
in Italian Painting," *Studies in Art, Architecture and Design,* London, 1968, I,
p. 61.) For documentation see V. Ruffo, "La galleria Ruffo nel XVII secolo a
Messina," *Bollettino d'Arte,* X, 1916, p. 255; and L. Montalto, "Gli Affreschi
del Palazzo Pamphilj in Valmontone," *Commentari,* VI, 1955, p. 297, docu-
ment XXII; and for illustrations, E. Waterhouse, *Baroque Painting in Rome,*
London, 1937, figs. 16, 18-19.

2 J. Bean, *17th Century Italian Drawings in the Metropolitan Museum,* New York,
1979, p. 238, no. 314, repr.; W. Vitzthum, *Cento Disegni Napoletani,* Gabinetto
Desegni e Stampe degli Uffizi, XXVI, Florence, 1967, pp. 50-51, nos. 77-79,
repr.

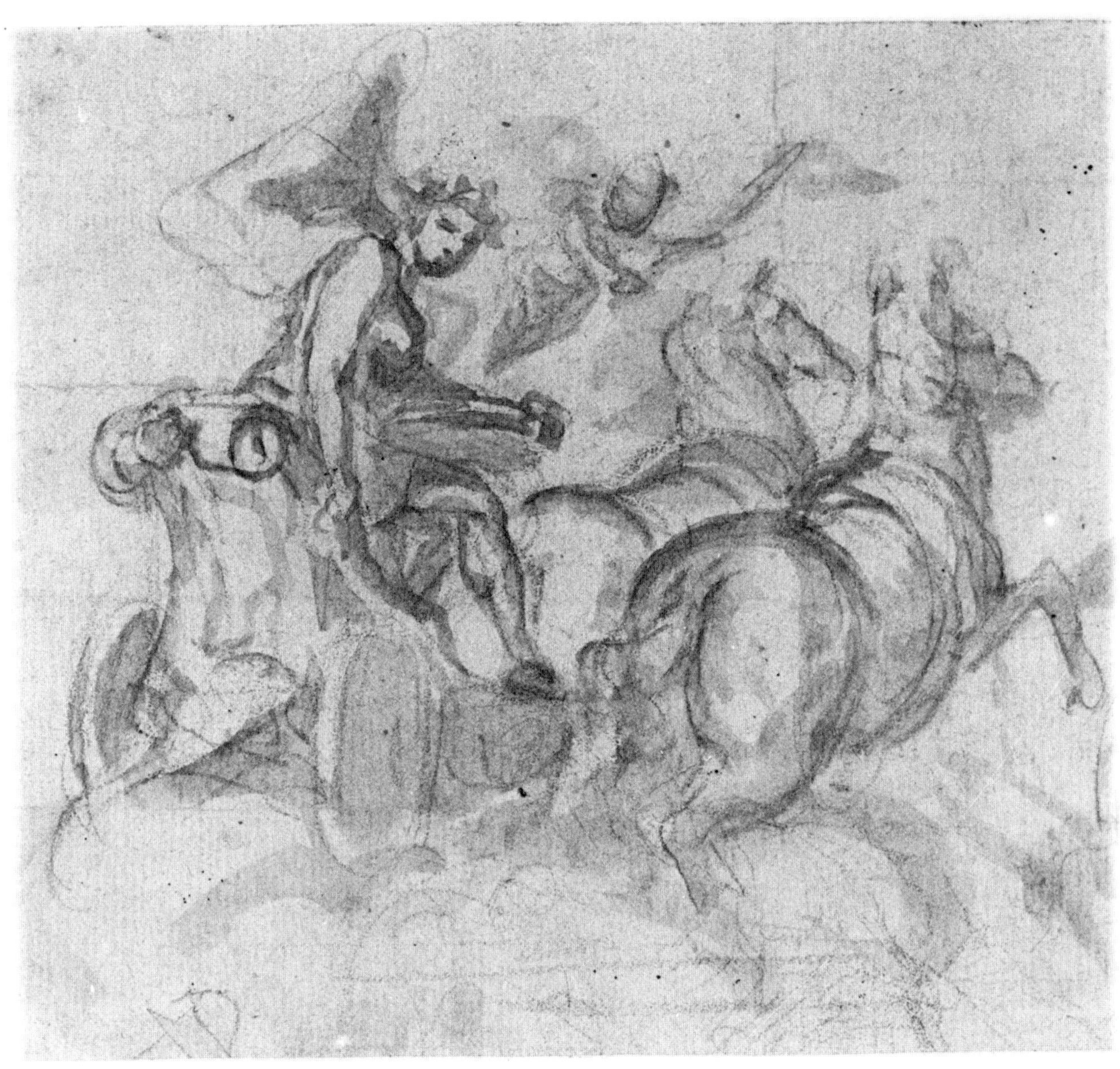

Gian Lorenzo Bernini

Naples 1598 – 1680 Rome

46 *Fame or Victory*

Black chalk. Watermark with an anchor in a circle, a six-pointed star above, and the letter J (?) below. 268 x 197 mm. On the *verso* a label inscribed: *55*

Provenance: A. Viggiano (Lugt Suppl. 191a).

This drawing of a winged allegorical figure who wears a laurel wreath around her head and is writing on a ceremonial scroll can be connected with a neglected drawing in the Victoria and Albert Museum which has been ascribed to the school of Bernini (fig. 46a).[1] Probably a copy of a lost drawing, the London sheet shows the allegorical figure standing in front of a large sarcophagus; she is flanked by various trophies including cannons, cuirasses, standards, and a crown and baton, and is supported on a three-sided base with a flat front, either a rectangular door or a recessed panel for the epitaph, and concave sides. According to the drawing this funerary monument was located in a large alcove, framed by an arch. The figure of Fame or Victory is remarkably similar in the two drawings, although in the London sheet, there is the addition of a sash fluttering down from her waist to the left, while in the present sheet, there is included a shallow rectangular base beneath the figure.

The purpose of the drawing in the Victoria and Albert Museum is not known, although the sheet has been compared to a drawing by Bernini, formerly in the collection of Anthony Blunt, which in turn has been interpreted as an unexecuted project for the tomb of Doge Giovanni Cornaro in the church of San Nicolò da Tolentino, Venice.[2] While it is true that both drawings not only show sepulchral monuments in large arched spaces, but also include three-sided bases sharing many features, there is little justification for concluding that the two projects were alternative solutions for the same commission. The back wall in the ex-Blunt project is flat, whereas the one in the drawing in the Victoria and Albert Museum is curved; and the tripartite base is a type frequently used by Bernini, as can be seen in more rudimentary form, for instance, in the tomb of Cardinal Pimentel in Santa Maria sopra Minerva (ca.1653), or in the pedestal for the Constantine monument in St. Peter's (at

the latest, 1666). More significant, the drawing in the Victoria and Alberta Museum does not include any of the usual imagery of the Venetian doge, such as his ceremonial cap (*corno*); and the trophies which are so prominently displayed would be inappropriate for Giovanni Cornaro, who was not known for his involvement in military affairs.[3] It is most likely then that the drawing in the Victoria and Alberta Museum and hence the present sheet were undertaken for another sepulchral monument which still awaits exact identification. The tomb must have been that of a distinguished military commander, whose valorous deeds the winged figure is here conscientiously inscribing.

In the present drawing the chalk has been used in ways consistent with Bernini's flexible late style. In places the chalk has been lightly and deftly put on; in others it has been deliberately smudged so as to produce a middle tone; and finally, it has been applied in a few abrupt strokes that form powerful accents. The long and straight limbs have only been faintly outlined, but the drapery with its angular ridges and deep pockets has received a good deal of the artist's attention. Some of the same features are to be found in Bernini's drawings for the Altar of the Holy Sacrament in St. Peter's (finished in 1674) or for the engraving of the *Feeding of the Five Thousand* (ca. 1677).[4]

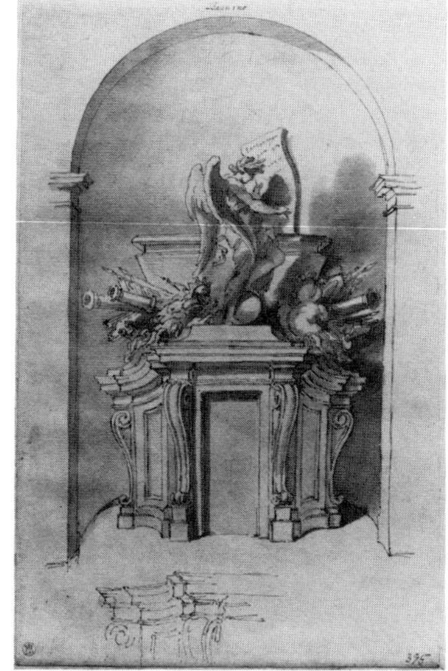

fig. 46a After G.L. Bernini, *Design for a Tomb*, pen and brown ink and wash over black chalk, Victoria and Albert Museum, London.

1 CAI 395; P. Ward-Jackson, *Italian Drawings, Volume Two: 17th-18th century,* Victoria and Albert Museum Catalogues, London, 1979, p. 24, no. 633, repr. The connection was first made by Roberto Ferretti.

2 R. Wittkower, *Gian Lorenzo Bernini,* London, 2nd ed., 1966, pp. 216-18, fig. 63; A. Blunt, "Two Drawings for Sepulchral Monuments by Bernini," *Essays in the History of Art Presented to Rudolf Wittkower,* London, 1967, pp. 230-32, repr.

3 Cf. the use of trophies in Bernini's drawing in the British Museum for the catafalque (1669) of the Duc de Beaufort, the French naval commander who died in the war with the Turks. H. Brauer and R. Wittkower, *Die Zeichnungen des Gianlorenzo Berini,* Berlin, 1931, reprint 1970, I, p. 161-62, II, pl. 121.

4 See Brauer and Wittkower, *op. cit.,* II, pls. 132a-141b.

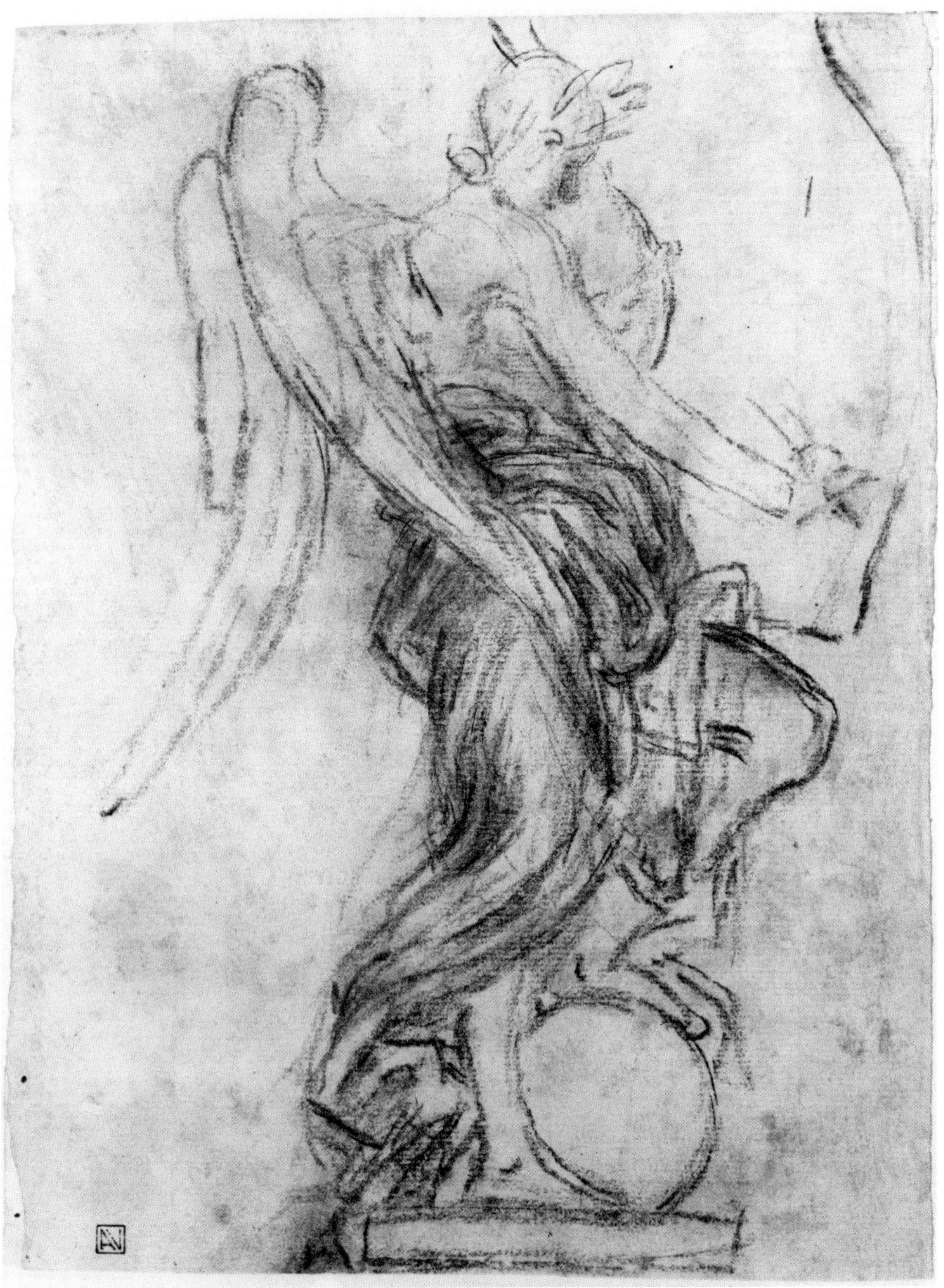

Claude Gellée
called Claude Lorrain

Champagne, Lorraine 1600 – 1682 Rome

47   *A Pastoral Landscape*

Pen and brown ink and wash, and some greyish wash, heightened with white (slightly oxidized in places) and black chalk, on paper tinted with light brown wash, except for an area at the horizon in the middle. Central vertical fold. Some damage along left and right edges. 263 x 405 mm.

Exhibited: Old Master Drawings, Colnaghi's, London, 1950, no. 46, repr.; *L'Ideale Classico nel Seicento in Italia e la Pittura di Paessaggio,* Palazzo dell'Archiginnasio, Bologna, 1962, pp. 431-32, no. 213, repr. (catalogue entry by M. Kitson).

Literature: Burlington Magazine, XCII, May, 1950, p. ii, repr; M. Röthlisberger, *Claude Lorrain, the Drawings,* Berkeley and Los Angeles, 1968, p. p. 335, no. 899, repr.

Provenance: Duke of Sutherland; L. G. Duke; Colnaghi; Nigel-Warren; property of a lady (according to Christie's as follows); Christie's 13 December 1984, lot 147.

This drawing by the great French landscape artist, Claude Lorrain, is included in an exhibition of Italian drawings not just because the artist spent most of his creative life in Rome, and derived abiding inspiration from the Roman *campagna,* but because his landscapes also represent the apogee of a tradition to which several other drawings shown here belong (see nos. 53, 64, and 65). The cowherds returning with their herds the towering tree, and the carefully organized recession into a luminous distance are all elements frequently found in Claude's works. Marcel Röthlisberger has pointed to the presence of these features in Claude's drawings from the 1630s and 1640s,[1] but the freedom and grandeur of this drawing have led both Michael Kitson and Röthlisberger to date it to the early 1660s.[2] As is usual with Claude's mature work, there is a compelling delicacy and sensitivity in the handling of details here, yet there is a masterful coherence of the whole. In this case, the artist has washed the entire sheet, except for a small area at the horizon in the middle, with a warm brown tone, and has strengthened the principal tree with added black chalk. Although the freedom of the execution reminds Kitson of studies done by Claude out-of-doors, he concludes that because of its size the drawing was no doubt executed in the studio.[3]

The drawing does not relate to any known painting.

An old imitation of the drawing is in the museum at Besançon.[4]

1   Röthlisberger, *op. cit.,* specifically referring to drawings in the École des Beaux-Arts, Paris, and the Louvre (Röthlisberger, nos. 181 and 493).

2   *L'Ideale Classico, op. cit.,* p. 432; and Röthlisberger, *op. cit.,* p. 335.

3   *L'Ideale Classico,* p. 432.

4   No. D.1, 325; Röthlisberger, *op. cit.,* p. 335.

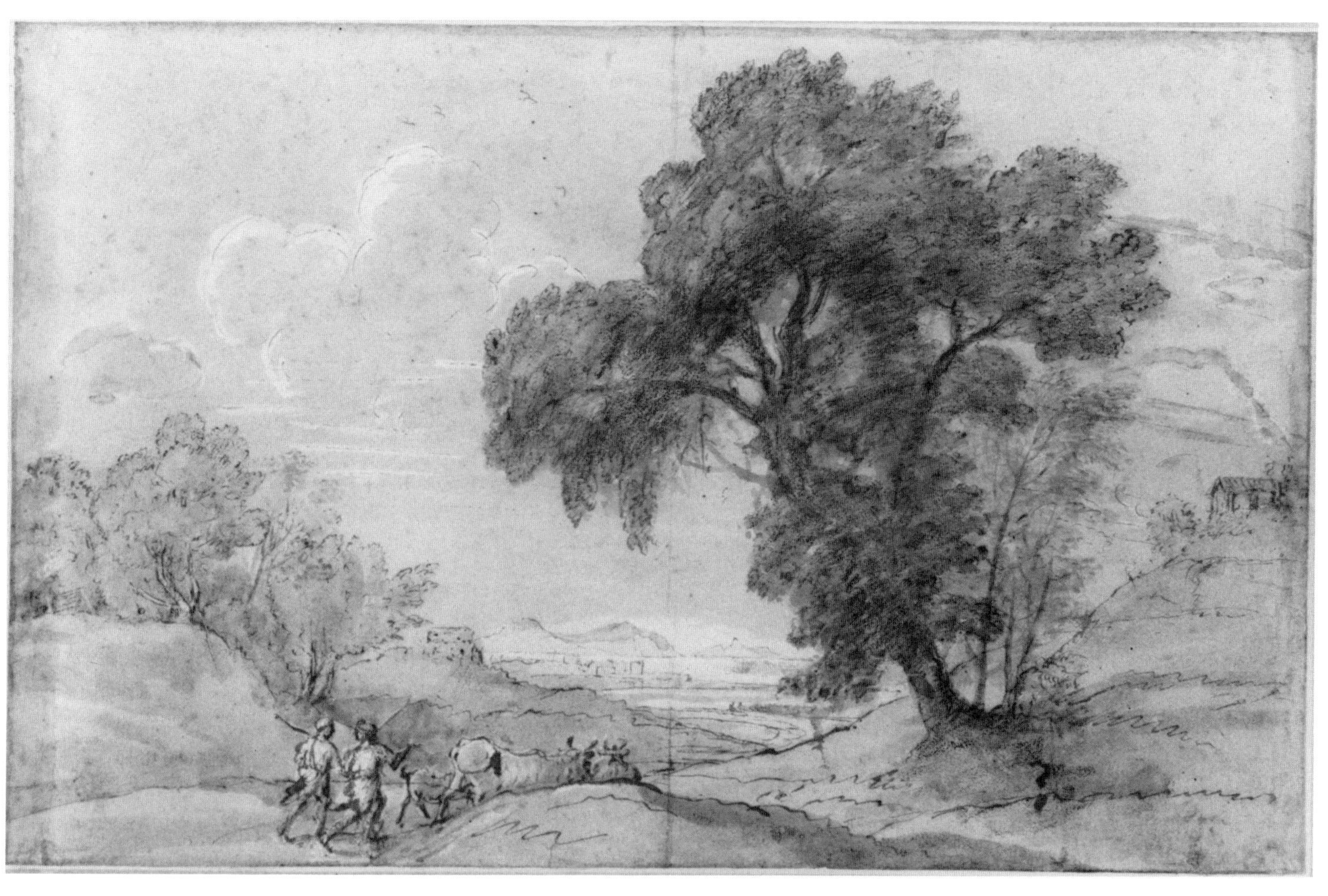

Giulio Carpioni

Venice 1613 – 1679 Verona

48 *Bacchus Punishing the Maenads*
    for the Death of Orpheus

Red chalk. 426 x 280 mm.

Exhibited: Disegni veneti di collezioni inglesi, catalogue entries by
J. Stock, Fondazione Giorgio Cini, Venice, Vicenza, 1980,
p. 52, no. 61, repr.

Provenance: A. Neerman; private collection, London;
Christie's, London, 12 April 1983, lot 87.

Only a small number of Carpioni's carefully worked drawings
in red chalk have survived. This fine example, first published by
Julien Stock,[1] may be compared to such red chalk drawings by
Carpioni as *A Blind Old Man Talking to Listening Women* (in
Stockholm), *The Mystic Marriage of St. Catherine,* of which there
are versions in the Ashmolean Museum, Oxford (with red
wash), and the National Gallery of Canada, and in particular,
The Eliades at the Tomb of Phaëthon, in the Albertina, Vienna.[2] As
Terisio Pignatti has remarked, the linear use of red chalk must
be related to Carpioni's considerable activities as an etcher.[3]

Although the subject of the present drawing was interpreted
by Pilo as the *Metamorphosis of the Eliades,* Felton Gibbons has
convincingly suggested that it is Bacchus changing the Thracian
women into oak trees, as punishment for their having wantonly
slain Orpheus (Ovid, *Metamorphoses,* XI, 1-84).[4]

1 *Disegni veneti di collezioni inglesi,* Fondazione Giorgio Cini, Venice, Vicenza,
   1980, p. 52, no. 61, repr. Before the discovery of this sheet a very similar
   drawing in the collection of Felton Gibbons had been published as
   the original: G. M. Pilo, *Carpioni,* Venice, 1961, pp. 57, 130, fig. 177; and
   T. Pignatti, *Venetian Drawings from American Collections,* International
   Exhibitions Foundation, Washington, 1974-75, p. 24, no. 42, repr.

2 P. Bjurström, *Italian Drawings,* Stockholm, 1979, p. 129, no. 128, repr. in col-
   our, p. xii; K. T. Parker, *Catalogue of the Collection of Drawings in the Ashmolean
   Museum, Volume II, Italian Schools,* 1956, p. 422, no. 805; *Annual Bulletin, 2,
   National Gallery of Canada,* 1978-79, pp. 105, 124, pl. 19; A Stix and L. Fröhlich-
   Bum, *Beschreibender Katalog der Handzeichnungen in der Graphischen Sammlung
   Albertina, Die Zeichnungen der Venezianischen Schule,* Vienna, 1926, p. III,
   no. 225, repr.

3 Pignatti, *op. cit.,* p. 24, under no. 42.

4 Pilo, *op. cit.*; Pignatti, *op. cit.*

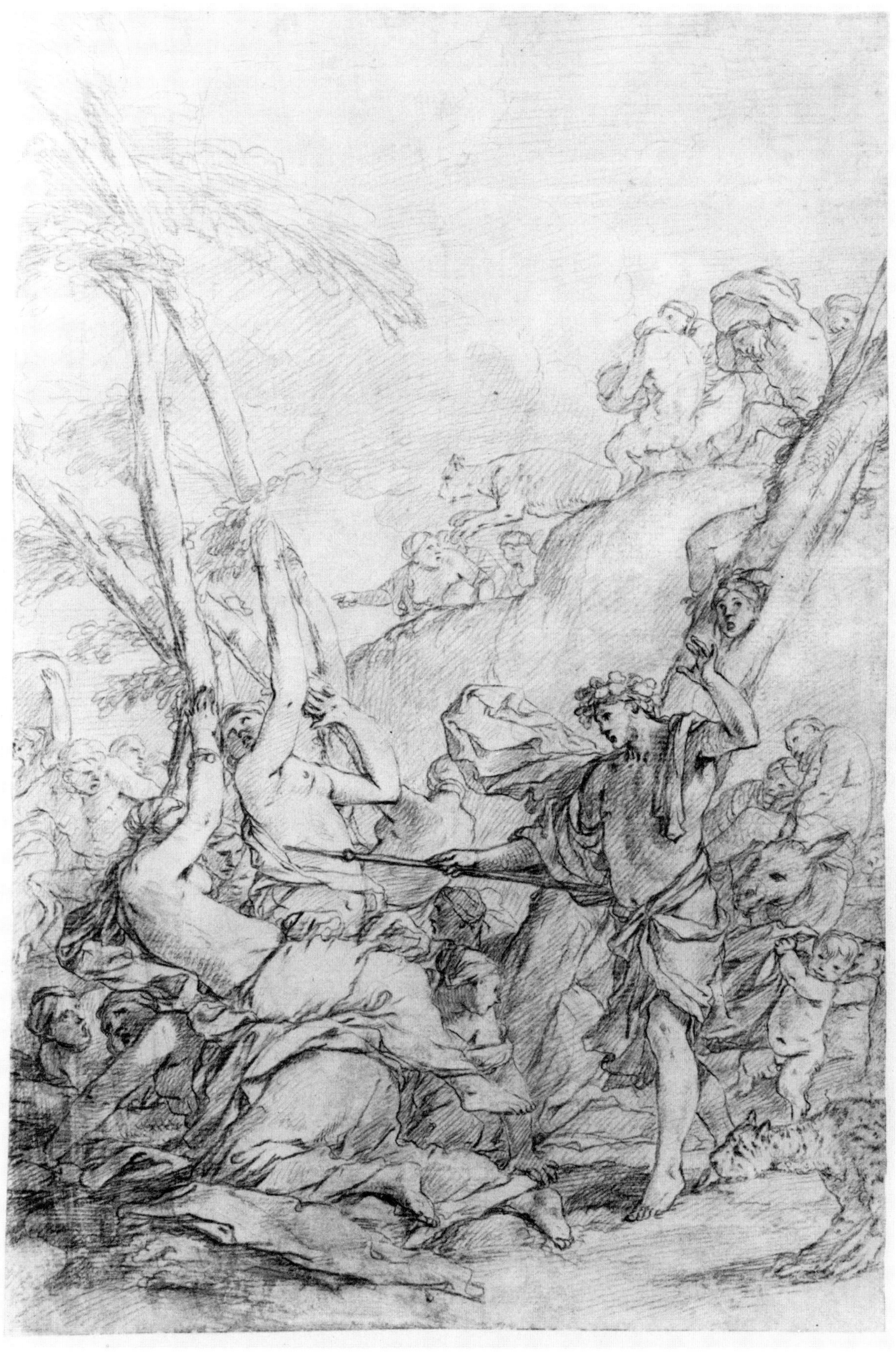

Carlo Maratta

Camerano 1625 – 1713 Rome

49 *Diana Hunting*

Red chalk. Two sheets of paper joined along a vertical line in
the middle. 227 x 327 mm

*Exhibited: Italian 17th-Century Drawings from British Private
Collections,* Edinburgh Festival Society, Edinburgh, 1972,
p. 31, no. 79, repr. p. 92.

Literature: S. Rudolph, ''The Toribio Illustrations and Some
Considerations on Engravings after Carlo Marratti,'' *Antologia
di Belle Arti,* 7-8, 1978, p. 203, under no. 37.

Provenance: Private collection, England.

This drawing can be connected with an engraving in reverse by
Andrea Procaccini (fig. 49a).[1] The engraving is inscribed *Eques
Carolus Maratta invent.,* but since no painting by Maratta is
known of the subject, it is likely that the present drawing played
a direct part in the preparation of the print. In a list dated 1711 of
prints made after Maratta's paintings and drawings, a *Hunt of
Diana* is included, and an annotation by the artist's daughter
Faustina states that the print was after a drawing.[2] Probably a
finished drawing was then prepared by Procaccini, who is
known to have produced a number of engravings under the
direct supervision of the aged Maratta.

Stella Rudolph dates the drawing to the last decade of the
seventeenth century.[3]

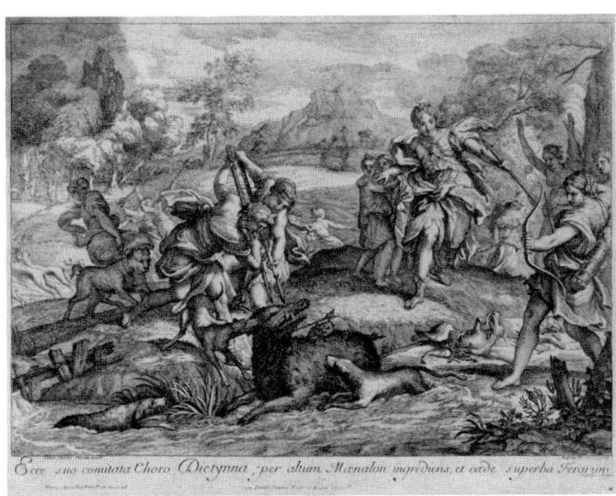

fig. 49a Andrea Procaccini after Maratta,
Diana Hunting, engraving.

1 C. Le Blanc, *Manuel de l'Amateur d'Estampes,* Paris, 1854-90, III, p. 256, no. 9.

2 Rudolph, *op. cit.*

3 Private communication to Roberto Ferretti.

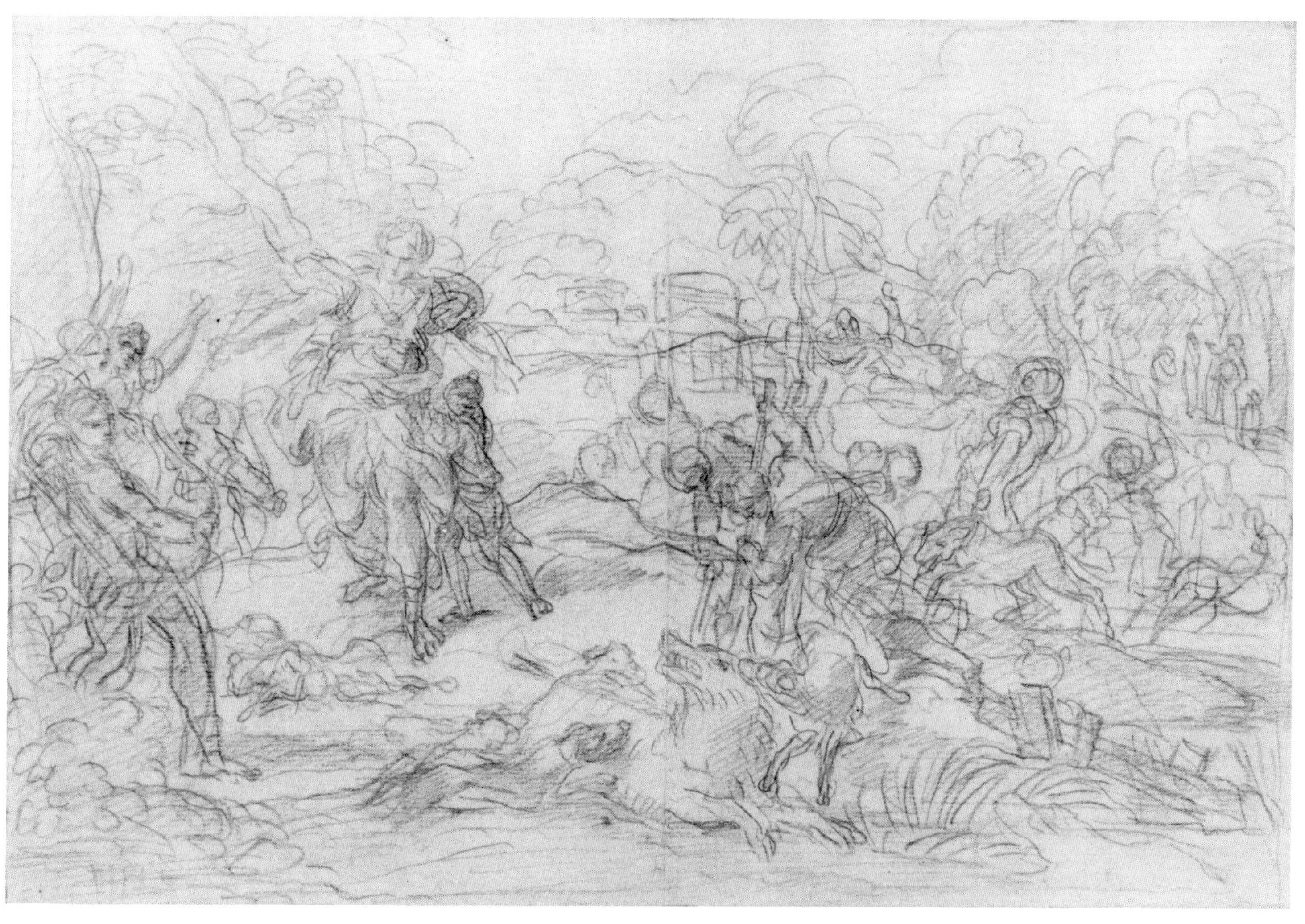

Carlo Maratta

Camerano 1625 – 1713 Rome

50 *A Gentleman Playing the Harpsichord (recto);
A Dog Asleep (verso)*

Black chalk. Some slight stains. 267 x 201 mm. Inscribed in
black chalk at lower centre (*verso*): *Tenerino il Poltrone* and at
lower right: *fatto dal re delli Poltroni;* at lower left in black chalk
in a different hand: *Cav. Carlo Maratti.*

Provenance: Marchese Giovan Giorgio Costaguti; his daughter
Teresa, married to Conte Giovanni Battista Ferretti.

Both sides of this sheet reveal Maratta in an unusually intimate
vein. Two of the inscriptions are probably autograph and amus-
ingly identify the sleeping dog as *"softy the lazybones"* and the
artist as the *"king of the lazybones".*

The drawing of the musician is freely executed – in an almost
rococo manner – which belies the solidity of the overall design.
This and the fact that the composition is carefully enclosed in
framing lines suggest that the drawing may have been an idea
for a painted or engraved portrait, yet none has been discovered.

Stella Rudolph dates the drawing to the 1690s or to the early
years of the next century.[1]

1 Private communication to Roberto Ferretti.

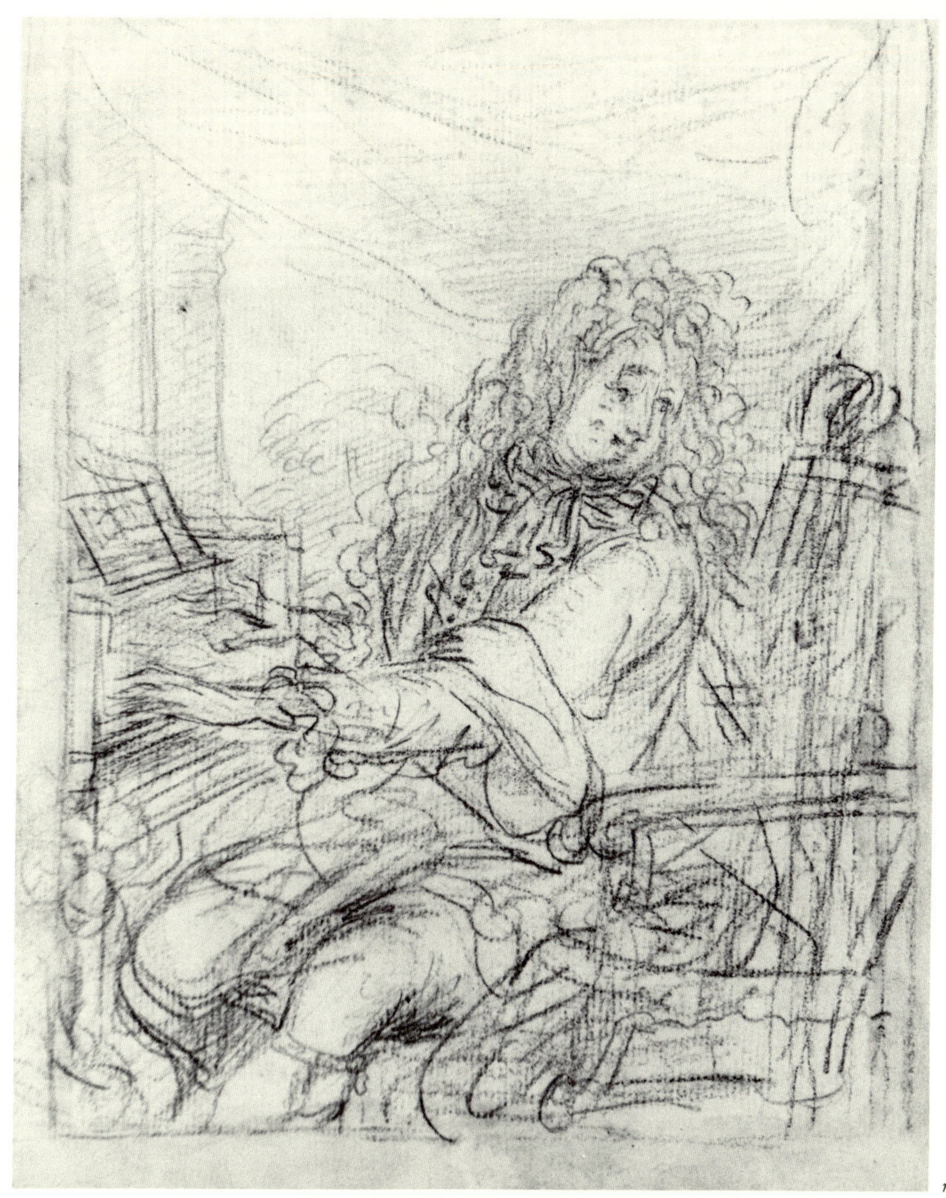

recto

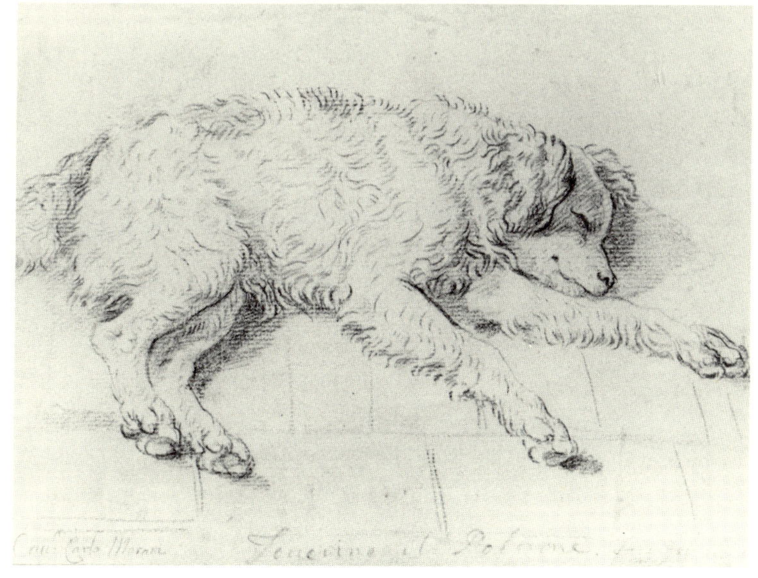

verso

III

Giuseppe Passeri

Rome 1654 – 1714 Rome

51 *Samuel Anointing David*

Pen and brown ink, brown and grey wash, heightened with white over red chalk. Laid down. 188 x 249 mm. Inscribed on the old mount: *Passari*

Provenance: Sotheby's, London, 3 July 1980, lot 36.

Executed in Passeri's highly pictorial technique – with ample use of red chalk and much wash and white heightening – this drawing has not been connected with any known commission by the artist.

The subject is Samuel anointing David as Saul's successor, in fulfilment of the Lord's instructions (I Samuel 16:13). To either side David's seven older brothers, each of whom had been passed over, react to this unexpected turn of events in agitated surprise. The subject is not especially common in Italian art, although Raphael, the idol of Passeri's teacher Carlo Maratta,[1] had included it among the Old Testament scenes on the vault of the Vatican Loggia, and as such it was engraved in the seventeenth century by Pietro Aquila. Passeri's drawing may indeed be seen as a baroque re-working of Raphael's composition.

---

1 For Passeri and Raphael, see L. Pascoli, *Vite de' Pittori, Scultori ed Architetti Moderni,* Rome, 1730, I, pp. 218-19.

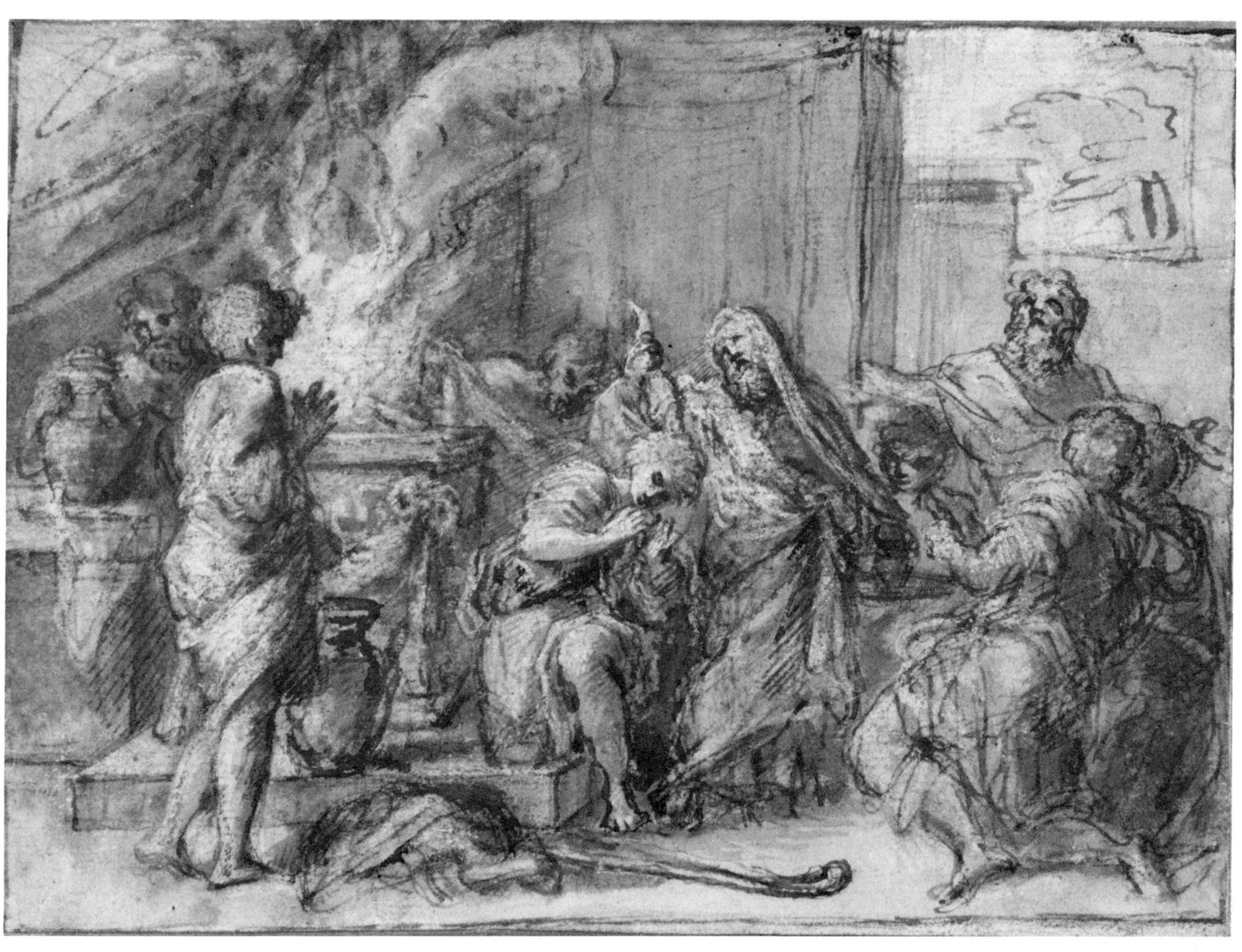

Luca Giordano

Naples 1634 – 1705 Naples

52 *Saint Anthony of Padua and Ezzelino (recto); Saint Anthony of Padua raising a man from the Dead (verso)*

Brown wash over black chalk (*recto*); black chalk (*verso*). 219 x 297 mm. Inscribed lower right: *242;* on the mount: *Luca Giordano*

Exhibited: Civiltà del Seicento a Napoli, Museo di Capodimonte, Naples, 1984, II, p. 97, no. 3.42 a-b, repr. (entry by J. Stock).

Literature: H. Leporini, *Die Handzeichnungen der Sammlung Török,* Vienna, 1927, no. 126 (as Paolo de Matteis).

Provenance: Benno Geiger?; Wilhelm Koenig (Lugt Suppl. 2653b); Johann Török.

This drawing is a preliminary study for parts of Luca Giordano's fresco decorations in the circular church of San Antonio de los Portugeses in Madrid. In 1692 Giordano had travelled to Spain where he stayed ten years. According to Antonio Palomino, who knew the artist in Spain, the frescoes in San Antonio were the last important commission undertaken by Giordano before the death of King Charles II in November 1700.[1] Palomino further relates that the frescoes in the dome of the church had already been completed by the Spanish artists Francisco Rizi and Juan Carreño, but only after modifying these frescoes did Giordano begin to paint the wall between the windows and altars, immediately below.

Giordano solved the problems arising from the awkward wall areas by inventing an elaborate illusionistic scheme which includes six scenes from the life of St. Anthony of Padua between the windows on the upper part of the wall, and eight seated saints between the altars below. The episodes from the life of St. Anthony are shown as if on tapestries held by angels. The present drawing of St. Anthony and Ezzelino is for one of these feigned tapestries, although no indication of either the tapestry or of the supporting angels is present. Nor do these elements appear in a related drawing by Giordano in the University of Michigan Museum of Art, Ann Arbor, of St. Anthony miraculously re-attaching the leg of the irascible son for one of other feigned tapestries.[2] In contrast, a number of oil sketches (on canvas) of the narrative scenes include not only indications of the tapestries and their supporting angels but also the allegorical figures seated in the spandrels below.[3] The *bozzetto* for St. Anthony and Ezzelino is in the City Art Gallery, Auckland, New Zealand (fig. 52a).

In the drawing, St. Anthony of Padua (ca. 1190/95-1236), in the habit of the Franciscan order, is seen at the left, preaching during a storm; while Ezzelino III da Romano (1194-1259), lord of Verona, Vicenza, and Padua, appears at the right. In 1230 St. Anthony, the *Malleus hereticorum* (hammer of the heretics), travelled to Verona to appeal the release of Guelph prisoners held by the heretical and, in legend at least, ruthless despot, Ezzelino. According to apocryphal accounts, St. Anthony's mission was entirely successful.

It is likely that the more summary black chalk study on the *verso* is for the scene of St. Anthony resurrecting the boy. Both drawings are typical of Luca Giordano's late style, wherein black chalk is used for defining the major forms, and a luminous pale brown wash is usually added to establish patterns of light and shade.

The correct attribution to Giordano is prominently inscribed on the front of the old mount. Similar mounts and related numbers inscribed at the lower right corner of the drawing itself are found on several Neapolitan drawings, but the collector responsible for the inscriptions has not been identified. The present drawing bears the number *242*, while the sheet at Ann Arbor, mentioned above, possesses the numer *243*. The number *241* appears on a drawing by Luca Giordano of the plague – evidently not connected with the frescoes in San Antonio de los Portugeses – now in the collection of the Art Gallery of Ontario.[4]

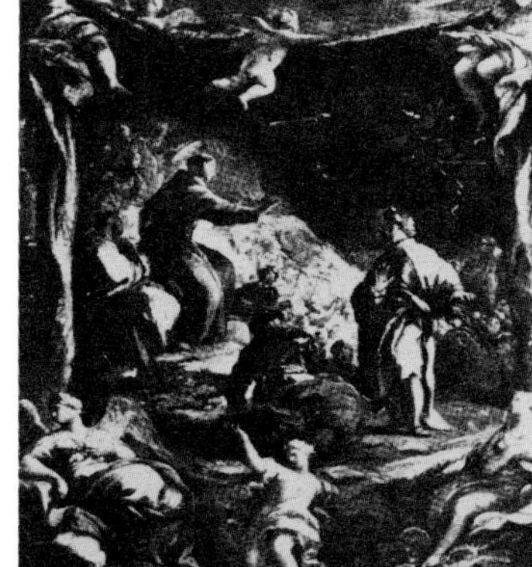

fig. 52a Luca Giordano, *St. Anthony of Padua and Ezzelino*, oil on canvas, City Art Gallery, Auckland, New Zealand.

1 *El Museo Pitórico y Escala Optica* (1724), ed. Madrid, 1947, pp. 11-13. For further details and illustrations, see O. Ferrari and G. Scavizzi, *Luca Giordano,* Naples, 1966, I, pp. 163-66; II, pp. 217-19; III, figs. 464-69, 658-60.

2 Identified by W. Vitzthum: *A Selection of Italian Drawings from North American Collections,* Norman Mackenzie Art Gallery, Regina, 1970, p. 70, no. 62, repr.

3 Ferrari and Scavizzi, *op.cit.,* I, pp. 165-66, pl. IX; II, pp. 218-19; III, figs. 470-73, 650. See also *Paintings & Sculpture of the Italian Baroque,* Summer exhibition, Heim, London, 1973, nos. 6-8, repr. A drawing in the British Museum (1950.11.11.6) by Giordano of St. Anthony and the believing donkey does, however, include the surrounding figures and indications of the window and altar niche (Ferrari and Scavizzi, *op.cit.,* I, p. 203, fig. XXXV; II, p. 255; N. Turner, *Italian Baroque Drawings,* British Museum Prints and Drawings Series, London, 1980, pp. 148-49, no. 65, repr.).

4 Vitzthum, *op.cit.,* pp. 70-72, no. 63 repr.

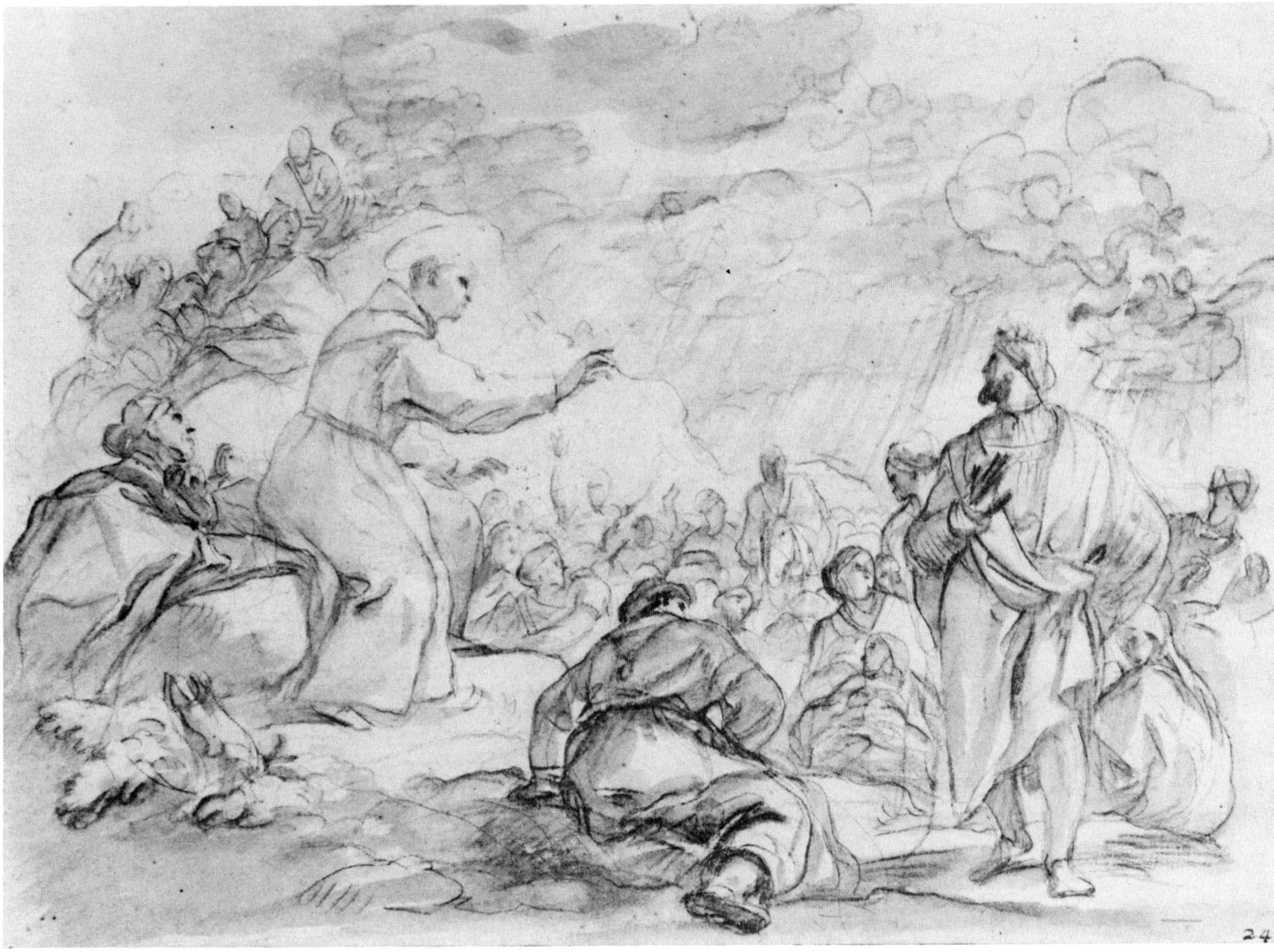

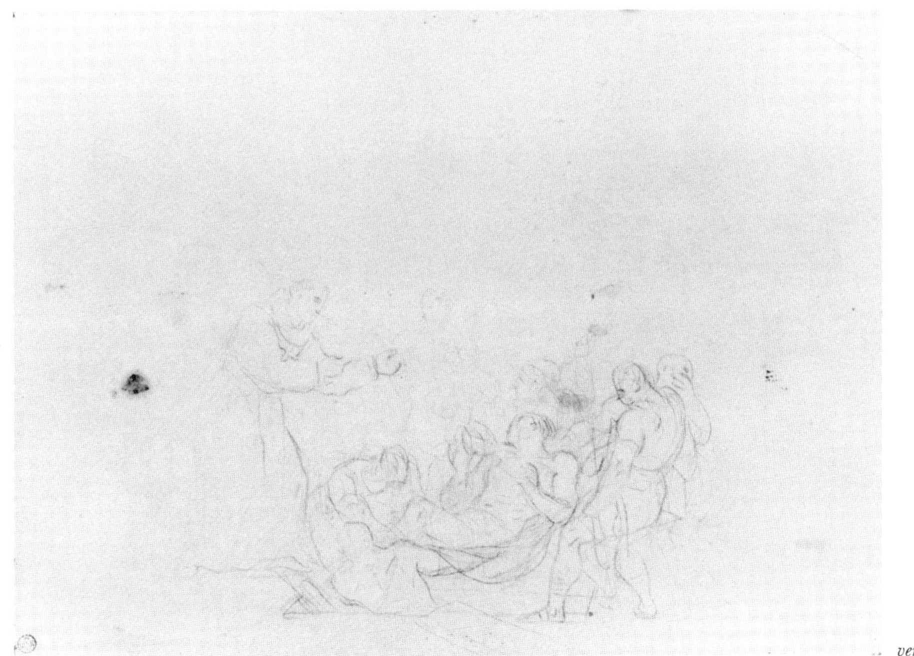

recto

verso

Gaspar Van Wittel
(Gaspare Vanvitelli)

Amersfoort (near Utrecht) 1652/53 – 1736 Rome

53   *Pastoral Landscape (recto);*
     Study of a Youth Seen from the Back (verso)

Pen and brown ink; grey, blue, green and white wash (*recto*);
pen and brown ink (*verso*) on greenish paper. Lower corners
replaced. 316 x 233 mm

Provenance: L. Grassi Junior (mark at lower right, not in
Lugt).

Like Claude before him, Van Wittel was a northerner who
journeyed early in his life to Rome, then made Italy his home
and Italian scenery the lifelong inspiration of his art. In the
present drawing the poetic evocation of an idyllic classical past
was no doubt directly inspired by the French landscape painter.[1]
The ruins of a Corinthian temple, the shepherd playing his
pipe, the framing trees, and the gentle but carefully organized
recession to the mountain-rimmed sea are all elements frequently found in Claude's landscapes.[2] With the careful
arrangement of all the parts and with subtle gradations of tone,
Van Wittel has also attained something of Claude's particular
serenity. The pen configurations for the foliage, however, are
unmistakably Van Wittel's own.

---

[1]   In this regard it is worth noting that probably in 1694 Van Wittel was
commissioned by the Grand Duke of Tuscany to paint two *vedute*, one as a
pendant to a painting by Claude: A. Zwollo, *Hollandse en Vlaamse
verduteschilders te Rome 1675-1725 ,* Assen, 1973, p. 162.

[2]   *E.g. Pastoral Landscape* (although without a vista to the sea), in the collection of
the Earl of Halifax (M. Röthlisberger, *Claude Lorrain: The Paintings,* New
Haven, 1962, pp. 142-44, no. 23, fig. 68).

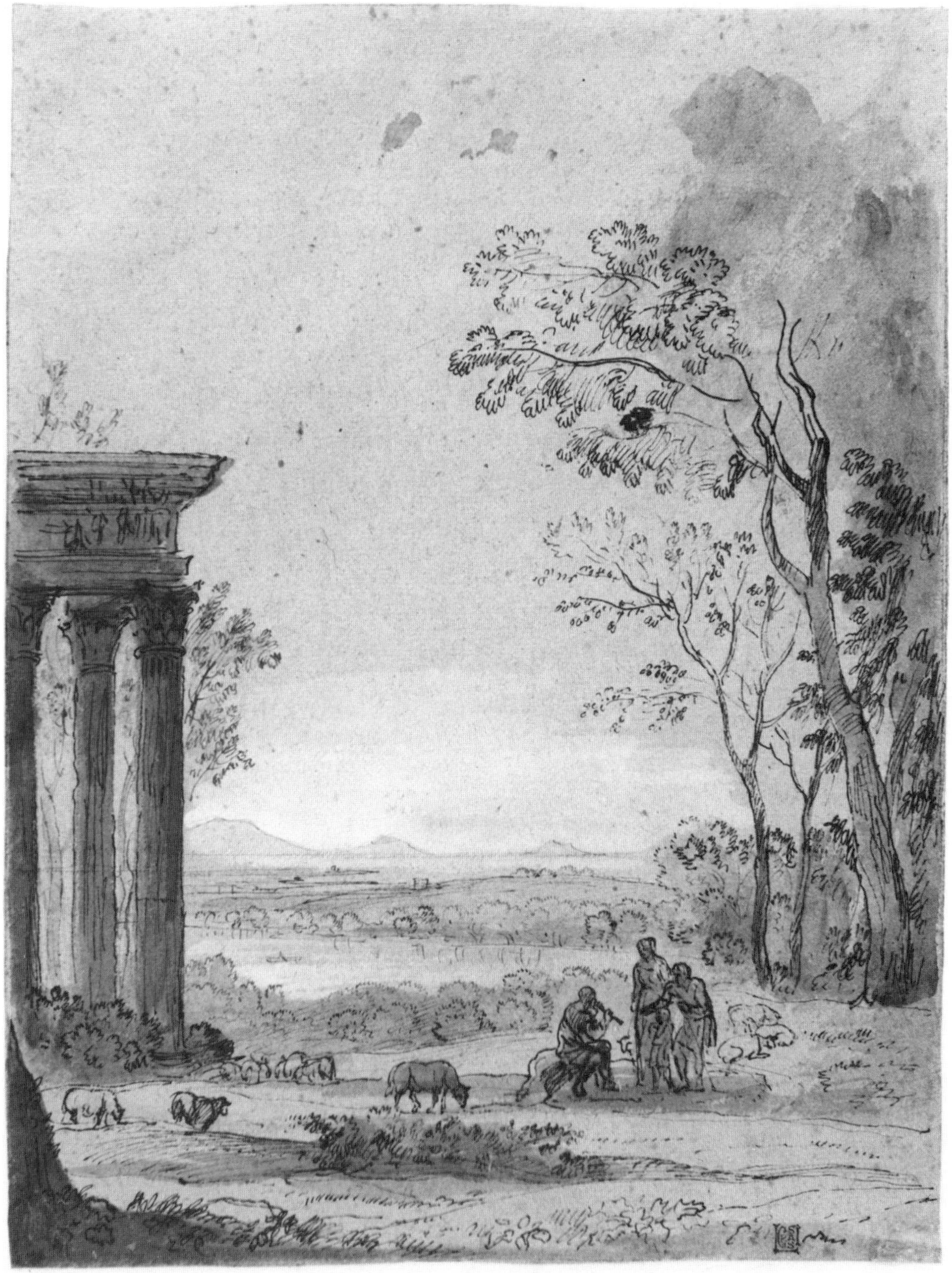

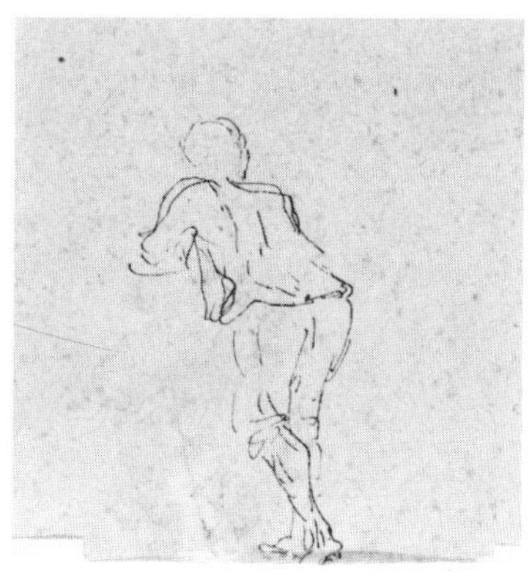

recto

verso

Gaspar Van Wittel
(Gaspare Vanvitelli)

Amersfoort (near Utrecht) 1652/53 – 1736 Rome

54 *The Falls at Tivoli (recto);*
A Reclining Peasant Girl (verso)

Pen and brown ink over black chalk; grey, brown and blue
wash, and red chalk, heightened with white on blue paper
(*recto*); black chalk (*verso*); encircled anchor watermark. Upper
right corner repaired. 379 x 263 mm

Exhibited: The Italian Scene, Drawings by Vanvitelli, Agnew's,
London, 1961, no. 5.

Literature: G. Briganti, *Gaspar Van Wittel e l'origine della veduta
settecentesca,* Rome, 1966, p. 278, no. 38d.

Provenance: B. Cavaceppi; V. Pacetti, P. Fatio; N. Rauch,
Geneva, 13 June 1960, lot 140; Stephen Richard Currier and
Audrey Bruce Currier (according to Christie's as follows,
p. 38); Christie's, London, 3 April 1984, lot 60.

Van Wittel did numerous drawings of both the urban and rural
areas of Italy, from the region around Naples in the south to
Lombardy and Venice in the north. Executed with a forceful
pen line and frequently with ample use of wash – or various,
coloured washes, as here – these drawings were both records of
his travels and points of reference for future paintings.

The exact location represented, which includes a secluded
hermitage in the foreground, has not been conclusively established. Many oils by Van Wittel of various aspects of Tivoli
survive, as do several drawings, but none corresponds to this
view.[1]

The study of a seated girl on the *verso* may be compared to a
similar black-chalk drawing, where the subject is dressed in a
comparable costume and is also seen in profile, on a sheet of
studies of a rocky landscape, now in the Royal Palace, Caserta.[2]

[1] For Van Wittel's views of Tivoli see G. Briganti, *Gaspar Van Wittel e l'origine
della veduta settecentesca,* Rome, 1966, pp. 225-31.

[2] Inv. 143; W. Vitzthum, *Drawings by Gaspar Van Wittel,* National Gallery of
Canada, Ottawa, 1977, pp. 26-27, no. 16, pl. 18.

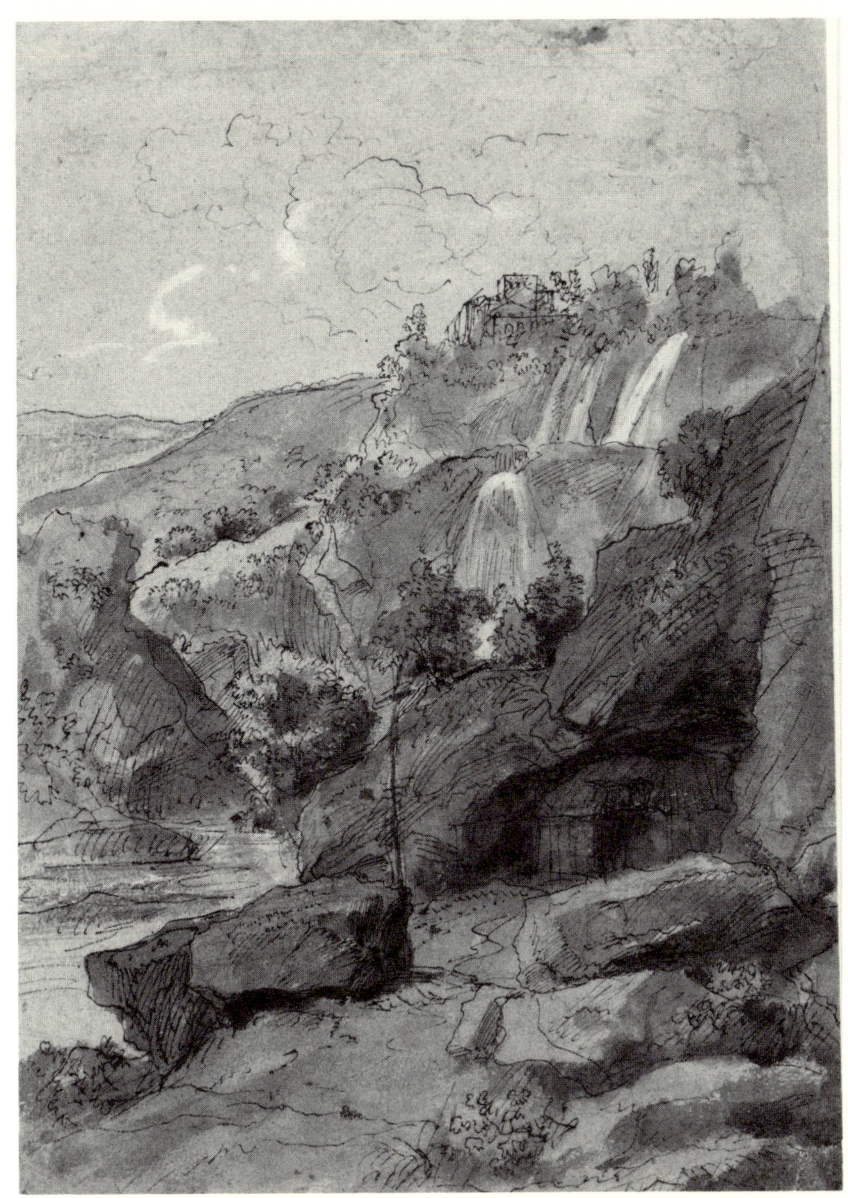

recto

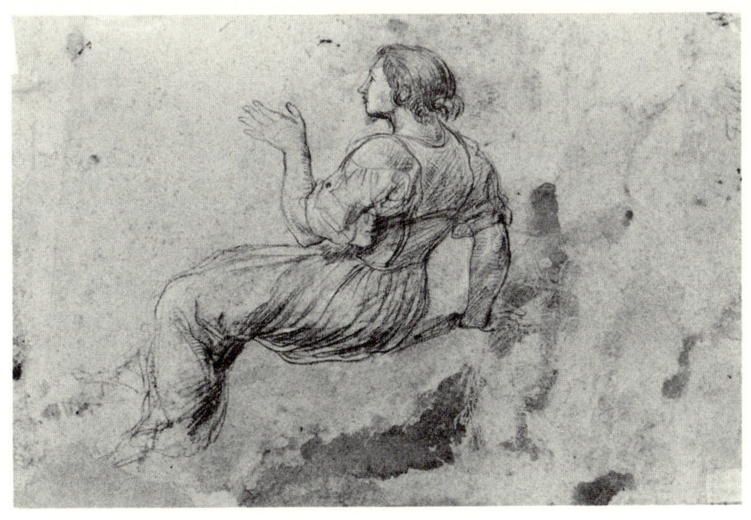

verso

Pier Leone Ghezzi

Rome 1674 – 1755 Rome

55   *The Grand Prior
Francesco Maria Ferretti (1652-1737)*

Pen and brown ink over black chalk. 324 x 225 mm. Inscribed
in brown ink on the *verso*: *Mr. Le G. prieur ferretti*

Provenance: (?) Cardinal Melchior de Polignac; acquired in
Paris in 1763 by Richard Neville Neville (according to
Sotheby's, which follows); his son, the Baron Braybrooke; by
descent to Rt. Hon. Lord Braybrooke; his sale, Sotheby's,
London, 10 December 1979, lot 109.

This portrait of an ancestor of the present owner comes from
one of two albums of caricatures (152 drawings altogether),
made by Pier Leone Ghezzi for the Cardinal Melchior de Polignac, or for someone in his immediate circle. The caricatures,
which feature members of the clergy, the papal court, and the
cardinal's own staff, in addition to distinguished French visitors
to Rome, must have been done during the 1720s, before the
Cardinal returned to France in 1730. The drawings are all executed in Ghezzi's distinctive pen technique, with much parallel
hatching; and most are inscribed in French in the same hand on
the *verso*. One inscription is dated 1729.[1]

Francesco Maria Ferretti, Grand Prior of England and the
Bali of Sant'Eufemia, was commander of the Papal fleet from
1696 until 1721. He carried out forty naval campaigns, including
the successful blockade and defeat of the Turks at Corfu. With
the death of Pope Clement XI he resigned his command, but for
some time he remained in Ancona and Rome, where he was a
well-known figure at the papal court. He died in Malta, aged
eighty-five; his tombstone is in the nave of St. John's at La
Valletta.[2]

1   *Caricature Drawings by Pier Leone Ghezzi,* Sotheby's, London, 10 December 1979,
    lot 148. See also Introduction, n.p.

2   Information from Roberto Ferretti di Castelferretto.

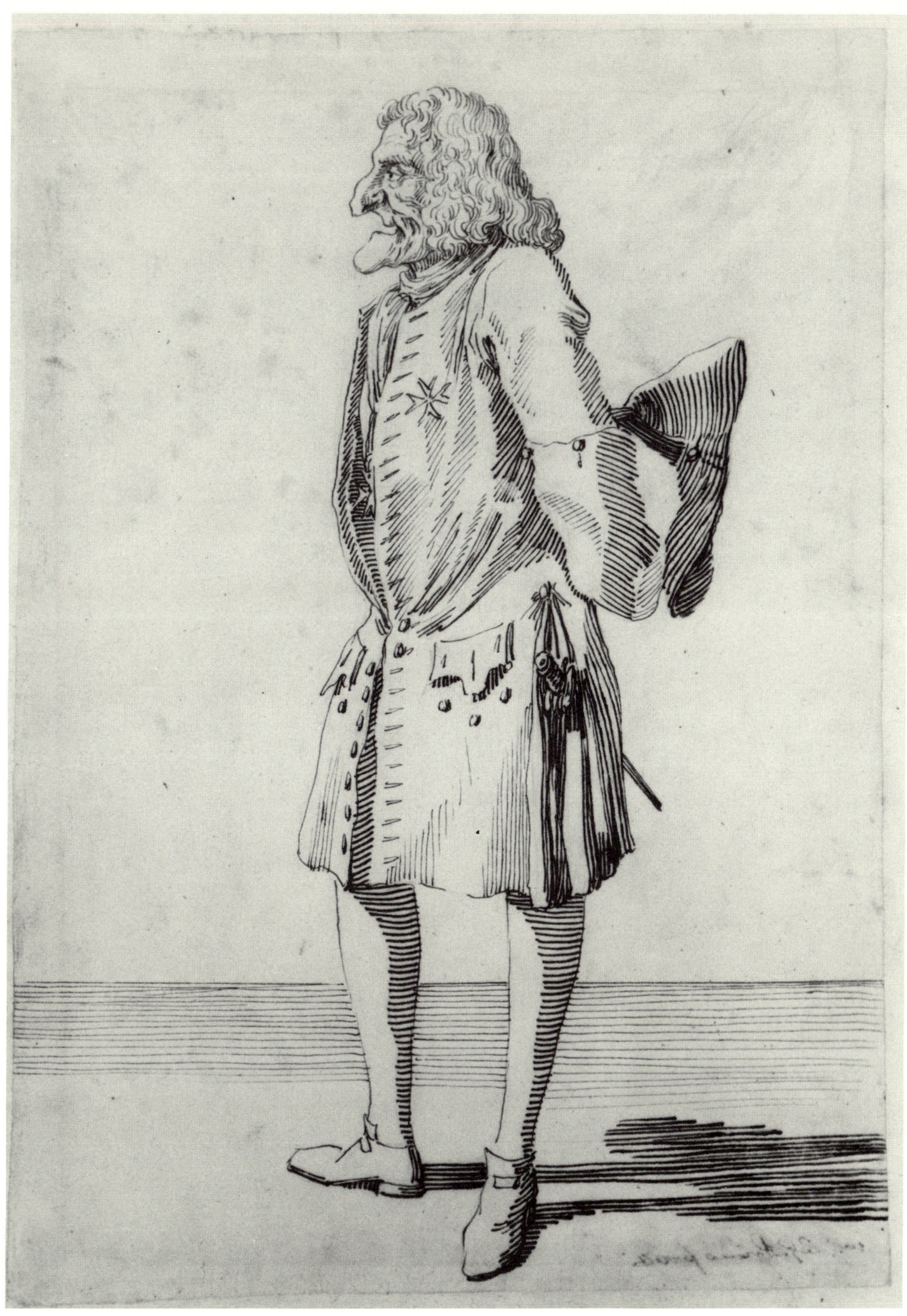

Sebastiano Ricci

Belluno 1659 – 1734 Venice

56   *Head of an Old Man*

Black chalk; greenish-brown wash on background.
221 x 171 mm. Inscribed in pen and brown ink at lower right:
B[astian]*Ricci* and below that: (?) *22*

Provenance: Pierre Crozat; Gabriel Huquier; sale, Amsterdam,
14 September 1761, lot 12; Dutch collector (according to
Christie's as follows); Christie's, London, 4 July 1978, lot 69.

The old inscription is manifestly correct; for confirmation the
drawing should be compared to a similar head, although much
larger in scale and executed in charcoal and coloured chalks on
grey paper, from the album of Sebastiano Ricci drawings in the
Accademia, Venice.[1] In both drawings, the type of bearded man
and the inclination of his head and shoulders are closely related.
Terisio Pignatti has detected in the Accademia drawing the
influence of Paolo Veronese, always a potent inspiration for
Sebastiano Ricci; while Alessandro Bettagno has referred to the
influence of Rembrandt, whose prints Ricci could have easily
studied in the extensive collections of his friend, Anton Maria
Zanetti.[2] Neither the Accademia nor the present drawing is
directly related to any known painting by Sebastiano Ricci,
although the physiognomic type is one that appears frequently
in his work. Most likely the drawings were done as ends in
themselves, and as such prefigure by some years the heads of
''orientals'' and other picturesque types by Giambattista Tiepolo. The Accademia head has been dated to the last decade of
the artist's life.[3]

An all but illegible inscription on the *verso* furnishes the information that this drawing once belonged to the great French
collector, Pierre Crozat, and was sold in Amsterdam in 1761. A
sheet of studies by Ricci of various figures in a landscape, now
in the Museo Civico, Udine, was also once in the Crozat collection, and it too bears an inscription *B. Ricci* and a numbering
system at the lower right similar to that of the present drawing.[4]

1 Inv. S.R. p. 23; T. Pignatti, *I Grandi Disegni Italiani nelle Collezioni di Venezia*,
Milan, n.d. [1974], no. 23, repr. in colour.

2 Pignatti, *op. cit.;* A. Bettagno, *Venetian Drawings of the Eighteenth Century*, Heim
Gallery, London, p. 22, no. 3.

3 F. Valcanover, *18e eeuwse venetiaanse tekeningen*, Groningen, 1964, no. 81.

4 *Sebastiano Ricci disegnatore*, ed. A. Rizzi, Sala Aiace del Comune, Udine, 1975,
no. 14, repr.

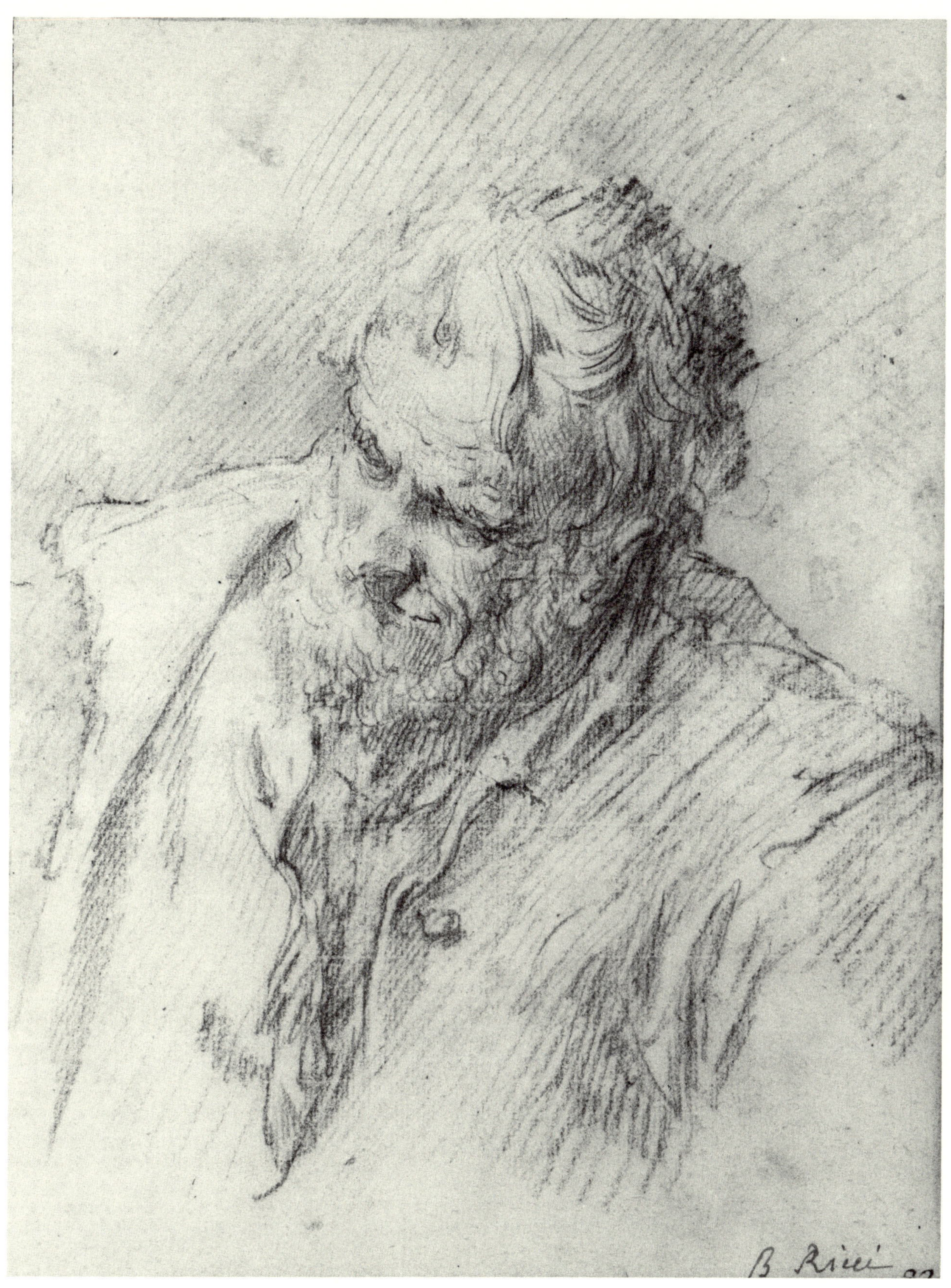

B. Ricci

Giovanni Battista Tiepolo

Venice 1692 – 1769 Madrid

57   *A Winged Deity and Other Figures on Clouds*

Pen and brown ink and wash over black chalk. 262 x 214 mm

Provenance: Drury; Tomás Harris; Sotheby's, London,
25 March 1965, lot 152; Hallsborough; Christie's, London,
8 December 1981, lot 46.

This drawing has not been connected with any finished work by
Tiepolo. Yet clearly it was not originally intended as an independent work of art, no matter how satisfactorily it may be
viewed as such today. In an engaging fashion, the drawing
permits a glimpse into Tiepolo's creative process, and reveals
altogether candidly his investigations and verifications of the
pose and position of the major figures. Thus it can be seen that
the head of the standing figure at the top was once inclined
downward to the left, and that (even more lightly sketched
under the left wing) the arm was raised at the elbow as if in
salutation.[1] Similarly, the head of the seated figure at the lower
left was initially placed at a higher level; moreover the entire
figure seems to have been studied again in the quick black-chalk
outlines in the foreground cloud. Only after he established the
position of the figures must Giambattista have added the delicately varied and luminous wash which partly masks the
rejected ideas for the figures.

The exact identification of the subject remains a mystery.
The winged figure appears to hold a small bowl or plate in its left
hand and what has been called, although not very convincingly,
a dagger in the right. The turbaned, ''oriental'' figures at the
left are a type frequently found in Tiepolo's *oeuvre* (see no. 58).
Since all the figures are seen from below, the composition must
have been intended for a decoration on a ceiling or a high wall.

George Knox dates this drawing to about 1740.[2]

1   The pose would then be akin to St. Helena's in Giambattista's *The Discovery of
the True Cross,* a canvas now in the Accademia, Venice, but painted for the
ceiling of the Cappuccine at Castello about 1740-45 (A. Morassi, *A Complete
Catalogue of the Paintings of G. B. Tiepolo,* London, 1962, p. 54, and fig. 121).

2   *Important Old Master Drawings,* Christie's, London, 8 December 1981, under
lot 46.

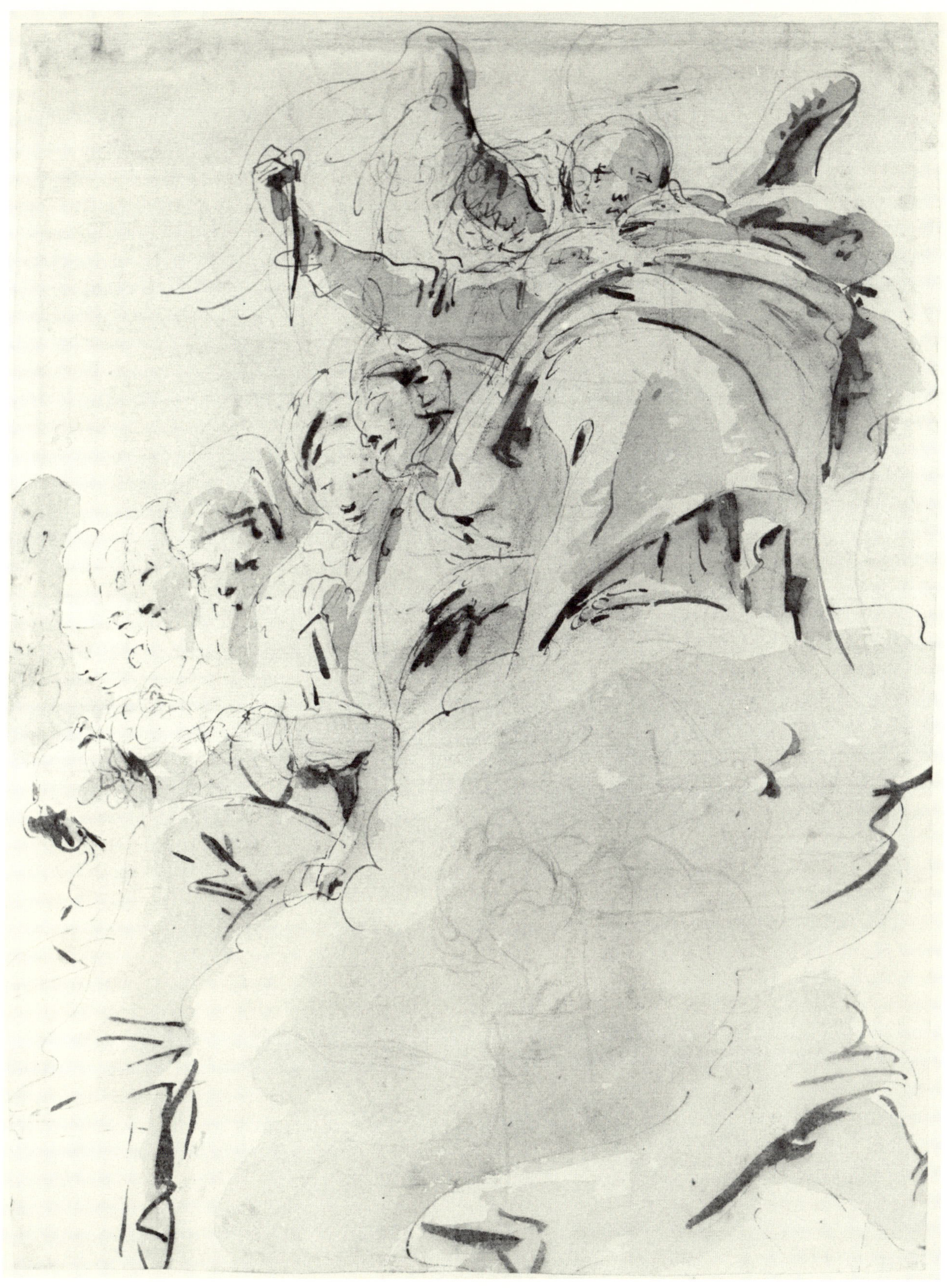

Giovanni Battista Tiepolo

Venice 1692 – 1769 Madrid

58   *Oriental Youth Wearing a Cloak and Hat*

Pen and brown ink and wash over black chalk. Corners
repaired. 235 x 136 mm

Provenance: M. Voggenauer; Christie's, London, 12 December
1978, lot 61.

This drawing is one of Giambattista's *sole figure vestite* (single
clothed figures), of which about two hundred examples survive.
The identification comes from the title of an album of eighty-six
of these pen and wash studies in the Victoria and Albert
Museum, London.[1] On the whole the drawings must have been
intended as ends in themselves, as very few of the sheets can be
directly connected with individual paintings. However, as
types, such figures appear frequently in Giambattista's paintings, especially pictures with biblical or historical subjects, and
they attest to the artist's fascination with "orientals" and their
exotic details of dress. The drawings are comparable to popular
engravings of standing figures dressed in local costume, but
with the *sole figure vestite* the dress is more often imaginative than
real, and the setting usually consists solely of a slight shadow on
the ground.

   This drawing has been dated by George Knox to about 1750.[2]

---

1   G. Knox, *Catalogue of the Tiepolo Drawings in the Victoria and Albert Museum,*
    London, 1960, pp. 3-4.

2   Private communication to the owner.

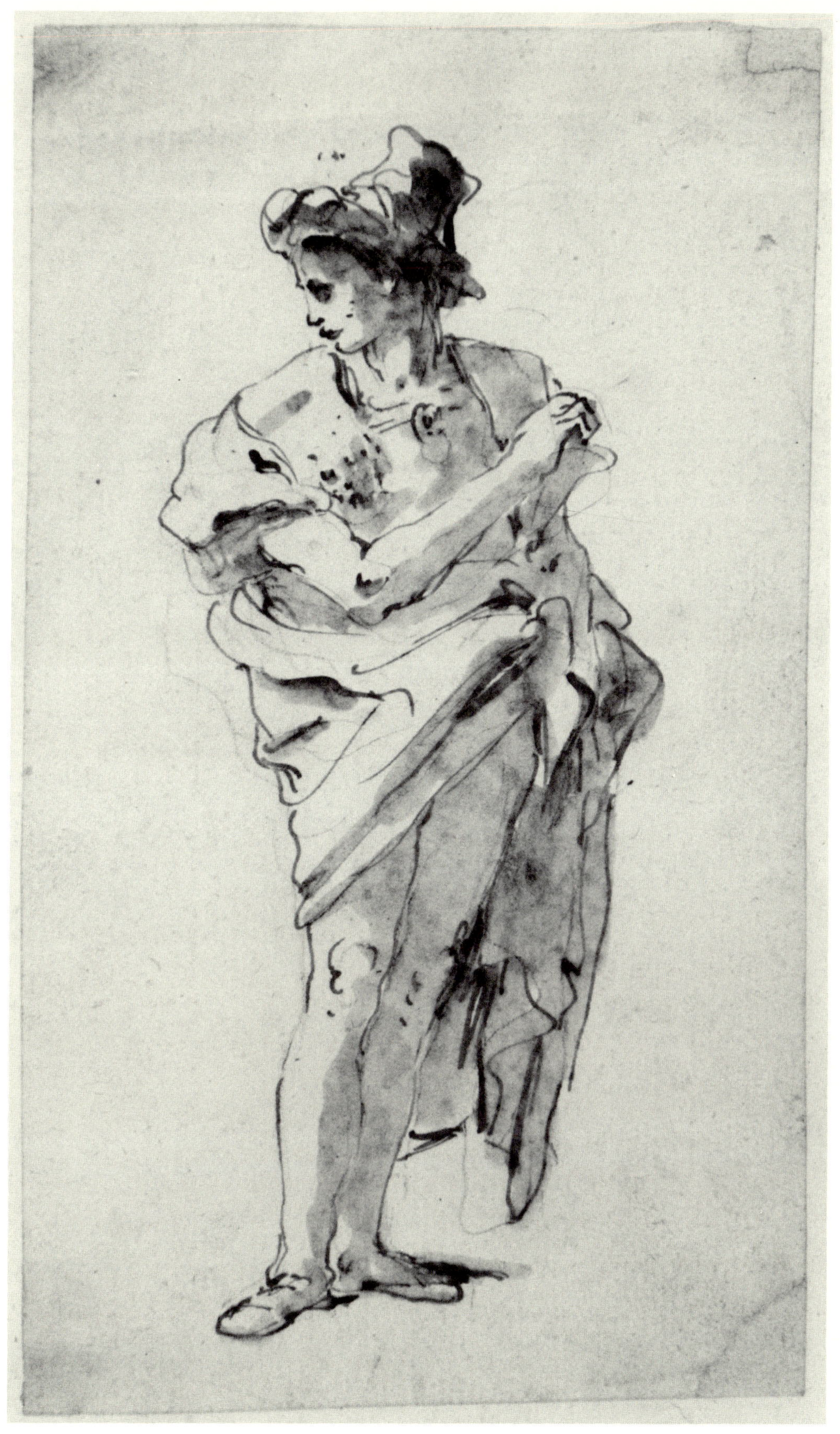

Giovanni Battista Tiepolo

Venice 1692 – 1769 Madrid

59 *Head of a Young Man, Turned to the Left (recto); Head Looking Upward to Left (verso)*

Red and white chalk on blue paper; indented for transfer *(recto)*; black and red chalk *(verso)*. 203 x 147 mm. Inscribed in ink on the *verso: X.ʳˢ 12* and *No 3242*. Also *386.*

Exhibited: Drawings by Old Masters, Savile Gallery, London, 1930, no. 32, repr.; *The Tiepolos: Painters to Princes and Prelates,* Birmingham Museum of Art and Springfield Museum of Art, Birmingham, 1978, no. 57, repr.

Literature: Detlev von Hadeln, *Handzeichnungen von G. B. Tiepolo,* Munich, 1927, I, p. 26, II, pl. 168; *The Bulletin of the Cleveland Museum of Art,* January 1930, p. 7, repr.; Detlev von Hadeln, *The Drawings of G. B. Tiepolo*, New York, 1970, p. 24, pl. 168; G. Knox, *Giambattista and Domenico Tiepolo. A Study and* Catalogue Raisonné *of the Chalk Drawings,* Oxford, 1980, I, p. 282, M.613.

Provenance: Dr. Hans Wendland; Dr. and Mrs. Malcolm Bick; Sotheby's, London, 3 July 1980, lot 67; Sotheby's, New York, 20 January 1982, lot 71.

From about 1740 onward, Giambattista Tiepolo made a practice of using chalk drawings, usually on blue paper, to investigate and to prepare such details as heads, hands and feet, and also pieces of drapery, for his major frescoes and oil paintings. This was a procedure with a prestigious history going back to the Renaissance; in a more novel vein Giambattista also at times used red chalk on blue paper for composition studies.[1]

The present sheet is a typical head study in chalk by Giambattista. In its execution, especially in the deft touches of chalk for modelling, the sheet reveals much of Giambattista's particular virtuosity, which is just as evident in his oils and frescoes as in his drawings.

The exact purpose of the drawing, which has been dated to about 1750-52, has not been established. A copy attributed to Giambattista's son, Lorenzo, is in the *Urlaub Sketchbook* of ca.1752 in the Martin von Wagner Museum, University of Würzburg.[2]

---

1 For a detailed discussion of the chalk drawings, see G. Knox, *Giambattista and Domenico Tiepolo. A Study and Catalogue Raisonné of the Chalk Drawings,* 2 vols., Oxford, 1980.

2 *Ibid.*, p. 177, H. 37. For the sketchbook, see pp. 174-75.

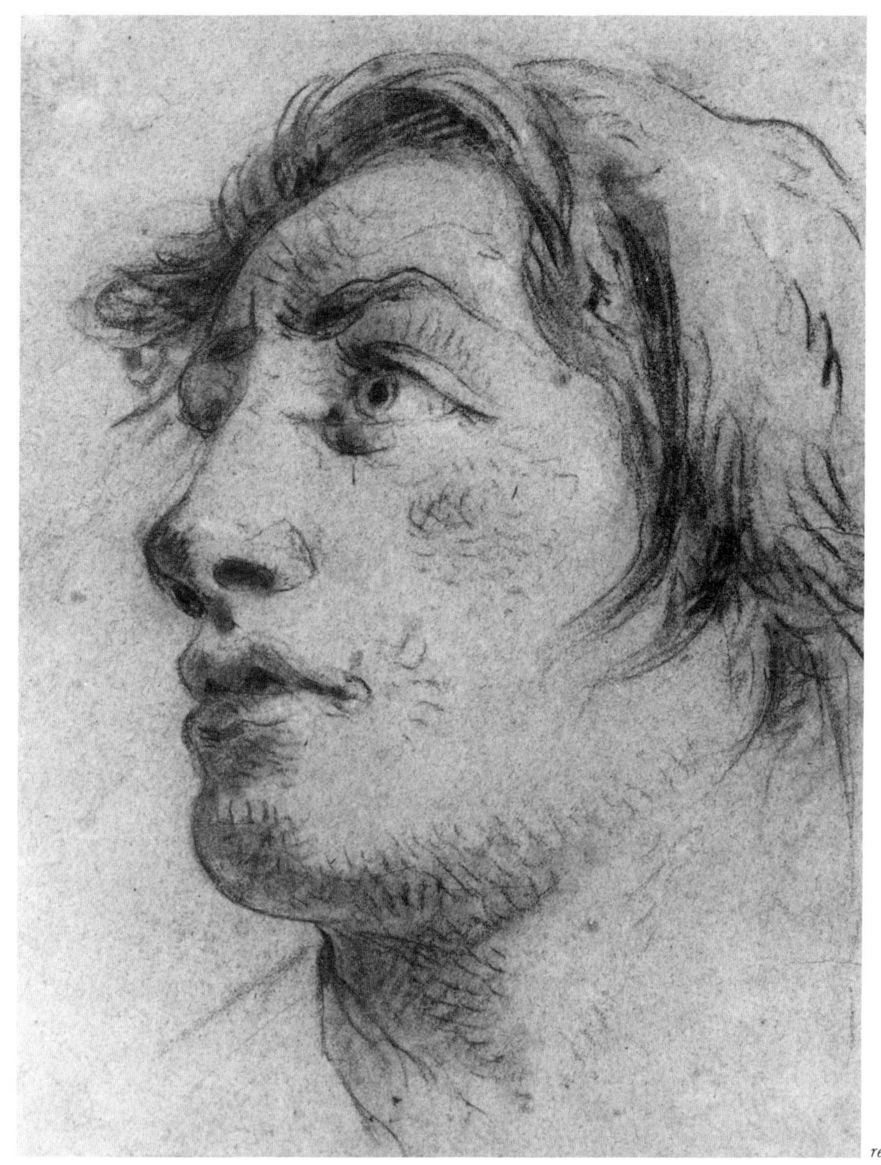

recto

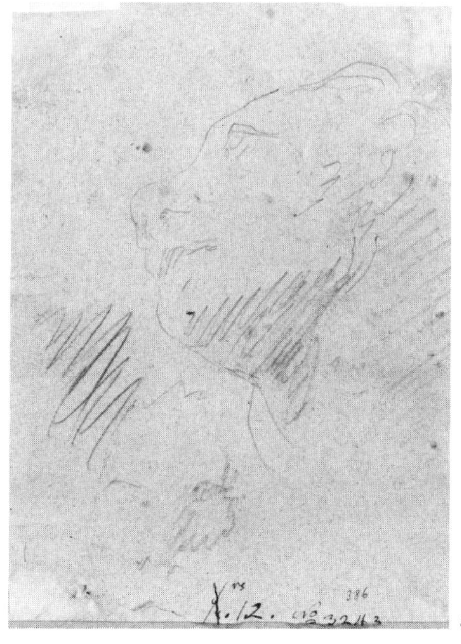

verso

Giovanni Antonio Guardi

Venice 1699 – 1760 Venice

60 *Two Studies of the Virgin and Child with St. Nicholas of Bari and other Saints*

Pen and brown ink and red wash, over red and black chalk; the central part ruled in pen and pale yellowish ink in parallel horizontal lines framed by two vertical lines. Vertical central fold. Stains along bottom. 222 x 272 mm

Exhibited: La peinture italienne au XVIIIe siècle, Petit Palais, Paris, 1960, no. 296; *Canaletto e Guardi,* Fondazione Giorgio Cini, Venice, 1962, p. 48, no. 52 (entry by J. Byam Shaw); *Mostra dei Guardi,* Palazzo Grassi, Venice, 1965, p. 307, no. 1, repr. (entry by P. Zampetti).

Literature: F.J.B. Watson, ''Moschini, Francesco Guardi'' (review), *Apollo,* 1957, p. 188; T. Pignatti, ''Un Disegno di Antonio Guardi donato al Museo Correr,'' *Bollettino dei Musei Civici Veneziani,* 1-2, 1957, pp. 25, 30, no. 13; T. Pignatti, ''Canaletto and Guardi at the Cini Foundation,'' *Master Drawings,* I, 1963, p. 50; A. Morassi, *Guardi, Tutti i Disegni di Antonio, Francesco e Giacomo Guardi,* Venice, 1975, p. 82, no. 15, fig. 14.

Provenance: L. Zatzka (Lugt 2672); Sir Francis Watson; Christie's, London, 9 December 1980, lot 104.

Francis Watson was the first to publish this sheet as a study related to an altarpiece in the parish church of Vigo d'Anaunia (Trento).[1] He tentatively ascribed the drawing to Francesco Guardi. In the same year the drawing was also published by Terisio Pignatti, but as a work by Giovanni Antonio Guardi.[2] Pignatti, however, supported the association with the altarpiece in Vigo d'Anaunia – a connection which has been repeatedly maintained since then. The painting is now generally given to Giovanni Antonio Guardi and has been dated to about 1742, at which time the altar was renovated.[3] Apart from the Virgin and Child seated on clouds, the painting includes Saints Nicholas of Bari and Roche at the left, and Saints Charles Borromeo and Anthony Abbot on the right. In the drawing St. Nicholas of Bari, dressed as a bishop and holding up the three gold balls, is easily identified in the lower centre of the right-hand project, and he may be the seated bishop saint in the left-hand project as well. Otherwise, the saints are difficult to distinguish, although the figure at the left of the right-hand project may be St. Peter, since a key seems to hang from his waist. It is certain, however, that in both projects there are only three saints, whereas in the altarpiece there are four. Since the number and identity of saints are not normally changed at will, it can be concluded that either the commission was substantially changed during the course of the preparatory work or that the drawing was undertaken for another altarpiece altogether. In the absence of further evidence, the latter conclusion is perhaps the more probable.

Whatever the case, this sheet provides engaging information about the genesis of a devotional image, carried out in a characteristically quirky use of pen and economical touches of delicate wash.[4]

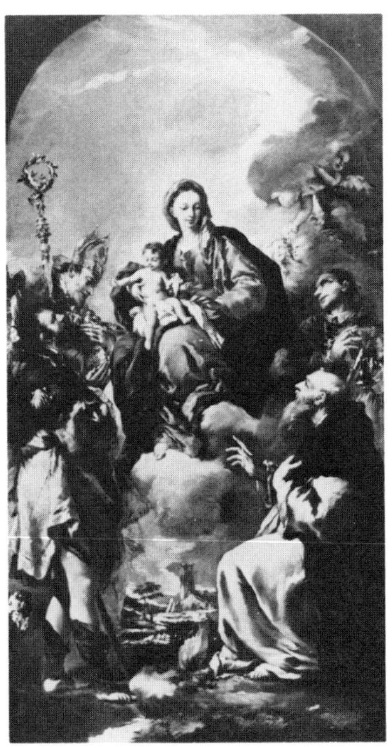

fig. 60a G.A. Guardi, *Madonna and Child and Four Saints,* oil on canvas, parish church, Vigo d'Anaunia.

---

1   F.J.B. Watson, *op.cit.,* pp. 188-89.

2   Pignatti, *op.cit.,* pp. 25, 30, no. 13.

3   A. Morassi, *Antonio e Francesco Guardi,* Venice, 1973, I, p. 318, no. 58, pl. III; II, figs. 60-61.

4   For a detailed analysis of the attribution to Antonio Guardi, see J. Byam Shaw in *Canaletto e Guardi,* Fondazione Giorgio Cini, Venice, 1962, p. 48, no. 52.

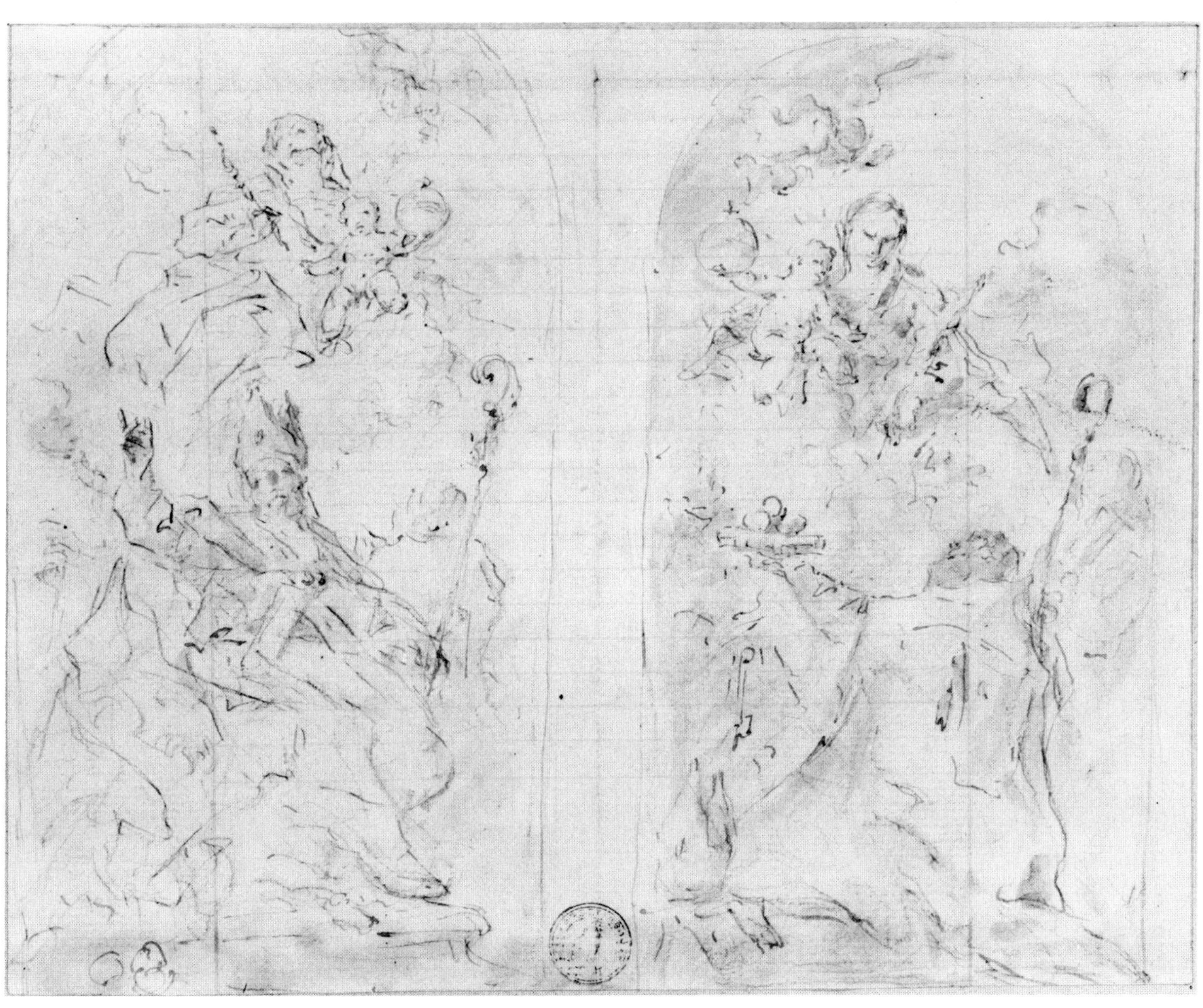

Luigi Vanvitelli

Naples 1700 – 1773 Caserta

61 *Project for Renovations to the Palazzo Ferretti, Ancona*

Pen and brown ink and wash over black chalk. Repairs for ink corrosion. 250 x 374 mm. Inscribed at the upper left: *disegno del Vanvitelli*; and along the lower margin: *Scala di 5 10 20 30 40 50 piedi Anconetani.*

Provenance: T. A. Heinrich

This unpublished drawing which was recently discovered in a Toronto collection shows plans for unexecuted renovations by Luigi Vanvitelli to the present owner's ancestral home, now the Museo Nazionale d'Arte Antica in Ancona.

In addition to the attribution to Vanvitelli in an anonymous hand, the drawing bears along its lower margin a scale in the architect's own hand explicitly stating the measurements to be *piedi Anconetani* (Ancona feet). Since this linear measurement was used only in Ancona and its immediate vicinity,[1] the building must have been located in a rather limited area. Luigi Vanvitelli undertook a number of important commissions in Ancona during the 1740s, and he has long been thought responsible for certain renovations to the Palazzo Ferretti at that time.[2] In fact, the measurements of the drawing correspond exactly to those of the original part of the *palazzo,* which was built for Angelo Ferretti, perhaps to the designs of Antonio da Sangallo the Younger, beginning about 1540.[3]

Like so much of Ancona, the Palazzo Ferretti is located on sloping ground, and enjoys a view from the back to the harbour below and the Adriatic Sea beyond. It is the rear façade which is shown in the present drawing. At this stage Vanvitelli's renovations were evidently focussed on a new entrance to the courtyard, approached by a handsome double stair, and related additions to the lower storeys of the façade at the left and the flanking walls above. In the event, these changes were not effected. In 1748 Cristoforo Ferretti, the owner, began to acquire adjacent properties, and a substantial addition, including an impressive formal staircase, was built to the palace – at the right in the drawing. Other changes involved joining the *palazzo* to the church of Santi Pellegrini e Filippo Neri or degli Scalzi, at the left in the drawing, and raising the level of the courtyard. On the other side of the street at the front of the palace two *palazzine* were built.

Thus, while it seems unlikely that any of the renovations of this project were ever realized, the sheet proves Vanvitelli's involvement in the rebuilding of the Palazzo Ferretti, and reinforces the supposition that he was responsible for the much more extensive renovations subsequently to occur.

1 F. Bartoli, *Contabilità preparatata contenente le Tavole di Ragguaglio fra le Misure, Pesi e Monete nei Comune della Provincia le Ancona...,* Ancona, 1866, pp. 2-3.

2 L. Serra, ''Le fabbricche di Luigi Vanvitelli in Ancona'', *Dedalo,* X, 1929, pp. 98-110, esp. p. 108; F. Fichera, *Luigi Vanvitelli,* Rome, 1937, pp.51-69, esp. p. 52.

3 For a general history of the palace and its decorations, see M. Ferretti Bocquillon, R. Ferretti and D. McTavish, ''Il Palazzo Ferretti di Ancona nell'opera di Antonio da Sangallo il Giovane – Pellegrino Tibaldi – Luigi Vanvitelli,'' *Ancona tra '500 e '700,* Cassa di Risparmio di Ancona, in press.

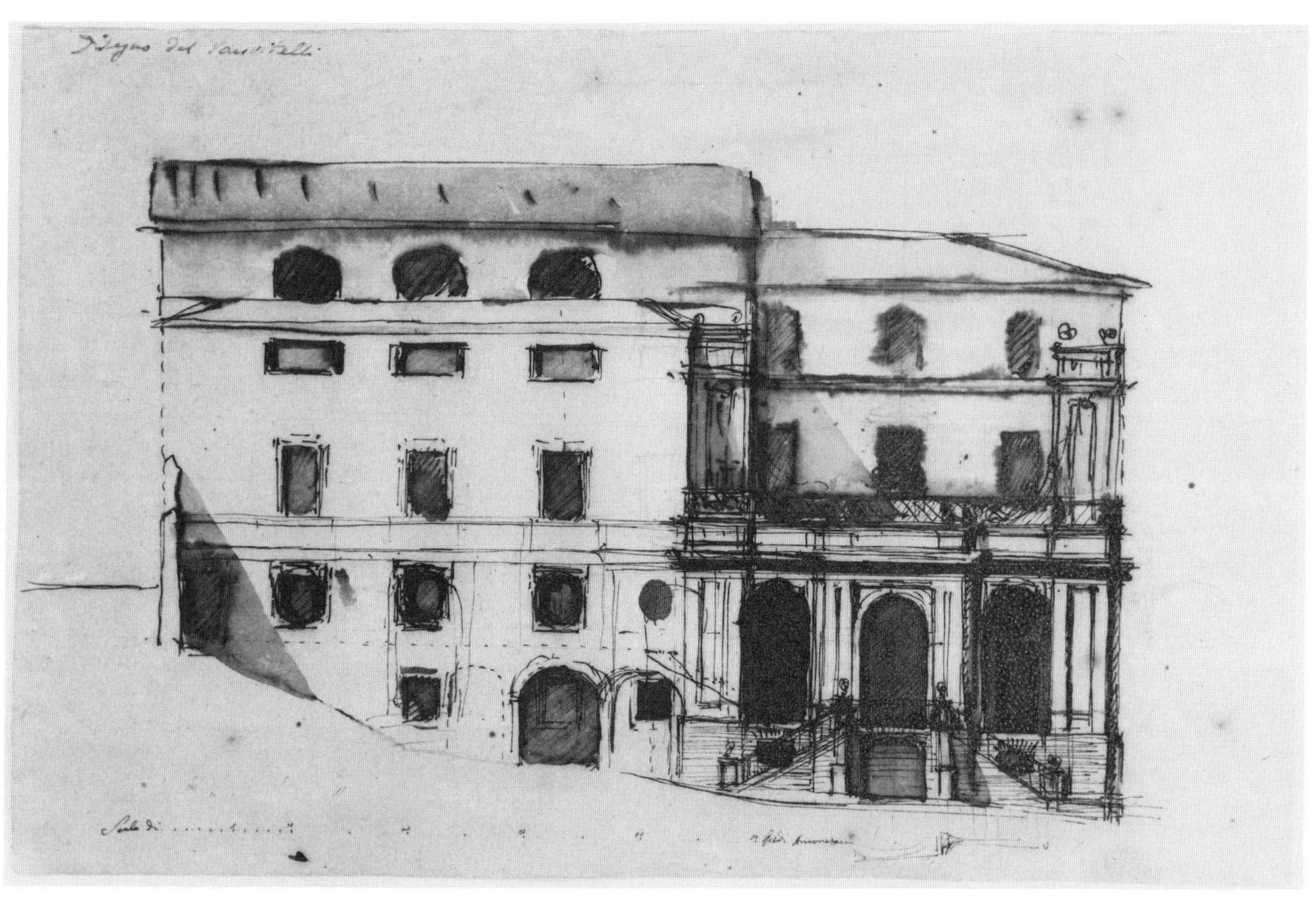
Disegno del Vanvitelli
Scala di ...
Piedi Romani

Giovanni Domenico Tiepolo

Venice 1727 – 1804 Venice

62 *The Magdalen Washing the Feet of Christ*

Brush and brown ink. Some restoration for ink corrosion;
the corners repaired. 222 x 350 mm

Literature: G. Knox, "*Primi Pensieri* by Domenico Tiepolo, and
a New Painting," *Master Drawings,* XVII, 1979, p. 30, pl. 17.

Provenance: Mrs. F. M. Humphreys; Sotheby's, London,
8 December 1972, lot 66.

George Knox has connected this drawing with a painting,
signed and dated 1752, now in the Mainfränkisches Museum at
Würzburg (fig. 62a).[1] The painting was one of four canvases
done by Domenico Tiepolo for the dining room at
Veitshöchheim, a country residence of the Prince Bishop
outside Würzburg. In the painting the arrangement of most of
the figures is approximately the same as in the drawing, but the
Veronese-like architectural backdrop has been re-arranged
somewhat. More significantly, the elongated composition of the
drawing has been considerably reduced at the right and to a
lesser extent along the top in the painting.

The drawing is a good example of Domenico's adroit use of
the brush alone to set down the general poses of the figures and
to organize larger areas of light and shade. As Knox has pointed
out, similar brush drawings, considered by James Byam Shaw
to date from the Würzburg years, are at Copenhagen, Princeton, and Besançon.[2]

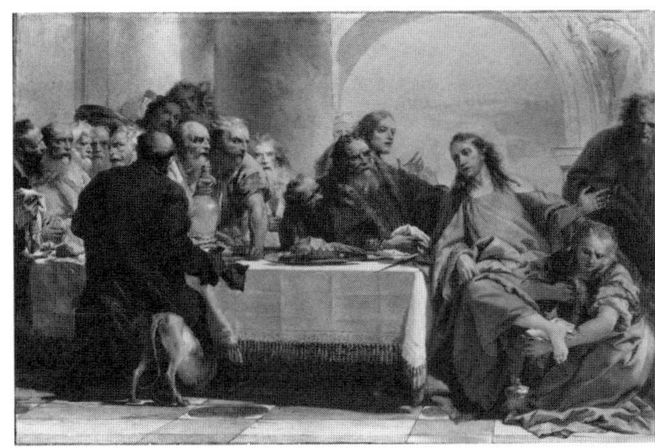

fig. 62a G.D. Tiepolo, *The Magdalen Washing the Feet of Christ*,
oil on canvas, on deposit Mainfränkisches Museum,
Würzburg.

1 Knox, *op.cit.* Also see A. Mariuz, *Giandomenico Tiepolo,* Venice, 1971, p. 127,
pl. 41.

2 *Ibid.*; J. Byam Shaw, *The Drawings of Domenico Tiepolo,* London, 1962,
pls. 6a, 6b, 7.

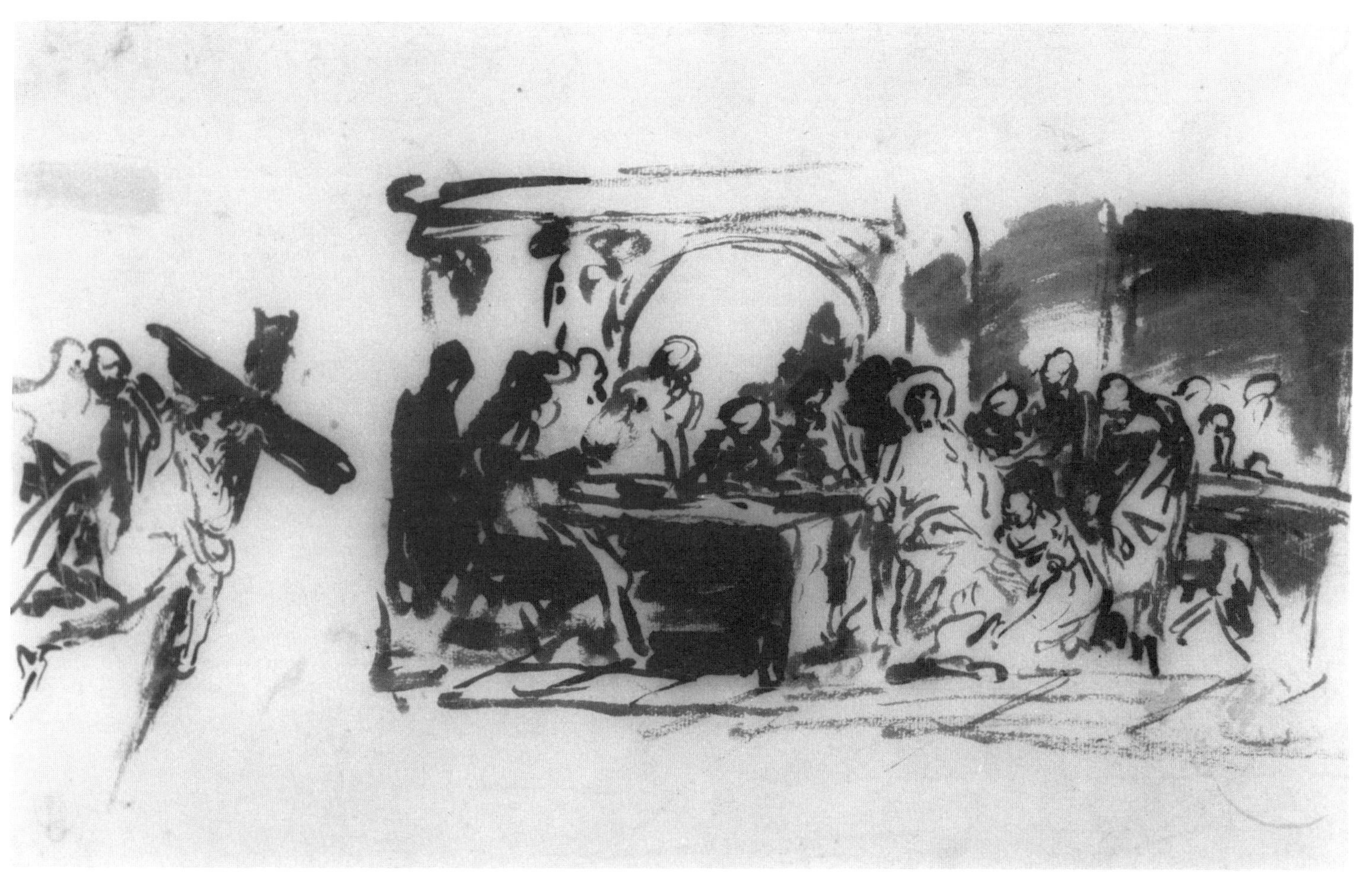

Giovanni Domenico Tiepolo

Venice 1727 – 1804 Venice

63 *Nessus Seizing Deianira, with a Satyr and Another Figure*

Pen and brown ink, brown and grey wash. The lower right corner repaired. 215 x 300 mm. Signed in brown ink at lower right: *Dom Tiepolo*

Literature: J. Cailleux, ''Centaurs, Fauns, Female Fauns and Satyrs among the Drawings of Domenico Tiepolo,'' *Burlington Magazine*, CXVI, June 1974, Supplement no. 31, pp. III, XVI, no. 36 (N D d 8), fig. 31.

Provenance: Linet, sale Paris, 15-16 May 1963; R.V. collection, Paris; Christie's, 8 July 1980, lot 50.

Domenico Tiepolo's best-known drawings belong to several series of variations on individual themes, both sacred and profane. Although these drawings may have connections with painted or etched works by Domenico or by his father, Giambattista, the drawings were normally conceived as ends in themselves and are frequently signed.

James Byam Shaw has called the drawings of satyrs and centaurs ''the most delightful and original of all Domenico's allegorical and mythological subjects.''[1] As with the other serial drawings, many of the sheets of satyrs and centaurs are inscribed with numbers, including one sheet with the number *144*. There is no certainty that this number indicates that one hundred and forty-four drawings were executed, but since about one hundred sheets have been located with this theme the total number may well have been at least that high.[2]

Jean Cailleux has divided the entire series of drawings of satyrs, fauns, and centaurs into various sub-categories, including one group of eight drawings dealing with Nessus and Deianira in the company of satyrs.[3] In the present drawing the centaur Nessus, the son of Ixion, is seen as an old man, but otherwise the sheet is typical of that group.

In various forms and formats the Tiepolo family treated satyrs and centaurs throughout much of the eighteenth century. Giambattista had represented satyrs and female fauns in various media from the mid-1730s onwards. Domenico, upon returning from Würzburg, undertook a Camera dei Satiri in the Palazzo Panigai at Nervesa; later in the family villa at Zianigo, he frescoed one small room with satyrs and another with centaurs (both now in the Ca' Rezzonico), while in the Palazzo Caragiani, Venice, he painted Nessus seizing Deianira.[4] Although there may be points of contact between these fresco decorations and the drawings under discussion,[5] the drawings are generally uniform in size and medium, and seem on the whole to have been independently conceived. The execution of the entire series of drawings may have extended over a considerable period of time; Cailleux, however, is inclined to see the majority of these drawings as having been done in the years between Domenico's return from Würzburg in 1753 and his departure for Spain in 1762.

---

1 J. Byam Shaw, *The Drawings of Domenico Tiepolo,* London, 1962, p. 41.

2 Cailleux, *op.cit.*, pp. iii.

3 *Ibid.*

4 A. Mariuz, *Giandomenico Tiepolo,* Venice, 1971, pp. 37, 113 (Palazzo Volpato-Panigai, dated 1754; Giambattista was also involved here); pp. 73, 141-42, pls. 240-44 (Camera dei Satiri, Zianigo; dated 1771); p. 141, pls. 354-63 (Camerino dei Centaurs; frescoes formerly part of the Stanza di Rinaldo e Armida); pp. 37, 145, pl. 340 (Palazzo Caragiani, ca. 1790-95).

5 See Cailleux's illustrations: figs. 11-12, 13-14, 20-21, 44-45, 48-49, 50-51, 62-63, 82-84.

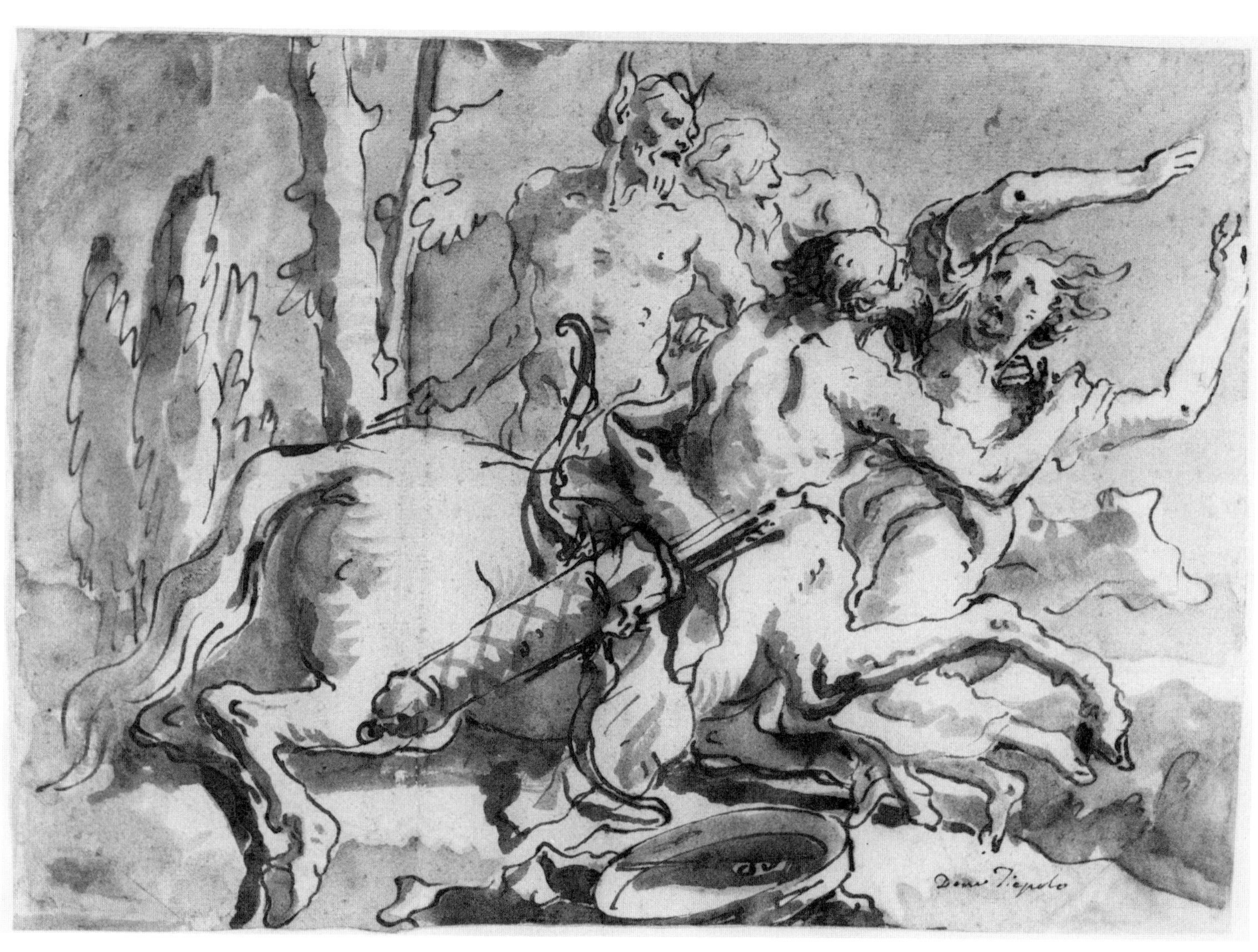

Dom. Tiepolo

Francesco Zuccarelli

Pitigliano (Tuscany) 1702 – 1788 Florence

64 *A River Landscape with Fisherfolk and Drovers, a Farm on a Bluff Beyond*

Pen and brown ink, grey and brown wash, heightened with white over red chalk. 201 x 308 mm. Signed with monogram lower left: *FZ.*; inscribed on the backing: *Zoffani, very valuable* and *signed left corner.*

Provenance: Christie's, London, 7 July 1981, lot 158.

Although born in Tuscany, Zuccarelli spent much of his life in Venice and in England, where he was a founding member of the Royal Academy (1768) and where his landscapes were much admired. This typical example was clearly intended as an independent work of art – it is signed at the lower left – yet it is also closely related to the artist's paintings on canvas. Composed according to a formula, Zuccarelli's landscapes comprise the *coulisse* of trees, the bucolic figures, the stretch of water, the rustic buildings perched on small promontories, and the birds wheeling overhead – all familiar to pastoral landscapes from the time of Claude on.[1] In addition, Zuccarelli's manner of recording natural detail follows a convention, as is seen in the rapid loops of pen line for foliage in the trees at the left and the grass in the foreground. These features notwithstanding, Zuccarelli effectively combines his pen and various coloured washes to produce a landscape of considerable charm.

1 For many of the same features, compare another signed landscape in the Castello Sforzesco, Milan: repr. G. Rosa, *Zuccarelli,* Milan, 2nd ed., 1952, n.p.

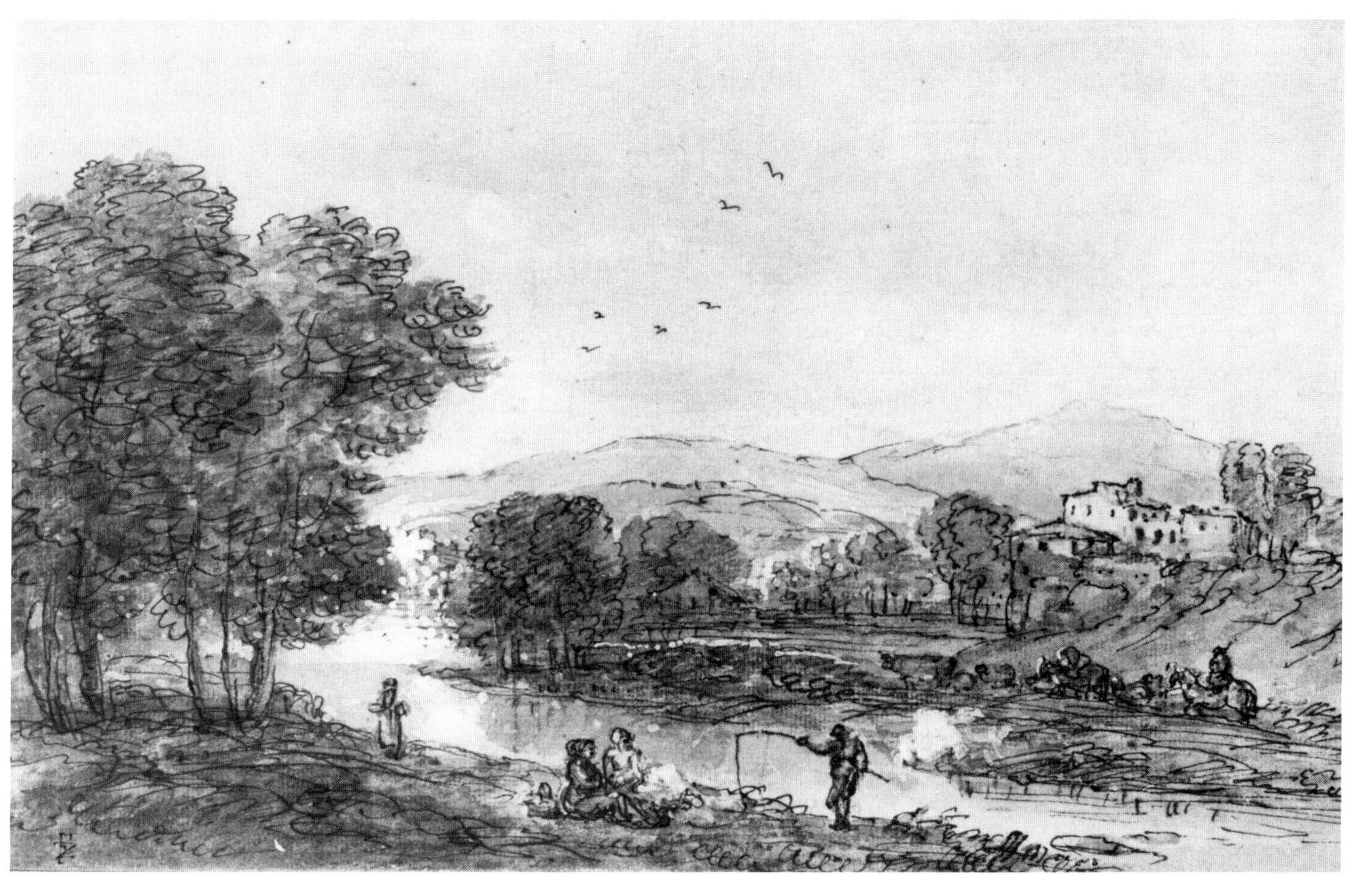

Giuseppe Zais

Forno di Canale 1709 – 1784 Treviso

65 *A River Landscape with Figures by a Small Waterfall*

Pen and brown ink, grey and black wash, heightened with
white, over traces of black chalk on beige paper. Framing lines
in brown ink. 225 x 336 mm

Much less well known in his own time than Zuccarelli, Zais
shared with him many of the same predilections toward
landscape painting. Zais was no doubt influenced by the slightly
older artist from Tuscany, and also by the Venetian Marco
Ricci. Although composed of many of the same elements as
Zuccarelli's landscapes, Zais's own work is more solidly
organized, frequently with stronger and more sudden contrasts
of light and shade. In the present instance the landscape, which
is probably imaginary, is also more rugged, and includes
gnarled trees and overhanging rocks, perhaps influenced by
Marco Ricci's paintings and drawings. Like the drawing by
Zuccarelli (no. 64), this sheet must also have been undertaken
as a finished work of art in itself.

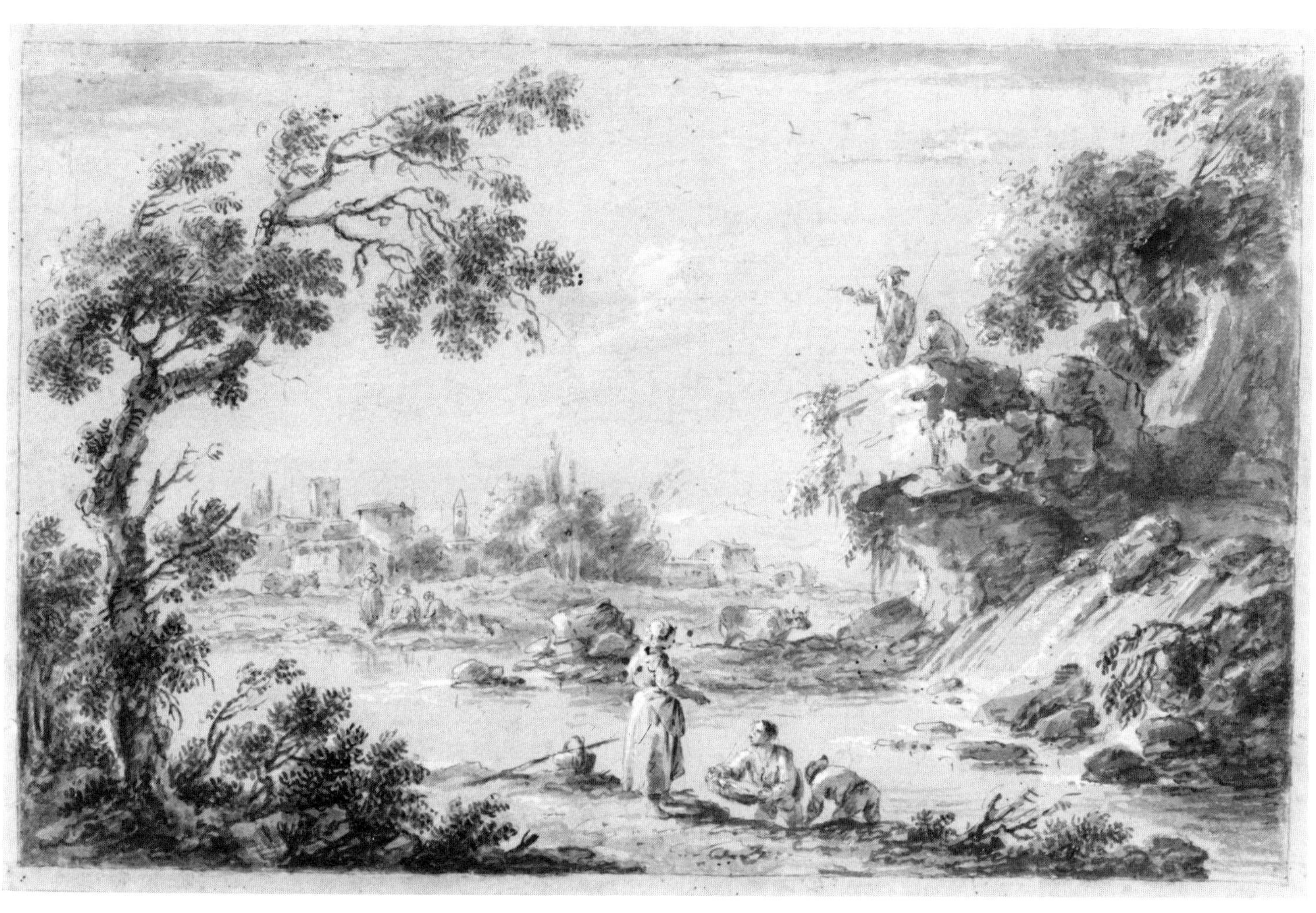

Francesco Guardi

Venice 1712 – 1793 Venice

66 *A Campo with the Lagoon in the Distance (recto); Hills above Lake Garda (verso)*

Pen and brown ink and brown wash over red chalk *(recto)*; pen and brown ink *(verso)*. 138 x 188 mm. Signed lower left *(recto):* *F*co *Guardi*; hills on *verso* identified as *Fasan* and *Maderno.*

Provenance: Christie's, London, 9 December 1982, lot 207.

Realized with Francesco Guardi's personal calligraphy and slight applications of wash, the quick but telling sketch on the *recto* can be directly connected with two late paintings by the artist, one in the National Gallery, London (fig. 66a), and the other formerly in the R. Makower collection.[1] A related gouache by Giacomo Guardi, Francesco's son, appeared at auction in 1980.[2] The exact site has not been identified and it may well be imaginary.[3]

The quick sketch on the *verso*, which looks west from the Lago di Garda toward Fasano and Maderno, just north of Gardone, was probably made on a trip Guardi took to the Val di Sole in the Trentino, north of the Lago di Garda, in October 1778.[4] Drawings in private collections of the Borgo di Valsugana in the Trentino include the same sort of decorative mountain peaks.[5]

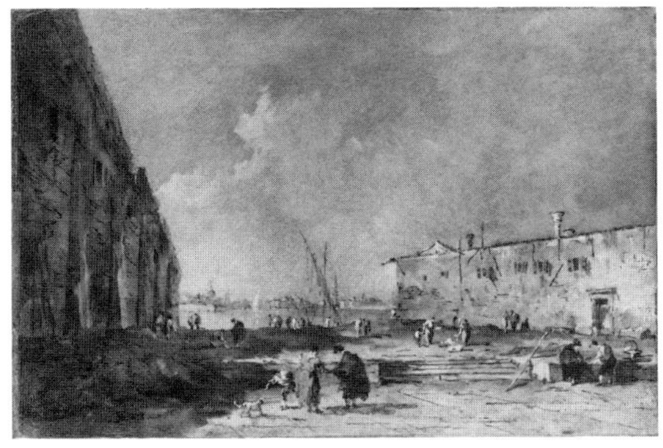

fig. 66a Francesco Guardi, *A View in Venice (?)*, oil on canvas, National Gallery, London.

1 A. Morassi, *Antonio e Francesco Guardi,* Venice, 1973, I, pp. 453-54, no. 772, fig. 708 (London version). M. Levey, *National Gallery Catalogues, The Eighteenth-Century Italian Schools,* London, 1956, p. 55 (no. 2520), dates the painting in London to ca.1775-80. The picture formerly in the Makower collection now belongs to The Cancer Research Campaign; *Venetian Eighteenth-Century Painting,* Thos. Agnew & Sons Ltd., London, 1985, pp. 30-1, no. 14, repr.

2 *Fine Old Master Drawings,* Sotheby's, London, 3 July 1980, lot 86, repr.

3 The painting in London has been called a *capriccio* by Morassi, *op.cit.*, but Levey, *op.cit.*, is inclined to see it representing a specific, although unidentified site.

4 F. De Maffei, *Gian Antonio Guardi pittore di figura,* Verona, 1951, p. 42; cited in Morassi, *op.cit.*, p. 519. Francesco Guardi may have made another trip to the Trentino in 1782, *ibid.*

5 See A. Morassi, *Guardi, Tutti i Disegni di Antonio, Francesco e Giacomo Guardi,* Venice, 1975, pp. 152-53, nos. 416-18, figs. 417, 419-420a.

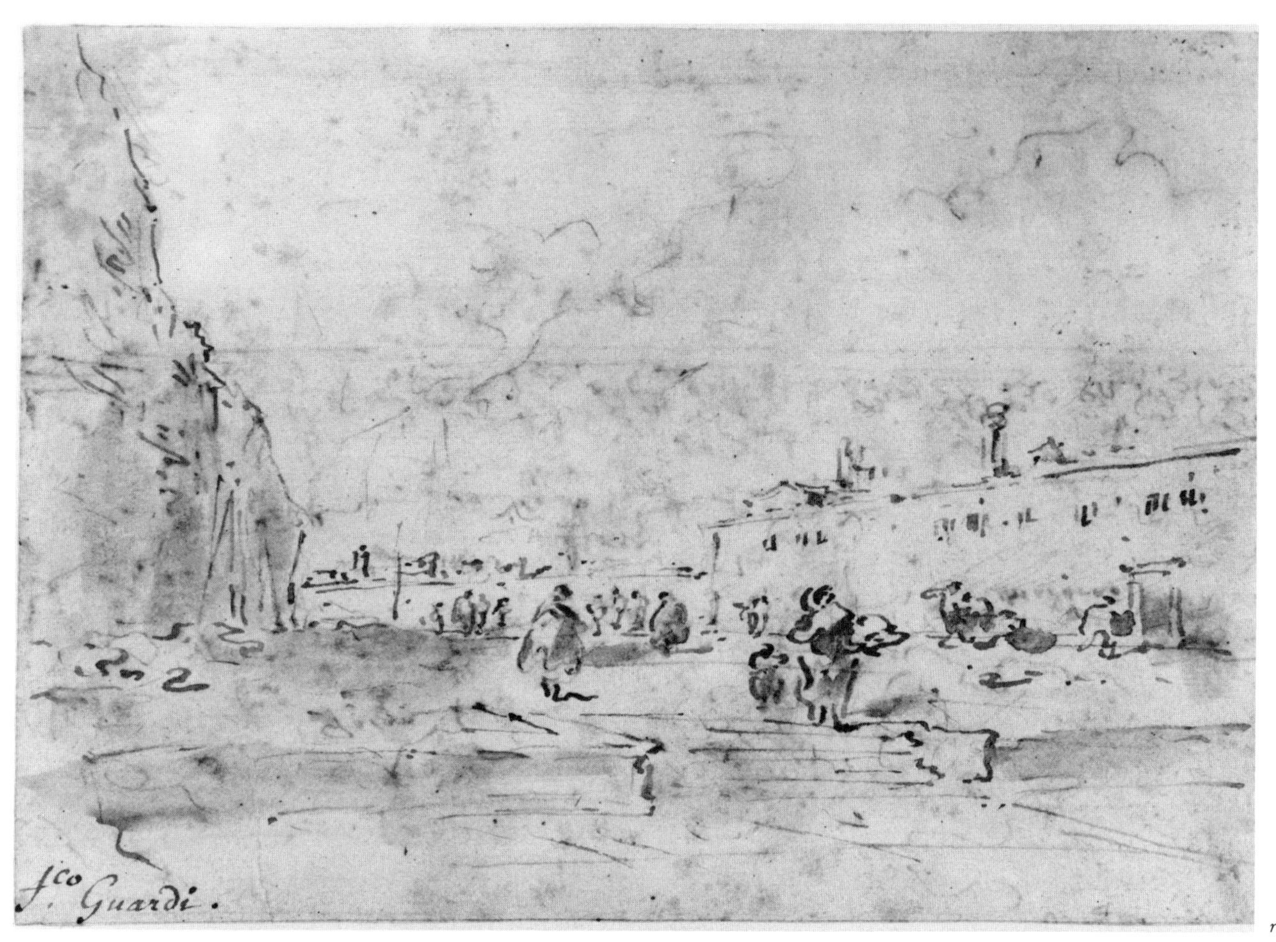

recto

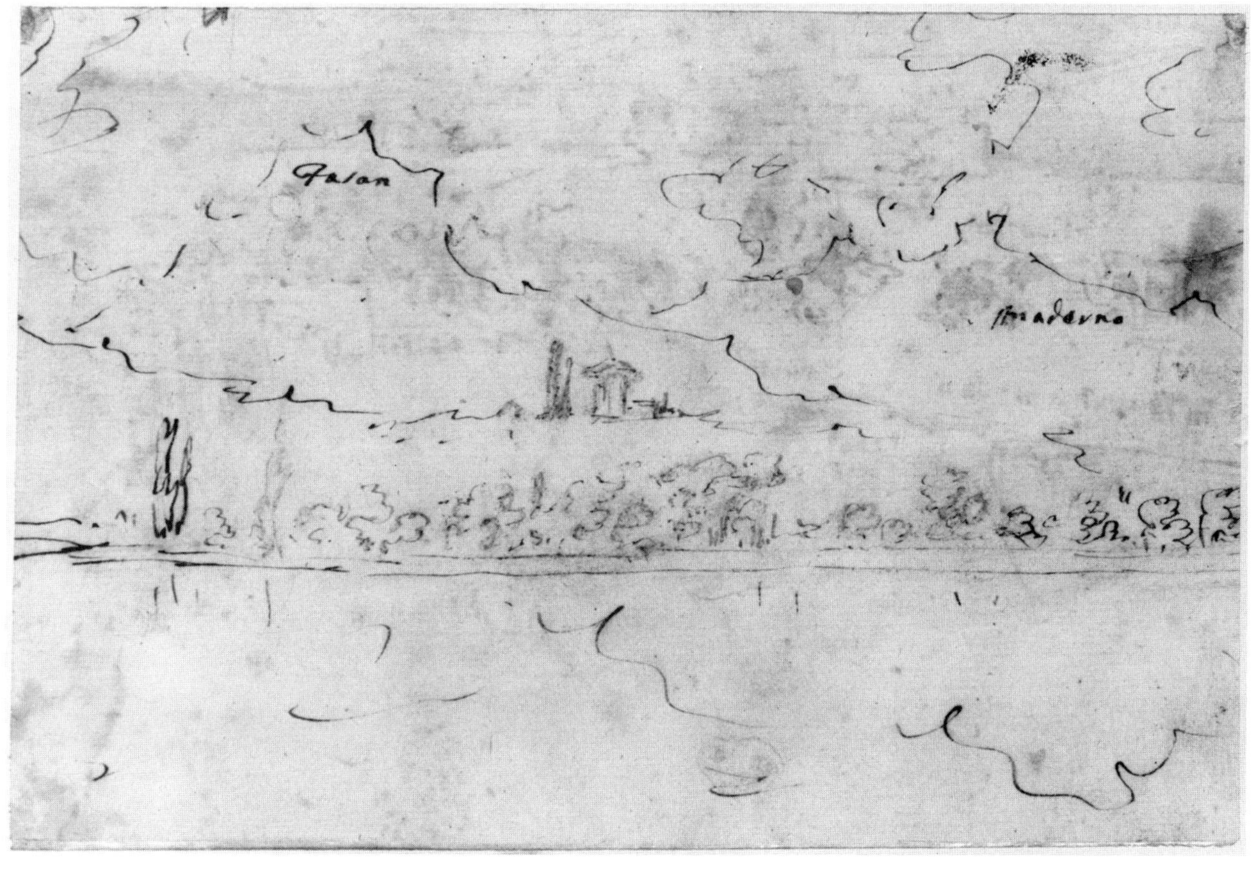

verso

Gaetano Gandolfi

San Matteo della Decima 1734 – 1802 Bologna

67 *Pluto and Proserpina by the Stix*

Black chalk on white paper. 333 x 392 mm. Strip of paper,
approximately 30 mm, added along upper margin. Inscribed
in black chalk on the *verso*: *G. Gfi f 1798*

Provenance: Sotheby's, London, 25 March 1982, lot 51.

Among the last works of one of the Bolognese school's last
exponents, Gaetano Gandolfi, is a series of large black-chalk
drawings of narrative subjects. Many of these drawings,
including the present example, are dated – from the late 1790s
until 1802 – in what may well be the artist's own hand. Although
evidently not always meant as ends in themselves,[1] the drawings
are in a sense Bolognese equivalents to the finished drawings by
Domenico Tiepolo in Venice. They are a *cadenza* to the
Bolognese school, and fittingly reflect the example of the
Carracci, and even in some details the idiosyncrasies of
Pellegrino Tibaldi almost two and a half centuries before.

Most of the drawings feature mythological or historical
figures in dramatic situations. The terrified Proserpina, here,
could well be the sister of an equally distraught Eurydice in
Gandolfi's drawing of Orpheus and Eurydice, dated 1802, in the
collection of David Rust.[2] In all of these drawings, the heroic
nudes are modelled in soft gradations of black chalk, accented
by sinuous contour lines.

The conspicuous presence of the boatman may recall Charon
in Giuseppe Maria Crespi's *Aeneas, the Sibyl and Charon* in
Vienna.

1 For a number of these drawings, related to paintings, see M. Cazort in *L'Arte del Settecento Emiliano, La Pittura, L'Accademia Clementina,* Palazzo del Podestà e di Re Enzo, Bologna, 1979, p. 135, under no. 285.

2 Repr. *Bolognese Drawings in North American Collections 1500-1800,* National Gallery of Canada, Ottawa, 1982, no. 114.

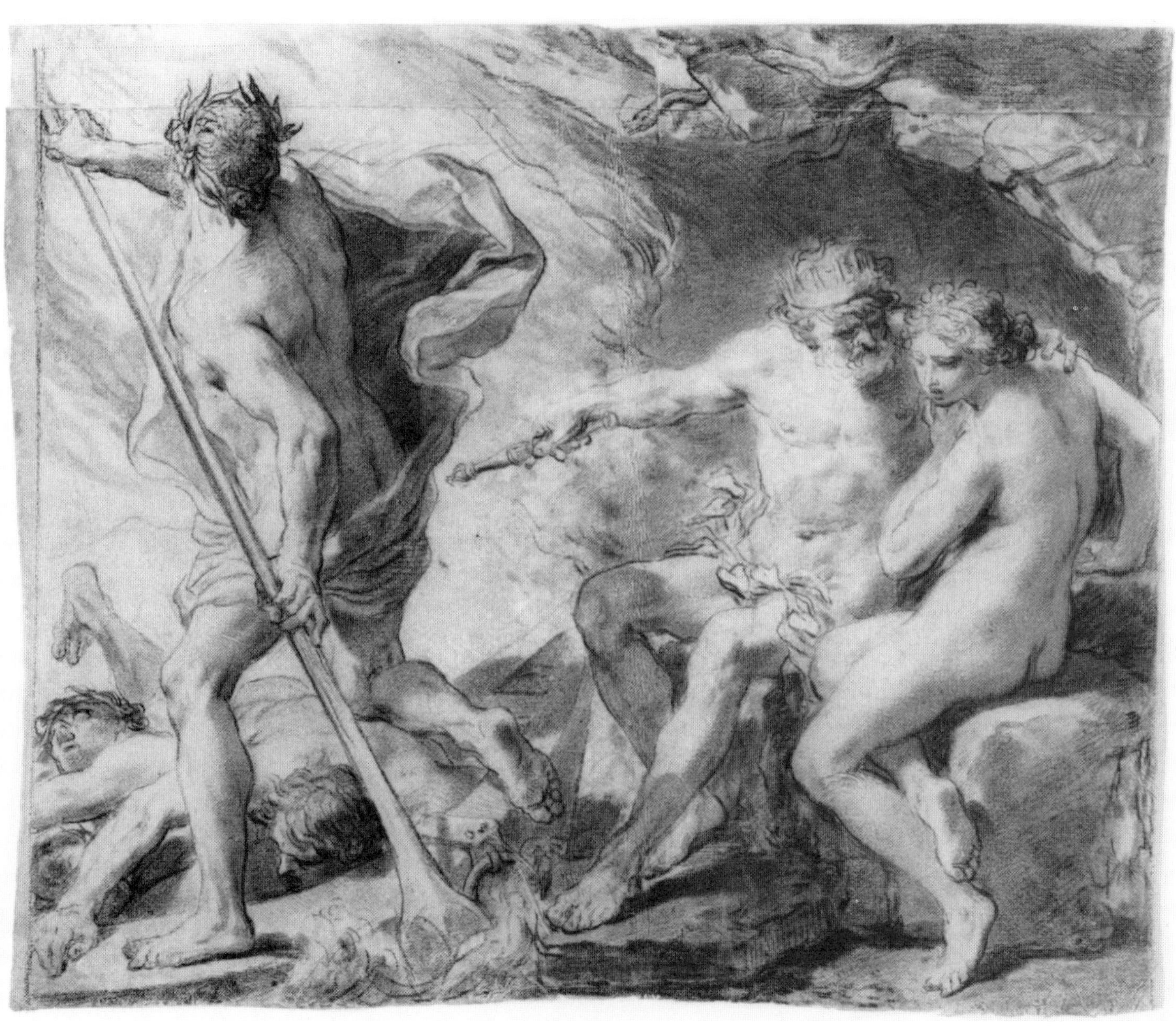

BALDINUCCI

F. Baldinucci, *Notizie dei Professori del disegno…*[1681-1728],
ed. P. Barocchi, 7 vols., Florence, 1974-1975.

BARTSCH

A. Bartsch, *Le peintre graveur,* 21 vols., Vienna, 1803-21.

LUGT

F. Lugt, *Les Marques de collections de dessins et d'estampes…*,
Amsterdam, 1921.

LUGT, SUPPL.

F. Lugt, *Les Marques de collections de dessins et d'estampes…
Supplément*, The Hague, 1956.

RIDOLFI

C. Ridolfi, *Le Maraviglie dell'Arte…*[1648], ed. D. von Hadeln,
2 vols., Berlin, 1914-24.

SANSOVINO-MARTINIONI

F. Sansovino, *Venetia città nobilissima et singolare* [1581],
with additions by G. Martinioni, Venice, 1663.

THIEME-BECKER

U. Thieme and F. Becker, *Allgemeines Lexicon der bildenden
Künstler,* 37 vols., Leipzig, 1907-50.

TIETZES

H. Tietze and E. Tietze Conrat, *The Drawings of the Venetian
Painters in the 15th and 16th Centuries*, New York, 1944.

VASARI

G. Vasari, *Le vite de' più eccellenti pittori scultori ed
architettori* [1568], ed. G. Milanesi, 9 vols., Florence, 1878-85.

VENTURI

A. Venturi, *Storia dell'arte italiana*, 11 vols. in 25 parts,
Milan, 1901-39.

Graphic Design: Richard Male Design Associates
Photography: Photographic Services, Art Gallery of Ontario
Composition: Cooper & Beatty, Limited
Printing: MacKinnon-Moncur Ltd.
Separations: Graphic Specialties Ltd.
Typeset in Baskerville and printed on Monadnock Caress